D0064797

Nicknames of Cities and States of the U.S.

By

Joseph Nathan Kane

and

Gerard L. Alexander

The Scarecrow Press, Inc.
New York and London 1965

L. C. Card No. 65-13550

Preface

Joseph Nathan Kane in his book "1,000 Facts Worth Knowing" published in 1938, out of print for more than a score of years, devoted a small section to nicknames. Thirteen years later, Gerard L. Alexander compiled "Nicknames of American Cities, Towns and Villages (Past and Present)", published by the Special Libraries Association, which is also out of print.

A mutual friendship and interest of the authors resulted in this larger and more complete list to which explanatory text has been added. The idea was broached to Scarecrow Press, and here is the result.

Contents

Introduction

Practically all the states, cities and towns in the United States, regardless of location, size or age, have nicknames. Some of them are well known, others are seldom used and rarely printed. Very few nicknames of states, cities and towns are official or adopted by legislative action. Often it is usual for a locality to have more than one definite nickname.

Nicknames have been conferred in numerous ways by chambers of commerce, literary sources, advertising executives, publicity representatives and by rival cities.

Over the years, some cities have acquired so many nicknames that each has lost its importance. These may be completely diversified and bear no relation to each other. New York City, for example, is called America's Leading Tourist Resort, The Babylonian Bedlam, The Capital of the World, The City of Skyscrapers, The Coliseum City, The Empire City, The Entertainment Capital of the World, The Front Office of American Business, The Metropolis, The Money Town, The Nation's First City, The Seat of Empire, The World's Fair City, The World's Metropolis, just to mention a few.

In the same vein, nicknames of one locality may be so similar in meaning to others that they may be easily interchanged with little loss. Boston, for example, is known as Beantown, the City of Baked Beans, the City of Bean Eaters or the Home of Baked Beans.

The most common form of nicknames is the descriptive one: The Battlefield City, The Border City,

The Classic City, The Cockade City, The College City, The Crescent City, The Druid City, The Dynamic City, The Empire City, The Executive City, The Exposition City, The Family City, The Frosty City, The Golden City, The Historic City, The Lookout City, The Prison City, The Stone City.

Industry

Another form of nickname associates the city with its most prominent industry: The Aluminum City, The Atomic Energy City, The Auto City, The Automobile City, The Beer City, The Bituminous City, The Bran Town, The Brass City, The Brewing City, The Butter City, The Camera City, The Canoe City, The Car Shop City, The Cash Register City, The Celery City, The Celluloid City, The Cement City, The Ceramic City, The Cereal Food Center, The Chemurgic City, The Clay City, The Chair City, The Chemical City, The Chocolate City, The Cigar City, The Circus City, The Clipper City, The Clock City, The Coal City, The Coke City, The Collar City, The Copper City, The Cordage City, The Cream City, The Crystal City, The Dairy City, The Electrical City, The Flour City, The Flower City, The Furniture City, The Granite City, The Gypsum City, The Hardware City, The Hat City, The Insurance City, The Iron City, The Kodak City, The Lock City, The Lumber City, The Marble City, The Missile City, The Motor City, The Nail City, The Oil City, The Paper City, The Pearl City, The Plow City, The Pottery City, The Pretzel City, The Railroad City, The Rubber City, The Salmon City, The Salt City, The Sawdust City, The Ship-building City, The Shoe City, The Shovel City, The Silk City, The Silver City, The Smelter City, The Spindle City, The Sponge City, The Steel City, The Sweatshop Capital, The Tannery City, The Textile City, The Thread City, The Tube City, The Wool City.

Geography

Geographical attributes often account for the nicknames of cities. Examples are: The Bay City, The Bayou City, The Bluff City, The Canal City, The Canyon City, The Cavern City, The City by the Lake, The

City by the Sea, The City on the Gulf, The Falls City, The Hill City, The Lake City, The Mile-High City, The Mound City, The Mountain City, The Natural Gas City, The Port City, The Scholarship City, The Science City, The Windy City.

Local

Nicknames are often specifically limited to locality: Arizona's First Capital, Arkansas' Only Seaport, Benton County's Fastest Growing City, Colorado's Second City, Delaware's Summer Capital, Idaho's Farm Market, Iowa's Own City, Maine's Fastest Growing Industrial and Recreational Area, Michigan's Most Famous Summer Resort, Montana's Largest and Friendliest City, New York's First Capital, Rhode Island's Most Historic Town, South Arkansas' Busy Port City, South Carolina's Capital City, South Dakota's City of Opportunity, Tallest Town in Oregon, Tennessee's Beauty Spot, Tip of Cape Cod, Trade Center of Southwest Georgia.

Botany

Flowers, trees and shrubs lend their influence to nicknames: The Camellia City, The Christmas Tree City, The Dogwood City, The Elm City, The Evergreen City, The Floral City, The Flower City, The Forest City, The Holly City, The Iris City, The Lawn City, The Lilac City, The Magnolia City, The Maple City, The Oak City, The Oleander City, The Orchard City, The Palm City, The Palmetto City, The Peony Center, The Rose City, The Sycamore City, The Tulip City.

Sports

Sports and games often serve as the nucleus for nicknames: Golf Capital, Hockey Capital of the Nation, Home of Baseball, Home of the Packers, Packer's Town, Polo Capital of, Ski Capital of.

Nationality - Religion

Nationality and religion have inspired nicknames for some cities: Czech Bethlehem, Deutsch Athens, Dutch City, Dutchtown, German Athens, Mormon City, Polish City, Quaker City, Quaker Town.

Meaningless

Many cities have adopted nicknames so bland and colorless that they have lost their importance and original individuality and are no longer distinctive or meaningful, such as: The Capital City, The City Beautiful, The City of Churches, The City of Homes, The City of Opportunity, The City of Roses, The City of Trees, The City With a Future, The Convention City, The Friendly City, The Gate City, The Gateway City, The Gem City, The Hub City, The Magic City, The Progressive City, The Queen City.

Hyperbole

Many nicknames are inspired by wishful thinking and hyperbole, such as: The Best Known City, The Cleanest Beach in the World, The Cleanest Big City in the World, The Closest State to Heaven, The Dancingest Town in the U. S., The Fastest Growing City, The Finest Beach in the World, The Friendliest Town, The Most Beautiful City, The Most Historic City, The Nation's Most Beautiful City, The Proudest Small Town in America, The Safest Spot in the World, The South's Fastest Growing City, The South's Greatest City, The South's Most Beautiful and Interesting City, The Tourist's Paradise, The Town Where Summer is Air Conditioned, The Town With the Most to Offer Industry, The West's Most Western Town, The Winter Playground of America.

Slander

Just as proud local citizenry are eager to accent these encomiums, there are jealous or hostile groups who swing the pendulum in the opposite direction to foster such slander as: Bad Birmingham, Hangtown, Mobtown, The Modern Gomorrah, The Murder Capital of, Sin City, Sinema City, The Sodom of, The Wickedest City of.

Geography (Foreign)

Many cities resort to associations with European countries and cities for their nicknames, such as: The Alexandria of, The Athens of, The Birmingham of, The Carlsbad of, The Eden of, The Edinburgh of, The

Essen of, The Gibraltar of, The Heidelberg of, The Lyons of, The Manchester of, The Naples of, The Paris of, The South Sea Island of, The Switzerland of, The Thermopylae of, The Venice of.

Geography (United States)

Some cities claim a fancied or non-existant relationship with a better known community, such as: The Atlantic City of, The Boston of, The Brooklyn of, The Chicago of, The Coney Island of, The Denver of, The Detroit of, The Greenwich Village of, The Hartford of, The Hudson of, The Kansas City of, The Las Vegas of, The Lexington of, The Little Louisville of, The Lowell of, The Minneapolis of, The Newport of, The Niagara of, The Pittsburgh of, The Plymouth of, The Saratoga of, The Spokane of, The West Point of.

Picturesque - Fanciful

Other cities prefer a picturesque or fanciful name, such as: Buckle on the Kansas Wheat Belt, City Built on Oil, Soil and Toil, City Where Mexico Meets Uncle Sam, City Where Oil Flows, Gas Blows and Glass Glows, City Where Progress and Pleasures are Partners, City Where Summer Winters, City Where There are no Strangers--Just Friends, City Where Work and Play are Only Minutes Away, Land of Cheese, Trees and Ocean Breeze, Magic Mascot of the Plains, The Peerless Princess of the Plains.

Food

Foods often serve as the basis of cities' nicknames. Here is a partial list roughly subdivided into classifications: The Honey Capital, The Pretzel City, The Rice City, The Scrapple City.

FRUITS: The Apple City, The Berry City, The Blueberry Capital, The Cherry City, The Citrus Center, The Home of the Tangerine, The Lemon Center, The Orange Capital, The Peach Bowl, The Peach Capital, The Pear City, The Raisin Capital, The Strawberry Capital, The Watermelon Capital.

MEAT: The Bratwurst Capital, The Broiler Capital, The Holstein Capital, The Pheasant Capital, The Pork City, The Turkey Capital.

NUTS: The Filbert Center, The Land of Hazel Nuts, The Maple Center, The Peanut City, The Pecan Capital, The Walnut City.

SEA FOOD: The Clam Town, The Crawfish Town, The Home of the Famous Silver King Tarpon, The Lake Trout Capital, The Sailfish Capital, The Salmon City, The Salt Water Trout Capital, The Sea Turtle Capital.

VEGETABLES: America's Carrot Capital, Bean Town, The Celery City, The Green Bean Center, The Lettuce Center, The Potato Capital, The Pumpkin Capital, The Spinach Capital, The Tomato Capital.

Book Titles

Nicknames are often taken from the title, the subtitle, the text or characters in books and stories: Green Felt Jungle, Money Town, Sodom by the Sea.

Made-Up Names

Coined names, made-up words and meaningless combinations of letters are sometimes used: Arkopolis, Bostonia, Cornopolis, Dupontia, Gotham, Hogopolis, Jacksonopolis, Mushroomopolis, Pigopolis, Porkopolis, Soo, Squawkiewood, Touropolis, Tusselburgh.

Humorous

Humorous or facetious names often lampoon a town: Annie's Town, Betsytown, Bumgannon, Lunchburg, Tater Town, Taterville, Unsainted Anthony.

Towns often acquire nicknames based upon the birth of some outstanding individual: Birthplace of Calvin Coolidge, Birthplace of Daniel Webster, Birthplace of Harry S. Truman, Birthplace of McKinley.

Other birthplaces are commemorated such as the Birthplace of American Liberty, Birthplace of Aviation, Birthplace of California, Birthplace of Dixie, Birthplace of Liberty, Birthplace of Maine, Birthplace of Oklahoma, Birthplace of Radio, Birthplace of Speed, Birthplace of The Nation, Birthplace of The Republican Party, Birthplace of United States Naval Aviation.

Some cities have acquired their nicknames from some event associated with their history: The Home of the Apple Blossom Festival, The Home of the Boll Weevil Monument, The Home of the Comstock Lode, The Home of the Florida Derby, The Home of the Mining Barons, The Home of the Miss Universe Pageant, The Home of the Pacific Fleet, The Home of the Snake River Stampede, The Home of the World Famous Glass Bottom Boats.

Historical and literary allusions often account for some nicknames: The Cradle of Liberty, The Cradle of Secession, The Mission City, The Modern Phoenix, Paul Bunyan's Capital, The Rebel Capital.

Peculiarly, nicknames of some cities may be contrary and at cross purposes with each other such as The Sleepy Town and The World's Greatest Workshop; The Babylonian Bedlam and The Wonder City; The Crime Capital and The Metropolis of the West; The Gas House of the Nation and The Nation's Headquarters.

Joint - Collective

Many cities have jointly adopted the same nickname with neighboring cities which is often used individually or collectively: Dual Cities, Fall Cities, Quad Cities, Tri-Cities, Twin Cities.

Abbreviations and Nicknames

Abbreviations and word contractions often serve as nicknames: Alex City, Ark City, Billtown, Bison City, Chi, El-ay, Frisco, Jax, Jeff City, Jimtown, L.A., Philly, Sacto, San Berdoo.

In every state, one city bears the nickname "The Capital City" or "The Capitol City." Capital and capitol are often interchanged, either correctly or incorrectly, so that it is impossible to state which is correct or which was originally intended.

Another point of argument or dispute is the use of the article "a" and "the" in the nicknames. Both are often used, in some instances neither are used, and in other cases are interchanged: A City of Homes, The City of Homes, A City of Opportunity, The City of Opportunity, A City of Trees, The City of Trees.

In some instances, both the "a" and the "the" are omitted.

In similar vein, an identical situation arises with regard to the use of "of" and "to." The Gateway of the South, The Gateway to the South, The Gateway of the West, The Gateway to the West.

Another variation is the use of the singular and the plural; City of Diversified Industry, City of Diversified Industries.

When a locality has a particular designation, it is possible that it may also have an unlimited number of variations. To illustrate the point, a city might be called The Celery Capital, The Celery Capital of Michigan, The Celery Capital of the United States, The Celery Capital of the World, The Celery City, The Celery City of Michigan, The Celery City of the United States, The Celery City of the World, Michigan's Celery City, The United States' Celery City, The World's Celery City. The ramifications may be extended indefinitely.

As the nuances are unlimited, a complete list of all the combinations of one city would be a mighty undertaking and when multiplied by the large number of places listed in this book, would make an encyclopedia minute by comparison. Furthermore, this overspecialization would decrease rather than increase the utility value of this book. Consequently, the temptation to strive for bulk has been disregarded, and no effort has been made to list all the existing possible names and combinations. However, exceptions have been made in instances where the deviations have become almost as commonplace and acceptable as the original name.

Often the publication of a brochure, map or publicity circular, the handicraft of word-outpouring by a promotion direction, tries to bring about a new image or concept. This is one of the prolific sources of nicknames and, being in print, remains for posterity.

Occasionally, nicknames are coined by some orator or political campaigner and find their way into the language.

Nicknames of cities often undergo a metamorphosis and revisions are made. Sometimes the change is proportionate to the inflated ego and exaggeration of the publicity director. Again, many nicknames have completely outlived their usefulness, or the purpose for which they were originally intended. The Town may become The City, The Hub of the Territory may change to The Hub of the State.

Where a city has more than one nickname, the nicknames have been listed alphabetically without attempting to grade them in importance or value.

The source or origin of many nicknames is unknown. In many instances, the authorities differ as to the reason of selection and consequently several versions exist. Where there are several different explanations, they have been listed without attempting to rate their importance.

When the nickname is descriptive or self-explanatory such as The Capital City, The City of Beauty, The Friendly City, The Progressive City, no attempt has been made to explain the obvious. Also, when no logical explanation can be given, it is likewise omitted.

The listing or inclusion of a nickname does not necessarily imply that it is official, in constant use or is approved by this book.

Certain nicknames are appropriate, others are not appropriate; others are sheer hyperbole, still others are misnomers while some have been judiciously named.

Some are grammatically incorrect, plurals being used for singulars and vice versa. Apostrophe marks are often applied in the wrong places. Hyphens are occasionally used unnecessarily and often omitted when required.

All known nicknames have been recorded impartially as this book is a record, not apologia or propaganda.

In addition to the informative material, this book portrays the field to the publicity departments and public relations executives of the various cities and enables them to revalue their efforts. It may stimulate them to strive for originality or adopt the platitudes of repetition if they desire. If this compilation serves to encourage the former, it will have well served its purpose.

The authors realize that this book is not the end-all on the subject. There are many places in the United States for which no nicknames are known. This may be because the place has none or that it is so limited that it has not escaped local confines, or that it is oral and has not been captured by print. If any of these sites have been omitted, or others inherit new nicknames, we would like to hear of them for inclusion in future editions. Advice from chambers of commerce and local officials will be especially appreciated.

It would be remiss not to thank the librarians, historians, public officials, city and state agencies and individuals whose assistance has been of inestimable value in the compilation of this book. As the authors primarily used the facilities of the New York Public Library, the Library of Congress and the Free Library of Philadelphia, special thanks are due their staffs who obligingly facilitated this work.

Geographical Index
Cities

ALABAMA

ALBERTVILLE	The Friendly City
ALEXANDER CITY	Alex City
	The City With a Great Civic Pride and a Sound Business Climate
ANDALUSIA	The Gem City of Southern Alabama
ANNISTON	Annie's Town (named for Mrs. Annie Scott Tyler)
	The Brooklyn of the South
	The City of Churches
	The Magic City
	The Model City (town laid out before plots were sold to the public)
	The Model City of Alabama
	The Pearl of the South
ATMORE	The City Where Industry Profits
	The City With Room to Stretch and Grow in
AUBURN	The Loveliest Village of the Plains
	The Village of the Plains
BESSEMER	The Iron City (steel furnaces)
BIRMINGHAM	Bad Birmingham
	The City Beautiful
	The City of Executives
	The City Where the Mighty Smith Stands (the Vulcan

BIRMINGHAM (Cont'd)	statue)
	The City With a Heart in the Heart of Dixie
	The Home of Vulcan (statue)
	The Industrial Center of the Great South (major iron and steel production center in the south)
	The Industrial Center of the Southeast
	The Industrial City Beautiful
	The Industrial City of Dixie
	The Industrial City of the South
	The Inland Metropolis
	The Magic City
	The Magic City of the South
	The Mineral City of the South
	The Murder Capital of the World (1932)
	The Pittsburgh of the South
	The Youngest of the World's Great Cities (settled in 1813, Jones Valley)
DECATUR	The City of Achievement
	The City of Hospitality
	The City Where River, Air, Rail and Highway Meet
	The City With Opportunity For All
	The Northern Gateway to Alabama
	The Saturday Town
	The Souths' Most Strategic and Distribution Center
	The Souths' Most Strategic Industrial and Distributional Center
	The Wonder City
DEMOPOLIS	The City of People
	The City of the People (founded in 1817 by Napoleonic exiles)

DEMOPOLIS (Cont'd)	The Peoples' City The Wine and Olive Colony
DOTHAN	The Home of the National Peanut Festival The Perfect Spot to Work, to Play, to Enjoy Life
ENTERPRISE	The Home of the Boll Weevil Monument (dedicated 1919) The Peanut Capital of the World (peanut oil mills, peanut butter factory, peanut shelling plants)
EUFAULA	The Bluff City (bluff rises 150 feet on the west bank of the Chattahoochee River)
FLORENCE	The City of Beautiful Churches, Homes and Buildings The City of Outstanding Educational Advantages The Home of Florence State College (the oldest teacher's institution in the south) The Tri-Cities (with Sheffield and Tuscumbia on the Tennessee River)
FOLEY	The Heart of the American Riviera (on the Gulf of Mexico)
GADSDEN	The Queen City of Alabama The Queen City of the Coosa (Coosa River)
GREENVILLE	The Camellia City
HUNTSVILLE	The City of Contrasts The City of Governors (Thomas Bibb, Gabriel Moore, Clement Comer Clay, Reuben Chapman, John Winston, David P. Lewis) The City of Gracious Living The First Capital of the State (1819) The Geographical Center of the South

HUNTSVILLE (Cont'd)	The Hub of the Powerful Tennessee Valley
	The Industrial City of North Alabama
	The Rocket City (The Jupiter "C" rocket was perfected here)
	Rocket City, U.S.A.
	The Space Capital of the Nation
JASPER	The Home of Hospitality
MOBILE	The Charm Spot of the Deep South
	The City of Five Flags
	The City of Six Flags
	The Gulf City (on the Gulf of Mexico)
	The Picnic City
	The Port City (the only seaport in Alabama)
	The Sportland of the Gulf
MONTGOMERY	The Birthplace of Dixie
	The Capital City (134, 393 population in 1960)
	The City of Beauty
	The City of Opportunity
	The Cow Town of the South
	The Cradle of the Confederacy (the first capital of the Confederacy)
	One of America's Most Interesting Cities
MUSCLE SHOALS	The Aluminum City (home of second largest producer of aluminum in U. S.)
	The Niagara of the South (the Tennessee River drops 134 feet in almost 40 miles)
OZARK	The Home of Fort Rucker, the Army Aviation Center
PHENIX CITY	The City of Progress and Opportunity

PHENIX CITY (Cont'd)	The Hub of the Chattahoochee Valley
	The Wickedest City in America (title of book by Edwin Strickland)
ROBERTSDALE	The Hub City
SHEFFIELD	The Iron City on the Tennessee River
	The Tri-Cities (with Florence and Tuscumbia)
SYLACAUGA	The Marble City (marble quarries)
TALLADEGA	The Bride of the Mountains (in the foothills of the Appalachian Mountains)
TRUSSVILLE	The City With Small Town Hospitality (1960 population 2,510)
TUSCALOOSA	The Athens of Alabama (University of Alabama)
	The City of Oaks
	The Druid City
TUSCUMBIA	The Home of Helen Keller ("Ivy Green" now a state shrine)
	The Tri-Cities (with Florence and Sheffield)

ALASKA

ANCHORAGE	The Air Crossroads of the World (SAS field on Europe-Orient flight)
	The Chicago of the North
	The Crossroads of the World
	The Front Door Entrance to an Alaska Vacation
	The Hub City
	The Largest City in the Largest State (1960 population 44,237)
	The Most Air-Minded City in the World

ANCHORAGE (Cont'd)	The Nerve Center of Alaska
CORDOVA	The Friendly City
FAIRBANKS	The Friendly Frontier City
	The Gateway to the Arctic
	The Golden Heart Metropolis of the Interior
	The Golden Heart of Alaska
	The Golden Heart of the North
	The Kansas City of Alaska
HAINES	The Strawberry Capital of Alaska
HOMER	The City Where People Like to Live (1960 population 1,247)
JUNEAU	Alaska's Capital City (1960 population 6,797)
	The Capital City
	The Capital of an Empire
	The Convention City
	The Gateway to Glacier Bay National Monument
	The Scenic City of Nightless Summer Days
KETCHIKAN	The First City
	The Gateway to Adventure
	The Salmon Capital of Alaska
KODIAK	The Home of the World's Largest Bear
	The King Crab Capital of the World
NOME	The Famed Gold Rush Town
PETERSBURG	Alaska's Little Norway
SEWARD	The Gateway City (on Resurrection Bay)
SITKA	The Portal to Romance (title of book by Barrett Willoughby)

ARIZONA

AGUILA	The Lettuce Center of the Nation

AJO	The Gateway to Sonoyta, Mexico and the Gulf of Lower California
BISBEE	Arizona's Copper Capital
	The Gateway to Fort Huachuca (U.S. electronic proving ground)
CHANDLER	The City Where Summer Winters
	The Five Star City in the Valley of the Sun
	The Green Spot in Arizona's Famous Valley of the Sun
DOUGLAS	The City Where Progress and Pleasure are Partners
	The Friendly City in the Heart of the Old West
FLAGSTAFF	Friendly Fabulous Flagstaff
	The Center of Everything in Northern Arizona
	The City in the Pines (ponderosa pine forests)
	The Home of Ten Thousand Friendly People (1960 population 18,214)
	The Hub of Arizona's Lumber Industry
	Touropolis of America (three major tour routes enter the city)
FORT HUACHUCA	The Electronic Center of the Southwest
GLENDALE	The City in the Valley of the Sun
	The Land of Perpetual Harvest
	The New Car Capital of Arizona (factory representatives of all major automobile concerns located here)
GLOBE	The Capital City of the County with a Copper Bottom (county seat of Gila County noted

GLOBE (Cont'd)	for its copper mines)
	The Gateway to Arizona's Scenic and Recreational Area
KINGMAN	The Gateway to "Wanderland" in Mohave County, Arizona
MESA	The City in the Heart of Arizona Vacationland
	The City Where It's June in January Along the Romantic Apache Trail
	The Gem City in Arizona's Valley of the Sun
	The Heart of the Romantic Southwest in the Valley of the Sun
	The Little City of Charm (1960 population 33,772)
MIAMI	The Concentrator City
PHOENIX	America's Favorite Sun and Fun Vacationland
	The Capital City (1960 population 439,170)
	The Capital City of Arizona (1889)
	The City in Arizona's Valley of the Sun
	The City Where Summer Winters
	The Heart of the Sun Country
	The Metropolis of the Desert
	The Palm City
	The Southwest's Sightseeing Center
	The Youngest Big City in the United States (settled 1870; 1960 population 439,170)
PORTAL	The Yosemite of Arizona (Cave Creek Canyon in Chiricahua Mountains)
PRESCOTT	Arizona's First Capital (first territorial legislature 1864, also 1877-1889)

PRESCOTT (Cont'd)	The Center of the Nation's Greatest Concentration of Varied Natural Attractions
	The Center of Yavapai (seat of Yavapai County)
	The Cowboy Capital
	The First Capital of Arizona (1864-65)
	The Mile High City (altitude 5,346 feet)
	The Mile High City of Health
	The Sentinel City in the Pines (in the Sierra Madre mountains)
SALOME	The City Where She Danced (town named for Mrs. Grace Salome Pratt)
SAN CARLOS	Hell's Forty Acres (on the San Carlos Indian Reservation)
SCOTTSDALE	The West's Most Western Town (new buildings simulate frontier structures)
TEMPE	The Home of the Fabulous Sun Devil Athletic Team and Arizona State University
	The Swell Place To Live
TOMBSTONE	The City of Health, History, Hospitality
	The City of Sunshine and Silver (famous mining center)
	The Town Too Tough To Die (water flooded the mines in 1886, but the people did not leave)
TUCSON	America's First City of Sunshine
	Arizona's Second Largest City
	The Ancient and Honorable Pueblo
	The City of Sunshine
	The Heart of the Old South-

TUCSON (Cont'd)	west
	The Heart of the Scenic Southwest
	The Home of the University of Arizona
	The Old Pueblo (oldest city in Arizona, first settlement 1776)
	The Retirement Center of the Nation
	The Sunshine Capital of the Southwest
	The Sunshine City
	The Western Gateway to Mexico (65 miles to Nogales, Mexico)
	The Wonderful Weather Land
WICKENBURG	A Bit of the Old West Transplanted in the Twentieth Century
	America's Dude Ranch Capital
	The Dude Ranch Capital of the World
WILLCOX	A Good Place to Know, Go, Visit, Stay
	The Cattle Capital and Agricultural Center of the Great Southwest
	The Cattle Capital of the Nation
	The Cattle Capital of the World
	The City in the Heart of the Southwest Wonderland
WINSLOW	The Center of Northern Arizona's Scenic Beauty
	The City in the Heart of the Nation's Sunniest State
	The Gateway to Hopiland and Navajoland (Hopi Indians and Navajo Indians)
YUMA	The City Where You Can Work, Live, Play, the

YUMA (Cont'd)	Western Way
	The Sunshine Capital of the United States

ARKANSAS

ALMA	The Crossroads for North-South, East-West Traffic
ARKANSAS CITY	Ark City
BERRYVILLE	The Turkey Capital of Arkansas (turkey farms)
BLYTHEVILLE	The City of Churches
BULL SHOALS	The Capital of the Big Lake (Bull Shoals Lake)
CAMDEN	South Arkansas' Busy Port City (on Ouachita River)
CONWAY	The City of Opportunity
DECATUR	The Community of Friendly People
DOVER	The Gateway to the Ozarks (between Little Rock and Fort Smith)
EL DORADO	The Oil Capital of Arkansas (oil discovered 1921)
EUREKA SPRINGS	America's Little Switzerland (mountain resort)
	The Capital Resort of the Ozarks (oldest resort in the Ozark Region)
FAYETTEVILLE	America's Little Switzerland (highest point in Arkansas Ozarks)
	The Athens of Arkansas
	The Gateway to Scenic Boston Mountains
	The City That Progress Built
FLIPPIN	The Gateway to Blue Shoals Lake and Dam
FORREST CITY	The Hoist Capital of America (Yale and Towne Inc. plant)
FORT SMITH	America's Industrial City
	Arkansas' Industrial Center
	The Center City

FORT SMITH (Cont'd)	The City of Balance The City of Your Future The Growing City of Industry and Recreation The Gateway to the Beautiful Ozark Playground The Leading Industrial City in Arkansas
GENTRY	The Typical Ozark Home Town
GRAVETTE	The World's Largest Black Walnut Factory
GREEN FOREST	The Tomato Capital of the Ozarks
HARRISON	The Hub of the Ozarks (in the Arkansas Ozarks) The Metropolis of a Fast Growing Commercial and Agricultural Area The Ozark Wonderland
HELENA	Arkansas' Only Seaport (on the Mississippi River) The City of Industrial Opportunity The Twin Cities (with West Helena)
HOT SPRINGS	America's Greatest Health and Resort Center America's Greatest Health and Rest Center America's Own Spa (The only health resort in the U.S. where the natural hot waters which flow from the earth are owned, controlled and endorsed by the U.S. government) Arkansas' Largest Health and Pleasure Resort The City Where the World Bathes and Plays The Nation's Health Resort (famous hot springs and

HOT SPRINGS (Cont'd)	spas)
	The Vapor City (steam from the hot springs)
JONESBORO	The City Ready for Tomorrow (home of Arkansas State College)
LITTLE ROCK	Arkopolis
	The Capital City (1960 population 107,813)
	The City of Roses
	The City of Three Capitals (three capital buildings remain, each of a different era)
MOUNTAIN HOME	The Center of the Most Popular Resort Section in the Ozarks
	The Fishing Capital of the Ozarks (White River, Norfork Lake, Bull Shoals Lake)
PARIS	The Gateway to Mt. Magazine
PINE BLUFF	The City of Gigantic Industries, Unparalleled Schools
	The City of Magnificent Churches, Beautiful Homes
	The City of Peace and Plenty
RUSSELLVILLE	The Home of Arkansas Polytechnic College
SPRINGDALE	The Agricultural and Industrial Center of Northwest Arkansas
	The Main Street of Northwest Arkansas
TEXARKANA	The Twin Cities (twin cities on the Arkansas-Texas border: Texarkana, Ark., and Texarkana, Texas)
WEST HELENA	The Twin Cities (with Helena)
WINSLOW	The Pioneer Resort Town

CALIFORNIA

ALAMEDA	The Isle of Pleasant Living (eastern shore of San Francisco Bay)

ALBANY	The City of Homes
ANAHEIM	The City of Good Living
	The Home of Disney Land
	The Ideal Year 'Round Community
ANGWIN	The City Set on a Hill
ATOLIA	The Sin City
AVALON	The Port of Friendliness
BALDWIN PARK	The Gateway to the Orange Empire
BANNING	The Gateway to the Desert and Idyllwild Mountain Resort
BENICIA	The Athens of California
	The City of Industrial Opportunity
BERKELEY	The Athens of the West (The University of California)
	The Balanced City
BISHOP	The World Gliding Center
CHOWCHILLA	A Nice Place to Live
	The City With a Big Future
CLAREMONT	A Bit of New England With a Sombrero on it
	Claremont, the Beautiful
	The City of Living and Learning
COALINGA	The Heart of the Westside of Fresno County
COMMERCE	The Modern City
COMPTON	The Hub City
CORONA	The Circle City (three mile circular boulevard surrounding the business district)
DEATH VALLEY	America's Bottom
	America's Low Spot
ELSINORE	The Scenic Health Resort of California
FONTANA	The Neighborly Friendly Community
FORTUNA	The City Where Nature Smiles the Year 'Round
	The Friendly City

FRESNO	The Bustling Center of Industry, Agriculture, Wholesale Trade and Shipping
GARDENA	The Little Las Vegas
	The Poker City
	The Poker-Playing Capital of the West
GLENDALE	The Jewel City
	The Queen of the Valley (San Fernando Valley)
HOLLYWOOD	The Big-Headed Burg
	The Celluloid City
	The Cinema Capital (moving picture studios opened 1911)
	The Cinema Village
	The Cinemaland
	The Cinematown
	The Circle City
	The City of Galloping Tin-Types
	The Fairyland
	The Film Capital
	The Film Capital of the World
	The Film City
	Filmdom
	Filmland
	The Flicker Capital
	The Flicker City
	The Flicker Lane
	The Land of Promise
	The Movie Village
	The Movieland
	The Screenland
	The Sinemaland
	The Squawkiewood
	The Stardom
	The Starland
	The Studioland
HOLTVILLE	America's Carrot Capital
INDIO	The Center of All Vacation Fun
	The Date Capital of the

INDIO (Cont'd)	United States (produces about 90% of all dates grown in the United States)
	The Desert Wonderland (Coachella Valley)
	Southern California's Desert Playground
INGLEWOOD	The Harbor of the Air (numerous aircraft plants)
ISLETON	The Asparagus Capital of the World
LAGUNA BEACH	The City of Serene Living
LAKE TAHOE	(see also Nevada)
	America's All-Year Playground
	The Cesspool for Gambling Joints
	The City With a Hole in the Middle
	The Coming Vegas
	The Recreational Slum
	The Sierra "Coney Island" (a pleasure resort in Brooklyn, N.Y.)
LANCASTER	The Heart of the Antelope Valley
LONG BEACH	The Home of the Miss Universe Pageant
	The Land of Industrial Opportunities
	The Pride of the Pacific
	The Proud Port of the Pacific
	The Queen of the Beaches
	The Star of the Southland
	The Year 'Round Playground of the Pacific
LOS ALTOS	The Garden Spot of the World Famous Santa Clara Valley
LOS ANGELES	A Circus Without A Tent
	A City of Flowers and Sunshine
	El-Ay

LOS ANGELES (Cont'd)	Elay
	L.A.
	Las Diablos
	Nineteen Suburbs in Search of a Metropolis
	The Angel City
	The Capital of Crackpots
	The Citrus Metropolis
	The City Built on Sand
	The City Metropolis
	The City of Angels
	The City of Dreadful Joy
	The City of Flowers
	The City of Liquid Sunshine
	The City of Sunshine
	The Detroit of Airplanes
	The Metropolis of Isms
	The Metropolis of the West
	The Movie City
	The Old Pueblo
LOS GATOS	The Gem City of the Foothills (Santa Clara County)
MANTECA	The Butter City (dairy production center, Spanish word for butter)
MARYSVILLE	The Peach Bowl of the United States
MILL VALLEY	The Gateway to Muir Woods
MODESTO	The City That Is Only Two Hours to the Sierras or the Sea (on the Tuolumne River)
MONTEBELLO	The City Between the Mountains and the Sea
	The City of Flowers
	The City of Gardens
	The City of Homes
	The City of Industry
	The Fastest Growing City in Los Angeles County (1960 population 32,097)
MONTEREY	The Capital of Old California (capital of old California from 1776 to the end of 1849

MONTEREY (Cont'd)	and de facto from 1770-1776)
	The City of History and Romance
	The City Where America Began in the West (site discovered in 1542 by Juan Rodriguez Cabrillo)
	The First American Capital West of the Rockies (capital of Alta California under the Spanish, Mexican and United States Flags)
NAPA	The Southeastern Entrance to the Redwood Empire (97% of the world's great redwoods)
	The Table Wine Center of the World (applied also to Napa County)
NORTH HOLLYWOOD	The Gateway to the San Fernando Valley (a part of the City of Los Angeles)
OAKDALE	The City in Central California Convenient to Everything
	The Ladino Clover Center of America (grazing for beef cattle, originally imported from Italy)
OAKLAND	The City of Progress and Prosperity
	The Detroit of the West (manufacturing center)
	The Western City of Ships (site of U.S. Army Port of Embarkation, Naval Supply Depot, etc.)
PALM SPRINGS	America's Foremost Desert Resort
	The Oasis in the Desert (in the Upper Colorado desert)
PALO ALTO	The Garden Spot of the Peninsular (at foothills of Coast Range Mountains)

PALO ALTO (Cont'd)	The Home of Stanford University
	The Ideal Home and Recreational Center
	The Ultra Modern City
PARAMOUNT	The City of Roses
PASADENA	The City of Roses
	The Crown City
	The Crown City of the Valley
	The Town That Roses Built (famous annual parade on January first, and football tournament)
PETALUMA	The Egg Basket of the World (egg production center)
PIEDMONT	The Queen of the Hills
PITTSBURG	The Industrial Capital of California
	The Industrial City of the West (steel plant, numerous factories)
PLACERVILLE	Hangtown (numerous hangings in pioneer days)
PORTERVILLE	The Friendly City
RICHMOND	The Fastest Growing Industrial Community (1960 population 71,854)
	The Largest City of Contra Costa County, California
RIVERSIDE	The City of Exceptional Beauty
	The City of Friendliness and Beauty
	The City of Individuality and Charm
SACRAMENTO	New Helvetia (founded August 12, 1839 by Captain John Augustus Sutter; first settlement of white men in interior California)
	Sacto (contraction of word, first and last syllable of Sacramento)

SACRAMENTO (Cont'd)	The Capital City (1960 population 191,667)
	The City of the Plains
	The City of Trees
	The City Where California Began (founded August 12, 1839 by Captain John Augustine Sutter; first settlement of white men in interior California)
	The Golden City
	The Heart of California
	The Land of Romance and Recreation
ST. HELENA	The City in the Heart of Colorful Napa Valley
	The Table Wine Center of the World
SAN BERNARDINO	The Gate City
	The Leading Inland City of the South (on the edge of the Mojave Desert at the base of the San Bernardino Mountains, about sixty miles inland)
	The Playground of Southern California
	San Berdoo
SAN BRUNO	The City With a Future
SAN CLEMENTE	The Spanish Village
SAN DIEGO	The Air Capital of the West
	The Birthplace of California (discovered 1542 by Cabrillo)
	The City Where California and Mexico Meet The Blue Pacific
	The City Where California Began (visited in 1539 by Father Marcos and his followers from the desert side)
	The Gateway to California

SAN DIEGO (Cont'd)	The Jewel City of California
	The Plymouth of the Pacific Coast (first permanent white settlement on the Pacific Coast)
	The Plymouth of the West
SAN FRANCISCO	Frisco
	The Bagdad by the Bay
	The Bay City
	The City Beautiful
	The City by the Golden Gate
	The City Cosmopolitan
	The City of a Hundred Hills
	The City of Bridges
	The City of Firsts
	The City of Many Adventures
	The City of One Hundred Hills
	The City of the Golden Gate
	The Cosmopolitan City
	The Cosmopolitan San Francisco
	The Exposition City
	The Financial Center of the West
	The Financial Center of the World
	The Gateway to the Far East
	The Golden City
	The Golden Gate City
	The Market of Three Barbarian Tribes
	The Mushroom City
	The Nation's Western Capital
	The Old Gold Hill
	The Paris of America
	The Poor Man's Paradise
	The Port O'Missing Men
	The Queen City
	The Queen City of the Pacific
	The Queen City of the Pacific Coast
	The Queen City of the West

SAN FRANCISCO (Cont'd)	The Queen of the Pacific
	The United Nations' Conference Center (United Nations Conference on International Organization of 46 nations opened April 25, 1945)
	The Western Gate
SAN JOSE	The Garden City
SAN LEANDRO	The Cherry City of California
SANTA BARBARA	California's World Famous All-Year Resort
	The City Where Hospitality is a Tradition
	The Queen of the Missions (Mission Santa Barbara founded 1786)
SANTA CRUZ	Scenic California's Scenic Playground
SANTA MARIA	The Valley of the Gardens (numerous seed farms)
SANTA MONICA	The City Where the Mountains Meet the Sea
SANTA PAULA	The Lemon Center
SAUSALITO	The Greenwich Village of the West (literary groups)
SELMA	The Raisin Capital of the World
SHAFTER	The Potato Capital
SOLVANG	Little Denmark (established in 1912 as a settlement for Danes; has Danish church, college and schools)
STOCKTON	A Variety of Recreational Opportunities
	California's Inland Harbor (on Stockton channel and San Joaquin River)
	The Center of California
	The City That Has Something for You
	The Gateway to the San Joaquin Valley
	The Industrial and Distribu-

STOCKTON (Cont'd)	ting Center of the Pacific Coast Empire
	The Industrial Hub of the West
	The Manufacturing City of the Pacific
UPLAND	The Western Shangri-La
WATSONVILLE	The Strawberry Capital of the World
WHITTIER	The Finest Home and Cultural Community in Southern California
	The Quaker City (founded in 1887 by Quakers)
WILMINGTON	The Heart of the Harbor
YUBA CITY	The Peach Bowl of the U.S.

COLORADO

ALAMOSA	The City at the Crossroads of Trans-Americas Highway and the Navajo Trail
BOULDER	The City Where Mountains and Plains Meet (at the foot of the Flatirons which rises 1,000 feet above the city)
	The Gateway to Colorado's Scenic Region
	The Wonderland of America
BRIGHTON	Brighton's Future is Bright
BRUSH	America's Sugar Bowl (Great Western Beet Sugar Factory, beet slicing capacity about 1,600 tons daily)
CENTRAL CITY	The Richest Square Mile on Earth
COLORADO SPRINGS	The City of Sunshine
	The Newport of the West
DENVER	The Capital City (1960 population 493,887)
	The Capital of the Rocky Mountain Empire
	The City of the Plains
	The Convention City

DENVER (Cont'd)	The Dynamic Metropolis of the Rocky Mountain Empire
	The Friendly City in the Sky
	The Little Capital
	The Mile High City (altitude 5,280 feet)
	The Queen City of the Plains
	The Queen City of the West
	The Western Capital
	The White Collar City
DURANGO	The Switzerland of America (altitude 6,505 feet)
ESTES PARK	Resort Town, U.S.A. (near Rocky Mountain National Park)
FORT COLLINS	Eden of the Closest State to Heaven
	The City of Beautiful Parks
	The City of Magnificent Mountains
	The City of Panoramic Boulevards
	The City of Plentiful Plains
	The Fascinating Foothills City (about 40 miles from Fort Collins Mountain Park)
	The Gateway to the Poudre (River)
	The Home of the Colorado Aggies (Colorado Agricultural and Mechanical College)
	The Lamb and Cattle Capital of the West (large lamb-feeding center)
	The Lilac City
	The Safest Spot in the World
GRAND JUNCTION	The Hub of the Scenic West (Grand Mesa National Forest)
LEADVILLE	The Cloud City (altitude 10,188 feet, claimed to be the highest incorporated city in the U.S.)
	The Magic City

LOVELAND	America's Sweetheart City (popular mailing address for valentines)
PUEBLO	Colorado's Second City The City of Homes and Industry The Fountain City The Manufacturing City of the Rocky Mountain Region The Steel City of the West (plant of Colorado Fuel and Iron Corp.)
SALIDA	Nature's Wonderland The City Atop the Nation's Roof Garden (altitude 7,038 feet) The City in the Valley of the Arkansas The City of Dreams The City on the Highway to Heaven (altitude 7,038 feet) The Closest State to Heaven The Crossroads to Wonderland The Gem City The Gem of the Ocean The Heart of the Rockies The Hospitality City of the Rockies The Lovely Gateway to the Passes The Portal to the Quint States The Roof Garden of America (altitude 7,038 feet) The Sportsman's Paradise The Town With a Heart

CONNECTICUT

BRIDGEPORT	The Essen of America The Industrial Capital of America The Industrial Capital of Connecticut

BRIDGEPORT (Cont'd)	The Park City
	The Recreation Center for Generations
BRISTOL	The Clock Center of the World (numerous clock factories, site of American Clock and Watch Museum)
CLINTON	The Truly Colonial Town
DANBURY	The City in the Country
	The Gateway to Candlewood Lake
	The Hat City (numerous hat factories; first one opened in 1780)
	The Hat City of the World
	The Space Age City
EAST HAMPTON	The Bell Town (site of bell factories since 1808)
	The Bell Town of America
FARMINGTON	The Mother of Towns (settled 1640)
GREENWICH	The Gateway to New England
GROTON	The World's Submarine Capital (the Nautilus first atomic-powered submarine built here and launched January 21, 1954)
GUILFORD	The Shore Village (on Long Island Sound)
HARTFORD	The Capital City (1960 population 162,176)
	The Charter Oak City (the constitution of Connecticut hidden in hollow of an oak tree)
	The City Beautiful
	The Convention City of the East
	The Insurance City (home office of about 40 insurance companies with combined assets over 12 billion)

MANCHESTER	A Village of City Charm (in the valley of the Connecticut River)
MERIDEN	The Silver City (home of International Silver Co. and other silverware manufacturers)
MIDDLETOWN	The Forest City
MYSTIC	The Cradle of Square Riggers (famous shipbuilding center about 1850's)
	The Home of Yachtsmen
	The Seaport Village (developed by Marine Historical Association)
	Williamsburg of the Sea
NEW BRITAIN	The Hardware City (production of builders' hardware)
NEW HAVEN	One of the First American Cities of the Industrial Age
	The City of Elms
	The City of the Future
	The Elm City
	The Yankee Athens (site of Yale University)
NEW LONDON	The Ideal City in All Seasons
	The Whaling City (industry centered here from 1784 to 1850)
NORWALK	The Clam Town
	The World's Oyster Capital
NORWICH	The Rose of New England (famous Memorial Rose Garden honoring World War II dead)
STAMFORD	The Lock City (Yale and Towne factory was located here)
	The Research City
STRATFORD	The Town With a Future (1960 population 45,012)
THOMASTON	The Clock City (Seth Thomas clocks made 1813)

WATERBURY	The Brass City (large brass industry)
	The Gateway to the Litchfield Hills
WESTPORT	The Town of Homes
WILLIMANTIC	The Eastern Connecticut Center
	The Thread City (mill of American Thread Company)
WINDSOR	The Heart of the New England Tobacco Farm Land
WINSTED	The Laurel City (mountain laurel)

DELAWARE

DOVER	The Capital City (1960 population 7,230, state capital in 1777)
	The Capital of the First State
	The First City of the First State (became capital May 12, 1777)
	The Home of Latex Rubber
REHOBOTH BEACH	Delaware's Summer Capital (popular summer resort on the Atlantic Ocean)
	The Nation's Summer Capital (because of the large number of vacationists from Washington, D.C.)
	Washington-By-The Sea (near Washington, D.C.)
WILMINGTON	Dupont Town (home of the E.I. du Pont de Nemours & Co.)
	Dupontonia (see above)
	Quaker Town (formerly used because of Quaker residents)
	The Chemical Capital of the World
	The First City of the First

WILMINGTON (Cont'd)

State (first settlement established by the Swedes in the territory which later was the first to ratify the Constitution)
The Heart of the Harbor
The Port of Personal Service (on Delaware River)

DISTRICT OF COLUMBIA

WASHINGTON

The Capital City
The Capital of a Great Nation
The Capital of America
The Capital of Miserable Huts
The Capital of the Vast Republic
The Center of History in the Making
The City Beautiful
The City in a Forest
The City of a Thousand Thrills
The City of Conversation
The City of Houses Without Streets
The City of Lost Footsteps
The City of Magnificent Distances (so-called by Jose Correo de Serra, once Minister from Portugal)
The City of Receptions
The City of Streets Without Houses
The City of Trees Without Houses
The City of Washington
The Commercial Empire of the United States
The Court City of a Nation
The Crossroads of the World

WASHINGTON (Cont'd)	The Embryonic Capital The Executive City The Federal Capital The Federal City The Federal Seat The Federal Site The Federal Town The Foundling Capital The Gas House of the Nation The Grand Emporium of the West The Grand Metropolis The Great Dismal The Great Serbonian Bog The Great White City The Heart of America The Metropolis of the Country The Metropolitan City The Mighty Capital The Most Beautiful City in America The Mud-Hole City The National Capital The Nation's Capital The Nation's Headquarters The Nation's State The New Capital The New City of Washington The New Settlement The Political Front The Second Rome The Virgin Capital The Wilderness City The World's Most Beautiful City The Young Capital Washington, B.C. -- Before Corn

FLORIDA

ANNA MARIA	The Choicest Spot in All

ANNA MARIA (Cont'd)	Florida
	The Island You'll Love
APALACHICOLA	The City of the Friendly People
	The Old City With a New Future
ASTATULA	The Center of Central Florida (on Lake Harris)
AUBURNDALE	The City in the Heart of the Citrus Belt and Holiday Highlands
BARTOW	The City of Oaks
	The City of Oaks and Azaleas
BELLEVIEW	The Progressive Community With a Bright Future
BLOUNTSTOWN	The Agricultural and Timber Empire (richest timber producing area of Florida)
	The Hub of the Great Apalachicola Valley
	The Kingdom of Opportunity
	The Paradise of Fishing, Hunting and Swimming
BOCA RATON	The Golden City of the Gold Coast
	The Water Polo Capital of Florida
BOYNTON BEACH	The Gateway to "Sailfish Alley"
BRADENTON	The Friendly City
BRANDON	A Good Place to Live--Better
BROOKSVILLE	The Home of the Tangerine
CAPE CORAL	The City of the Future
	The City With a Future
CAPE KENNEDY	The Spaceport, U.S.A. (rockets, satellites)
CHIEFLAND	The Watermelon Capital
CLEARWATER	Florida's Newest Convention City
	The City With a Sparkle
	The Home of the World Cham-

CLEARWATER (Cont'd)	pion Clearwater Bombers
	The Springtime City
	The Winter Home of the National League Philadelphia Phillies (baseball club)
CLERMONT	The Gem of the Hills (amid 17 lakes and hills)
CLEWISTON	America's Sweetest Town (sugar cane fields)
COCOA	The Citrus Center (shipping point for Indian River citrus fruits)
	The Salt Water Trout Capital of the World
COCOA BEACH	Missile Land, U.S.A.
	The World's Best Beach
CORAL GABLES	Florida's Showcase Community
	The City Beautiful (part of Greater Miami)
CRESCENT CITY	The Gateway to the Bass Capital of the World
CRESTVIEW	The Hub City in the Heart of Florida's West Country
	The Hub City of Northwest Florida
	The Real Paradise for Family Living
CROSS CITY	The City Way Down Upon the Suwannee River
DADE CITY	The Home of the Pioneer Florida Museum
DANIA	The City Where Life Is Worth Living
DAYTONA BEACH	Florida's Newest Metropolitan Industrial Area
	The Ideal Year-Round Resort
	The Summer Fun Capital of the South (founded 1870)
	The World's Largest Family Resort
	The World's Most Famous Beach (23 miles long, 500

DAYTONA BEACH (Cont'd)	feet wide at low tide)
DEERFIELD BEACH	The Heart of the Gold Coast The Miracle City of the Gold Coast The Northern Gateway to Broward County
DE LAND	The Athens of Florida (home of Stetson University) The Home of Stetson University The Land of Flowers The Land of Sunshine
DESTIN	The World's Luckiest Fishing Village (fishing area for red snapper, etc.)
DUNNELLON	Home of Rainbow Springs (largest in Florida) Home of the World's Largest Bass The Kingdom of the Sun (on the Withlacoochee River)
EAU GALLIE	The Gateway to the Missile Test Center The Gateway to the Space Program The Harbour City (Indian River) The Progressive City
EDGEWATER	The City of Progress The Gateway to Nova (Nova Industrial Area) The Place in the Sun to Visit, to Play, to Work, to Live
ENGLEWOOD	The City Where Life Is Lived Every Day Of the Year Your Tropical "Home Town"
EUSTIS	The Center of Our Nation's Playground (on east shore of Lake Eustis) The Orange Capital of the World

EUSTIS (Cont'd)	The Winter and Summer Vacation Center of Florida
EVERGLADES	The Fisherman's Paradise
	The Western Water Gate (the way to 2,100 square miles of Everglades National Park)
FERNANDINA BEACH	The Buccaneer City (favorite port for pirates)
	The Ocean City (on Amelia Island)
FORT LAUDERDALE	Florida's Tropical Paradise
	The All-Year Vacation City
	The Gateway to the Everglades
	The Home Town in the American Tropics
	The Place to Go in Florida
	The Tropical Wonderland
	The Venice of America (more than 165 miles of lagoons, canals and rivers flow within its boundaries)
FORT MYERS	The City of Homes
	The City of Palms (Thomas Alva Edison advocated the planting of palms throughout the city)
	The City Where the American Tropics Begin
	The Jewel City of the Florida West
FORT MYERS BEACH	The Tropical Island Wonderland in the Gulf of Mexico (on Estero Island)
FORT PIERCE	Florida's Finest Agricultural Industrial and Resort Community
GAINESVILLE	Florida's Center for Science, Education, Medicine
	North Central Florida's Shopping Center
	North Central Florida's Shopping Headquarters

GAINESVILLE (Cont'd)	The Home of the University of Florida
	The University City (University of Florida)
HALLANDALE	The Home of the Florida Derby
HIGH SPRINGS	The Ideal Living City in the Heart of Florida
HOBE SOUND	The Gateway to the Famous Gold Coast
HOLLYWOOD	Florida's Golfingest City
	The Dream City Come True
IMMOKALEE	The Watermelon Capital
JACKSONVILLE	Florida's Gateway City
	Florida's Hub of Fun
	Jax
	The City of Pleasant Memories
	The Colorful Key Center for Defense Activities
	The Communication Center of Florida
	The Deep Water Port
	The Distribution Center of the Southeast
	The Finance Center of Florida
	The Friendly City of Endless Charm
	The Gate City of Florida (world port and commercial center)
	The Gateway City
	The Gateway to All Florida
	The Hartford of the South (numerous insurance companies)
	The Hub of Fun
	The Hub of Progress
	The Ideal Year Round Vacation Spot
	The Insurance Center of the South

JACKSONVILLE (Cont'd)	The Key National Defense Center
	The Naval Center of the South
	The Popular Vacationland
	The Tourist and Convention Center
JENSEN BEACH	The Sea Turtle Capital of the World
KEY BISCAYNE	The Island Paradise
KEY WEST	America's Singapore
	America's Southernmost City (county seat of Monroe County)
	The Cigar Capital of the World (popular in the 1870's)
	The Island City of Old World Charm
	The Nation's Southernmost City (near extreme end of Florida Keys)
LAKE PLACID	The Caladium Capital of the World (a tropical American plant of the arum family)
LAKE WALES	Florida's Attraction Showcase
	The City of the Carillon (the Bok Tower, 71 bells weighing from 12 pounds to 11 tons)
LAKE WEIR	The Year Around Living At Its Best
	The Very Center of the Sunshine State
LAKE WORTH	The City Where The Tropics Begin
	The Heart of the Palm Beaches (south of Palm Beach)
LAKELAND	Florida's Eighth City
	Polk County's Largest City
	The City of Lakes (19 lakes)
	The Heart of the Citrus Industry
	The Hub of Florida's Scenic Wonderland (19 lakes within city limits)

LAKELAND (Cont'd)	The Imperial Polk (in Polk County)
	The World's Citrus Center (about 90% of the crop is grown here)
LANTANA	The Gem on the Ocean
LARGO	The Fair City (site of the Pinellas County Fair and Horse Show)
	The Hub of Pinellas County
LEESBURG	The Community With a Heart in the Heart of Fabulous Florida
	The Watermelon Capital of Florida
MACCLENNY	North Florida's Gretna Green (numerous marriages performed by judges)
MARATHON	The Heart of the Florida Keys (second largest community in Florida Keys)
MARGATE	The City That Started With A Plan
MELBOURNE	Crossroads to the Universe
	The Mid-Way City (midway between Jacksonville and Miami, Fla.)
MIAMI	Florida's Magic City
	The Air Capital of the World
	The City of Opportunities
	The Hub of All South Florida's Sun-Fun Vacationland
	The Magic City
	The Metropolis of Southeastern Florida
	The Paradise of the South
	The Playground of the Americas
	The South Sea Isles of America
	The Tropic Metropolis
	The Wonder City of the World
	The World's Largest Import-

MIAMI (Cont'd)	Export Air Cargo Terminal
MIAMI BEACH	America's Year Round Playground
	The City Where the Palms Meet the Sea
	The Fabulous City in the Sun
	The Playground of the Americas
	The Sister City of the Sun
	The Year Round Playground of the Americas
	Vacationland, U.S.A.
MONTICELLO	The Garden Spot of Northwest Florida (county seat of Jefferson County)
NAPLES	The City on the Gulf (Gulf of Mexico)
	The Gateway to the 10,000 Islands
	The Refuge From Resorts
NEW PORT RICHEY	The Gateway to Tropical Florida
NEW SMYRNA	The World's Largest Safest Bathing Beach (on the banks of the North Indian River)
OCALA	The Heart of Florida's Fun-Land(county seat of Marion County)
OKEECHOBEE	The Chicago of the South
	The Year-Round Sportsman's Paradise (on Lake Okeechobee)
ORLANDO	Florida's City Beautiful
	The City Beautiful
	The Very Heart of Florida (largest inland city in Florida)
ORMOND BEACH	The Birthplace of Speed (automobile races began about 1902)
PALATKA	The City Where Industry and Recreation Meet
	The City Where Work and

PALATKA (Cont'd)	Play Are Only Minutes Away
	The Gem City
PALM BEACH	The Center of a Sportsman's Paradise
	The Golden Coast of Florida
	The Mecca for Champions in Many Fields
	The World's Premier Winter Resort (a 14 mile island connected by several bridges to West Palm Beach)
PANAMA CITY	The City in Beautiful Bay County (on St. Andrew Bay)
	The City on the Cool Gulf Coast (an indentation of the Gulf of Mexico)
PENSACOLA	The Annapolis of the Air
	The Birthplace of U.S. Naval Aviation (naval air training school opened 1914)
	The City of Camellias
	The City of Pleasant Living
	The Cradle of Naval Aviation
	The Garden Spot of the South
	The Gateway to Florida
	The Gulf Coast City
	The Industrial Center of West Florida
	The Metropolis of West Florida
	The Panama Port
	The Pleasant All-Year Vacation Center
	The Typical Resort City
PERRY	The Gateway to All Florida (county seat of Taylor county)
PLANT CITY	The City Most Convenient to All Florida
	The Neighborly Satisfying Community for Living
	The Winter Strawberry Capital of the World

POMPANO BEACH	The Gem of the Gold Coast The Heart of the Gold Coast The New Playground of America (between Palm Beach and Miami)
PORT ST. JOE	The City With a Future The Constitution City (where the Florida constitution was drawn up in 1839)
PUNTA GORDA	The Home of the Famous Silver King Tarpon The Sportsman's Paradise (on Charlotte Harbor)
QUINCY	The Shade-Grown Tobacco Capital
RIVIERA BEACH	The Center of the Palm Beaches (on Singer Island on the Atlantic)
RUSKIN	The Area of Opportunity The Salad Bowl of the Nation
ST. AUGUSTINE	America's Oldest City (where Juan Ponce de Leon landed on April 3, 1513) The Ancient City The Fountain of Youth City The Nation's Oldest City (continuous existence since 1565) The Oldest City in the United States (permanent white settlement 1565) The Summer and Winter Year 'Round Resort (on Matanzas Bay)
ST. PETERSBURG	One of America's Greatest Playgrounds The City of Good Living The City of Homes The City with a Million Ambassadors The Sunshine City
ST. PETERSBURG BEACH	The City on the Gulf of Mexico

SANFORD	The Celery City
	The World's Celery Center (about 20% of celery production in the United States)
SEBRING	A Good Place to Visit
	A Wonderful Place to Live
	The Golfing Capital of Florida
	The Hub of the Florida Peninsula
SILVER SPRINGS	The Home of World Famous Glass Bottom Boats
STUART	The Sailfish Capital of the World
TALLAHASSEE	The Capital City (1960 population 48,174)
	The Capital City of Fabulous Florida
	The Southland at its Best
TAMPA	Florida's Convention Center
	Florida's Gulf Coast Metropolis
	Florida's Metropolitan Distributing Center
	Florida's Year 'Round City
	The Cigar City
	The City of Diversity
	The Gateway to the Caribbean
	The Hub of the Great Orange, Grapefruit and Winter Strawberry Producing Section in the United States
	The Spanish Town
TARPON SPRINGS	The Sponge City (sponge divers)
	The Venice of the South (bordered on three sides by water, the Gulf of Mexico, the Anclote River and Lake Tarpon)
TAVARES	The City Beautiful
	The City That Has Everything for Enjoyable Living

TITUSVILLE	The Gateway to the Galaxies (rocket sites)
	The Missile City
VERO BEACH	The City of Homes
WEST PALM BEACH	First on the Fun Coast of Florida
	Florida's All-Year Resort
	The City Where Pleasure Begins
	The Metropolitan Center of Tropical Florida's First Resort Area
	Tropical Florida's First Resort
WINTER HAVEN	The Citrus Center of the World
	The City of Homes
	The City of Hundred Lakes
	City of One Hundred Lakes
	The Heart of Florida's Citrus Industry
	The Prettiest Little Town This Side of Heaven
WINTER PARK	The City of Homes
	The Town That Has Become a University (Rollins College)

GEORGIA

AIKEN	One of the Most Favorable Resorts of the South
ALBANY	The Artesian City (numerous artesian wells)
	The Trade Center of Southwest Georgia (seat of Dougherty County)
AMERICUS	Georgia's Mobile Home Center
ATHENS	The Athens You Will Want To See
	The Classic City of the South (home of the University of Georgia, opened 1801, and named for the Greek City)

ATHENS (Cont'd)	The Home of the University of Georgia
ATLANTA	The Capital City (1960 population 487,455)
	The Citadel of the Confederacy
	The City of Homes
	The Dogwood City
	The Federal City
	The Gate City
	The Gate City to the South
	The Gateway of the South
	The Hub of the Southeast
	The Insurance City
	The Manufacturing and Industrial Metropolis of the Southeast
	The Metropolis of a New South
	The New York of the South
	The Railroad City
AUGUSTA	A Wonderful Place To Live
	A Wonderful Place To Live, To Work, To Play
	Georgia's Second Oldest City
	The Battlefield of the Revolution (American Revolution)
	The Center of a Rich and Highly Diversified Agricultural Empire
	The City of Beautiful Churches
	The City of Beautiful Homes
	The Distribution Center of the Southeast
	The Friendly City
	The Garden City of the South
	The Gateway of the Southeast
	The Golf Capital of America (site of the Masters Invitation Tournament)
	The Heart of Eastern Georgia and Western South Carolina
	The Leading Resort City
	The Lowell of the South

AUGUSTA (Cont'd)	(textile manufacturing)
	The Progressive City
	The Winter Golf Capital of the World
BARNESVILLE	The Home of Gordon College
BRUNSWICK	The City of Opportunities
	The Georgia Vacationland
	The Ideal Vacationland
CEDARTOWN	The Only Cedartown in the U.S.A.
COLUMBUS	The South's Oldest Industrial City (planned 1827)
DAWSON	The Spanish Peanut Center of the World
	The World's Largest Spanish Peanut Market
DOUGLAS	The Friendly City
EAST POINT	A Community Well Planned, Well Developed, Well Equipped For Commerce, Industry and Family Life
	A Good Place to Live, to Work and to Rear Your Family
	The City of Homes and Industry
	The City Where People Are Happy and Industry Flourishes
	The City You Can Be Proud to Live and Work In
	The South's Fastest Growing City
ELBERTON	The Granite Center of the World
FITZGERALD	The Colony City (settled in 1895 by a colony of Union veterans)
	The Heart of the South Georgia Empire
FORT BENNING	The West Point of the South
FORT VALLEY	The Best Pecan Producing Area in the South

JEKYLL ISLAND	America's Year-round Holiday Island
MACON	The Friendly City in the Heart of Georgia
	The Heart of Georgia (about six miles from the geographical center)
	The Heart of the Southeast
	The South's Most Beautiful and Interesting City
MIDWAY	Georgia's Cradle of the Revolution
	The Cradle of the Revolution
NEWNAN	The City of Homes
ROME	The City of Fine Educational Institutions (Shorter College)
	The City of the Seven Hills (like Rome, Italy, built on seven hills)
	The Hub of Northwest Georgia
	The Versatile City
ST. SIMONS ISLAND	The Georgia Vacationland
	The Golden Isles of Georgia
	The Land of the Old South
SAVANNAH	America's Most Beautiful City
	The City of Historical Charm
	The Cradle of Georgia (founded Feb. 12, 1773 by James Edward Oglethorpe, English nobleman, as a colony and buffer state against the Spaniards in Florida)
	The First City of the South (settled Feb. 12, 1773 by General James Edward Oglethorpe)
	The Forest City
	The Forest City of the South
	The Garden City
	The Mother City of Georgia
SEA ISLAND	The Georgia Vacationland
	The Golden Isles of Georgia
	The Land of the Old South

THOMASVILLE	The City of Roses The Famous Winter Resort for Northern Invalids and Pleasure Seekers (used in 1895) The Key Junction to the Southeast The Original Winter Resort of the South The Rose City (rose gardens and annual rose show)
VALDOSTA	The Airways of America (near Moody Air Force Base) The Naval Stores Capitol of the World (largest inland naval stores market) The Vale of Beauty
WARM SPRINGS	The Little White House City (home of Franklin Delano Roosevelt)
WAYCROSS	The Center City of Southern Georgia The Diversified City The Gateway to Okefenokee Swamp

HAWAII

HILO	The City of Orchards The Crescent City The Orchid Capital of Hawaii
HONOLULU	The Capital City (1960 population 294,179) The Exciting City of Welcome

IDAHO

AMERICAN FALLS	The Power City (second largest artificial reservoir in the United States)
BOISE	The Capital City (1960 population 34,481)

BOISE (Cont'd)	The City of Beautiful Homes
	The City of Trees
	The Nation's Largest Basque Colony
	The Pacific Northwest's Most Progressive Community
	The Tree City
	The Western Mecca for Enjoyment Unlimited
	The Woods
BURLEY	The Best Lighted Town in the West (light, power and water obtained from the Minidoka Project)
	The Jewel of the Gem State
CALDWELL	Idaho's Farm Market
COEUR D'ALENE	The Beautiful City by a Beautiful Lake
	The City by the Lake (Lake Coeur d'Alene)
	The Famous Playground of the Wondrous Northwest
	The Heart of the Emerald Empire in the North Idaho Scenic Land
	The Only Town in the U.S. with an Apostrophe in Its Name
GOODING	The Commercial Center of Irrigated Idaho
JEROME	The Geographical Center of Magic Valley
KELLOGG	The Home of Idaho's Greatest Mines
LEWISTON	Idaho's Oldest Incorporated City
	Idaho's Only Seaport (at the confluence of the Snake and Clearwater Rivers)
	The Banana Belt City
	The First Territorial Capital (of Idaho)

LEWISTON (Cont'd)	The Seaport for the Land-locked State of Idaho
MOSCOW	The City of Homes, Churches and Fine Schools (University of Idaho)
NAMPA	The City of Expanding Industry
	The Home of the Snake River Stampede (a rodeo staged during July)
POCATELLO	The Gate City to the Great Northwest
SUN VALLEY	America's Foremost Year 'Round Sports Center
TWIN FALLS	One of America's Fastest Growing Cities (1960 population 20,126)
	The Hub of the Magic Valley (headquarters for the Sawtooth National Forest)
WENDELL	The Center of Gooding County

ILLINOIS

ALTON	The City That Came Back (Anti-abolitionist riot 1837, abolitionist Elijah P. Lovejoy killed and printing presses destroyed)
	Tusselburgh (evidently referring to above)
BLOOMINGTON	The Prairie City
BYRON	The Hudson of the West (on Rock River)
CARBONDALE	The Crossroads of the Continent (division headquarters for the Illinois Central Railroad)
CENTRALIA	The Gateway to Egypt (name applied to southern quarter of Illinois, Egyptian motifs on several buildings)
CHAMPAIGN	The Twin Cities (with Urbana, Ill.)

CHICAGO

America's No. 1 Contrary City
America's Riviera
Chi
Hogopolis
Old Chi
Pigopolis
Porkopolis
The Big Town
The Breezy Town
The City Beautiful
The City by the Lake
The City of Extremes
The City of Big Shoulders
The City of the Lakes
The City of the Lakes and Prairies
The City of Winds
The City With Two Faces
The Cornopolis
The Country's Greatest Rail Center
The Crime Capital
The Gangland
The Garden City
The Gem of the Prairies
The Host City of the Nation
The Hub of American Merchandising
The Lake City
The Leading Convention City in the Country
The Metropolis of the West
The Midland Metropolis
The Mighty Metropolis
The Nation's No. 1 Convention City
The Phoenix City
The Pork City
The Prairie
The Western Metropolis
The White City
The Windy City
The World's Railroad Capital

CHICAGO (Cont'd)	The World's Railroad Mecca
DE KALB	The Barbed Wire Capital of the World (barb wire invented and manufactured there in 1873)
DECATUR	Playtown, U.S.A.
	The Soybean Capital of the World (numerous processing mills)
	The Soybean Center
EAST MOLINE	America's Farm Implement Capital (plant of International Harvester Co.)
	The Quad Cities (with Moline, Ill., Rock Island, Ill., and Davenport, Iowa)
EFFINGHAM	The Heart of the U.S.A.
EUREKA	The Pumpkin Capital of the World
EVANSTON	The Finest New England Village in the Middle West
	The Historical City of Homes
	The Ideal Home Community
GALENA	The City Time Forgot
	The Crescent City of the Northwest
GALESBURG	The College City (Knox College)
	The World's Greatest Mule Market
HARVARD	America's Milk Center (Starline Model Dairy Farm)
JOLIET	The Pittsburgh of the West (several hundred manufacturing plants)
LOMBARD	The Lilac Town
MACOMB	The World's Largest Art Pottery City (site of the Haeger Potteries, Inc.)
MOLINE	The Farm Machinery Capitol of America
	The Plow City (John Deere began the manufacture of

MOLINE (Cont'd)	plows in 1847)
	The Quad Cities (with East Moline, Ill., Rock Island, Ill., and Davenport, Iowa)
	The Tri-Cities (with Rock Island, Ill., and Davenport, Iowa)
MOOSEHEART	The City of Childhood (children's home of Loyal Order of Moose)
NAUVOO	The City Beautiful (on the east bank of the Mississippi River)
OAK PARK	The Saints Rest (settled in 1833)
PEKIN	The Celestial City
PEORIA	Illinois' Second City (1960 population 103,162)
	The Bright Spot of America
	The Progressive City
	The Whiskey Town (site of the world's largest distillery, Hiram Walker & Sons)
PULLMAN	The City of Brick (part of Chicago)
QUINCY	The Gem City
	The Gem City in the Heart of the Great Mississippi Valley
	The Gem City of the Middle West
	The Gem City of the West
	The Model City
ROCK ISLAND	The Quad Cities (with East Moline, Ill., Moline, Ill., and Davenport, Iowa)
ROCKFORD	Illinois' Second Industrial City
	The City of Beautiful Homes
	The Crossroads of the Middle West
	The Forest City
	The Nation's Second Largest Machine-tool Center

SPRINGFIELD	A Great American Shrine (Lincoln Tomb State Memorial)
	A Progressive American City
	An Important Convention and Conference City
	Illinois' Capital City (selected 1837)
	The Capital City (1960 population 83,271)
	The City of Flowers
	The Flower City
	The Home of Abraham Lincoln
URBANA	The Twin Cities (with Champaign, Ill.)
VANDALIA	Wilderness Capital of Lincoln's Land (capital of Illinois from 1820 to 1839)

INDIANA

BEDFORD	The Stone City (the Heart of the Indiana limestone district)
BLOOMINGTON	The Gateway to Scenic Southern Indiana
BOONVILLE	The Lincoln City
BRAZIL	The Clay City (about a dozen factories making clay products from local clay)
CARROLLTON	Tailholt (featured in James Whitcomb Riley's poem "The Little Town O'Tailholt")
CRAWFORDSVILLE	The Athens of Indiana
	The Hoosier Athens (Wabash College)
DANVILLE	The Gable Town (gabled roofs)
ELKHART	The Musical Instrument Capital of the World (band instruments manufactured)
EVANSVILLE	The Air Crossroads of America

EVANSVILLE (Cont'd)	The City in the Valley of Opportunity
	The City of Opportunity
FORT WAYNE	The Gateway to the Northern Indiana Lake Region
	The Hub of the Great North-Central Industrial and Agricultural America
	The Summit City
FRANKFORT	The City Substantial
FRENCH LICK	America's Greatest Health and Pleasure Resort (mineral waters, Pluto water bottled here, luxury hotels)
	America's Sports Mecca
	The Carlsbad of America
	The Home of the Famous Pluto Mineral Springs
GARY	The Center of Industry
	The Gateway to Indiana Dunes
	The Gateway to Vast Farm and Industrial Markets
	The Magic City
	The Playground of the Dunes
	The Steel City (U.S. Steel Corp. mill)
GOSHEN	The Maple City
GREENSBURG	The Tower Tree City (the tower of the courthouse contains a growing tree)
GREENWOOD	The Town of Happy Homes
INDIANAPOLIS	America's Greatest Inland City
	The Capital City (1960 population 476,258)
	The City That Has the Resources to Fit Your Business Needs
	The Crossroads of America
	The Hoosier Capital
	The Hoosier City
	The Hub of the Nation-wide Transportation System (7 interstate highways, 6 major

INDIANAPOLIS (Cont'd)	railroads, 6 airlines, 125 truck lines)
	The Railroad City
JEFFERSONVILLE	Indiana's Gateway City (terminal of the American Commercial Barge Line)
	The Falls Cities (with New Albany, Ind., and Louisville, Ky.)
LAFAYETTE	The Star City (on the Wabash River)
LEESBURG	The Gateway of the Lake Region (Tippecanoe Lake)
LOGANSPORT	The City of Bridges (situated at the confluence of the Wabash and Eel Rivers)
MADISON	The City 'Neath the Hills (on the Ohio River)
MARION	The Queen City of the Gas Belt (gas and oil discovered in 1880's)
MARTINSVILLE	The Artesian City (artesian wells supply mineral water)
MICHIGAN CITY	The Capital of Duneland (located in the famous sand dune country at the southern end of Lake Michigan)
MIDDLETOWN	The Typical American City
MISHAWAKA	The City in the Valley of Promise
MITCHELL	The Largest Small City in Indiana (1960 population 3, 552)
MORGANTOWN	The Gateway to Brown County
MUNCIE	The Typical American City (on the White River, 1960 population 68, 603)
NEW ALBANY	The Falls Cities (with Jeffersonville, Ind., and Louisville, Ky.)
NEW HARMONY	The Athens of America (on Wabash River)
NEWCASTLE	The City of Roses

PAOLI	The Crossroads of Southern Indiana
PERU	The Circus City (winter headquarters of numerous circuses)
	The Circus City of the World
PLAINFIELD	The Friendly Folk's Village
	The Village of Friendly Folk
RICHMOND	The Quaker City of the West (founded 1806 by the Society of Friends)
ROANOKE	The Athens of Indiana (Roanoke Classical Seminary, considered ultimate in culture in 1860's)
SEYMOUR	The Crossroads of America
	The Gateway of Southern Indiana (between the White River and the Vernon Fork of the Muscatatuck)
TERRE HAUTE	The Pittsburgh of the Big West
	The Switzerland of America
	The Sycamore City
VINCENNES	The Citadel of the Old Northwest (fort erected here in 1732)
WABASH	The Rock City (Wabash River over white stones and rocks)

IOWA

ALGONA	The Friendly City
BURLINGTON	The Orchard City
	The Porkopolis of Iowa
CEDAR FALLS	The Garden City
	The Lawn City
CEDAR RAPIDS	The Metropolis of Industry
	The Parlor City
	The Rapid City (swift rapids)
DAVENPORT	The City of Beauty
	The Progressive City With the Rich Heritage and Charm

DAVENPORT (Cont'd)	of the Old River Days
	The Quad Cities (with East Moline, Moline, and Rock Island, Ill.)
	The Queen City
	The Tri-Cities (with Moline and Rock Island, Ill.)
DES MOINES	Iowa's Own City
	The Capital City (1960 population 208,982; capital in 1857)
	The Center of the Midwest and the Country (250 miles from Minneapolis and St. Paul; 140 miles from Omaha; 340 miles from Chicago; 300 miles from St. Louis and 200 miles from Kansas City)
	The City of Certainties
	The Largest Insurance Center in the West (about fifty insurance companies)
DUBUQUE	Iowa's Industrial, Scenic and Cultured City
	The City of Progress
	The Heidelberg of America (Germanic influence in architecture and schools)
	The Queen City of the Northwest
FORT DODGE	The Gypsum City (one of the largest gypsum producing centers)
IOWA CITY	The Athens of America
	The Athens of Iowa
KEOKUK	The Gate City
	The Power City (Keokum Dam drains about 120,000 square mile area)
MUSCATINE	The Pearl City (pearl button production)
SIOUX CITY	The City Where the Industrial East Meets the Agricul-

SIOUX CITY (Cont'd)	tural West
	The Home Market for the Great Northwest
	The Industrial City of Iowa
	The Livestock, Grain and Industrial Capital of the Great Northwest
	The World's Central Livestock Market

KANSAS

ABILENE	The Biggest Little City (1960 population 6,746)
	The City of the Plains (on Smoky Hill River)
	The Greyhound City (about sixty percent of America's greyhound dogs born and bred here)
ARKANSAS CITY	The Ark City (on Mississippi River)
CALDWELL	The Queen City of the Border
CEDAR VALE	The Quail Haven
COFFEYVILLE	The Cow Town (settled in 1870, formerly used)
COLBY	The Golden Buckle on the Wheat Belt (the heart of the wheat belt)
DODGE CITY	The Biggest Little City in the U.S.A. (1960 population 13,520)
	The Buckle on the Kansas Wheat Belt
	The Cowboy Capital
	The Queen City of the Cow Towns
	The Queen of the Cow Towns
	The Wickedest Little City in America
EMPORIA	The Educational Center of the West (site of Kansas State Teachers College and College

EMPORIA	of Emporia)
FORT LEAVENWORTH	The City Where The History of the West Begins (fort erected in 1827 as protection from Indians)
GREAT BEND	The Oil Capital in the Heart of the Wheat Belt (oil wells)
HUTCHINSON	The Salt City (extensive salt beds underlying the city)
KINSLEY	Half Way and a Place to Stay (between Dodge City and Great Bend)
LEAVENWORTH	The Cottonwood City
NORTON	The Pheasant Capital of Kansas
OGDEN	The Last Place on the Map
OLATHE	The Cowboy Boot Capital (boot factories)
SALINA	The Metropolis of Central and Northwest Kansas
SHAWNEE	The Gateway of Kansas
TOPEKA	The Capital City (1960 population 119,484)
VICTORIA	The Cathedral of the Plains (St. Fidelis Church)
WICHITA	One of the World's Great Airplane Manufacturing Centers (Beech, Boeing, Cessna, etc.)
	The Air Capital of America
	The Air Capital of the World
	The Cow Capital
	The Magic Mascot of the Plains
	The Peerless Princess of the Plains
WILLIAMSTOWN	Billtown

KENTUCKY

ASHLAND	The City Where Coal Meets Iron (steel mill)
CAVE CITY	The Gateway to the Mammoth Cave

CORBIN	The Hub of the Valley of Parks (near Cumberland Falls, Lake Cumberland and Levi Jackson Wilderness Road State Park)
COVINGTON	The Dixie Gateway (at confluence of Ohio and Licking rivers opposite Cincinnati, Ohio)
FRANKFORT	The Bluegrass Capital (selected in 1792)
	The Capital City (1960 population 18,365)
	The Diversified Community
	The Heart of America
	The Heart of Kentucky
	The Historic Frankfort (founded in 1786)
LEXINGTON	One of the Nation's Largest Spring Lamb Producing Centers
	One of the South's Foremost Educational Centers
	The Athens of the West (University of Kentucky)
	The Belle City of the Bluegrass Regions
	The Bluegrass Capital
	The Capital of the Bluegrass Region
	The Chief City of the Bluegrass Region
	The Dimple of the Bluegrass
	The Heart of Kentucky's Blue Grass Region (about 1,200 square miles)
	The Retail, Wholesale, Industrial, Medical Institutional Center of Kentucky
	The Thoroughbred, Standardbred and Saddle Horse Center of America

LEXINGTON (Cont'd)	The World's Largest Loose-Leaf Tobacco Market
LOUISVILLE	The City by the Falls (Ohio River)
	The City of Beautiful Churches
	The City of Homes
	The City of the Falls
	The Convention City
	The Falls Cities (with Jeffersonville and New Albany, Ind.)
	The Falls City (on the Ohio River)
	The Gateway City (on the Ohio River)
	The Gateway to the South
	The Metropolis of the New South
	The Nation's Thoroughfare
MURRAY	The Birthplace of Radio (Nathan B. Stubblefield radio pioneer)
	The Friendliest Little "Big Town" in Kentucky (1960 population 9,303)
PADUCAH	America's Newest Industrial Center
	The Capital of Western Kentucky
	The Medical Center

LOUISIANA

ALEXANDRIA	The Crossroads of Louisiana (on the Red River)
	The Hub City (center of the industrial area of the state)
	The Twin Cities on the Red River in the Heart of Louisiana (with Pineville)
BATON ROUGE	The Capital City (1960 population 152,419)
BOGALUSA	The Magic City of the Green Empire (founded 1906)

BREAUX BRIDGE	The Crawfish Capital of the World
CROWLEY	The Rice Capital of Louisiana
	The Rice Capital of the World
	The Rice Center of America
	The Rice City of America
FORT JESSUP	The Cradle of the Mexican War (troops from the fort were sent to Texas during the Revolution from Mexico)
HAMMOND	The Strawberry Capital of America
INDEPENDENCE	Little Italy
LAFAYETTE	The Azalea Trail City
	The City in the Heart of South Central Louisiana (on the Vermilion River)
LAKE CHARLES	The Rice Capital of Louisiana
	The Sea Gate to the Southwest (on the Calcasieu River, 37 miles from the Gulf of Mexico)
MONROE	The Twin Cities (with West Monroe)
	The Twin Cities of the Ouachita (with West Monroe)
NATCHITOCHES	The Up-to-Date Oldest Town in Louisiana (French trading post established in 1714)
NEW IBERIA	The Queen City of the Teche (a stream flowing into the Atchafalaya Bayou)
NEW ORLEANS	America's Most Interesting City
	The Air Hub of the Americas
	The Alexandria of America
	The City Care Forgot
	The City of Charm
	The City of Contrasts
	The Crawfish Town
	The Crescent City (it curves around the Mississippi)
	The Gateway to the World
	The Great South Gate (en-

NEW ORLEANS (Cont'd)
trance to the Gulf of Mexico)
The Gulf City (on the Gulf of Mexico)
The Hub of the Americas
The Key of the Great Valley
The Old French Town
The Paris of America
The Queen of the South
The South's Greatest City (founded in 1718; 1960 population 627,525)
The Winter Capital of America

PINEVILLE
The Crossroads of Louisiana
The Twin Cities on the Red River in the Heart of Louisiana (with Alexandria)

RAYNE
The Frog Market of the Nation

ST. FRANCISVILLE
The Town Two Miles Long and Two Yards Wide (1960 population 1,661)

SHREVEPORT
The Capital City of the Land of Ark-La-Tex
The New City in the Old South (incorporated 1839)
The Pivot City of the Central South
The Pivot City of the South
The Queen City of the Ark-La-Tex Area

WEST MONROE
The Twin Cities (with Monroe, La.)
The Twin Cities of the Ouachita (with Monroe, La.)

MAINE

AUBURN
The City of Homes
The Industrial Heart of Maine
The Shoe City (about 15 shoe factories)
The Twin Cities (with Lewiston)

AUGUSTA
The Capital City (1960 population 21,680)

BANGOR	The Greatest Lumber Market in the World (not claimed now)
	The Lumber City
	The Metropolis of the Northeast
	The Queen City (1960 population 38,912)
	The Queen City of the East
	The Twin Cities (with Brewer; Bangor on the east bank, Brewer on the west bank of the Penobscot River)
BAR HARBOR	Maine's Most Famous Coast Resort (on Mount Desert Island, on Frenchman Bay)
BATH	The Shipping City (on the Kennebec River, claims to have launched more ships than any other place in the world)
BELFAST	The Broiler Capital of Maine
	The Shire City of Waldo County
BETHEL	The Gateway to Maine from the White Mountains
	The Ideal Place in Which to Live, Work and Play (in the Rangeley Lake area, on the Androscoggin River)
BIDDEFORD	The City Where Life Is Different
	The Gateway to Maine (on the Saco River)
	The Nation's Best Recreational Area - Four Season Fun
	The Twin Cities (with Saco, Me., opposite sides of the Saco River)
BINGHAM	The City Where Historic Yesterday Greets Dynamic Tomorrow
BREWER	The Twin Cities (with Bangor, Me., opposite sides of the

BREWER (Cont'd)	Penobscot River)
BRIDGTON	The Vacation Fun Spot of Western Maine (12 lakes in the town)
CALAIS	The International City (International Bridge to St. Stephens, New Brunswick, Canada)
CAMDEN	The City Where the Mountains Meet the Sea (on Penobscot Bay)
DAMARISCOTTA	The Twin Villages (with Newcastle; Damariscotta on the east bank of the Damariscotta River opposite Newcastle)
ELLSWORTH	The City at the Crossroads Down East
FARMINGTON	The Gateway to Rangeley and Sugarloaf
	The Gateway to the Rangeley Lakes
FORT KENT	The Gateway to Canada's St. Lawrence Seaway (at the junction of the Fish and St. John River)
	The Gateway to the Allagash Country
	The Gateway to the Fish River Chain of Lakes
FREEPORT	The Birthplace of Maine (where the commissioners of the District of Maine and the Commonwealth of Massachusetts signed an agreement for the separation)
FRYEBURG	The Friendly Prosperous Town
	The Place for Vacations Year 'Round and for Year 'Round Living
HOULTON	The Garden of Maine (Aroostook County agricultural center)

JACKMAN	The Gateway to Real Vacation Pleasure
	The Switzerland of Maine
KINGFIELD	The Little City in the Woods
KITTERY	The Gateway to Maine
LAKEWOOD	The Broadway Colony in the Heart of Maine (Lakewood Playhouse and Summer colony)
LEWISTON	The Industrial Heart of Maine
	The Spindle City (largest textile manufacturing center in Maine; the home of Bates Manufacturing Co.)
	The Twin Cities (with Auburn, Me.)
MONHEGAN	The Fortunate Island (in Knox County, island in the Atlantic Ocean)
MOSCOW	The City Where Historic Yesterday Greets Dynamic Tomorrow
MOUNT KATAHDIN	America's Alarm City
NEWCASTLE	The Twin Villages (on the west bank of the Damariscotta River opposite Damariscotta on the east bank)
NORWAY	Maine's Fastest Growing Industrial and Recreational Area
	The Fastest Growing Community in Maine
OGUNQUIT	The Beautiful Place by the Sea (scenic three-mile beach whose Indian name means "beautiful place by the sea")
OLD ORCHARD BEACH	The All-Round Playground (seashore resort)
	The Cleanest Beach in the World
	The Finest Beach in the World (700 feet wide at low tide)
	The Playground of Vacationland
OLD TOWN	The Canoe City (industrial

OLD TOWN (Cont'd)	city on the Penobscot River where world-famed canoes are manufactured)
PARIS	Maine's Fastest Growing Industrial and Recreational Area
	The City on the Hill
	The Fastest Growing Community in Maine (1960 population 3,601)
PATTEN	The Northern Gateway to the Natural Paradise Baxter Park
	The Unspoiled Beauty Spot of Northern Maine
PITTSFIELD	The Center of Progress in Maine (on the Sebasticook River)
PORTLAND	America's Sunrise Gateway
	The Beautiful City by the Sea
	The Beautiful Town That Is Seated by the Sea
	The Forest City
	The Hill City
	The Vacation City on Casco Bay
SACO	The City Where Life Is Different
	The Gateway to Maine (on the Saco River)
	The Twin Cities (with Biddeford)
SANFORD	The Up and Coming City (in York County, 1960 population 10,936)
SEARSPORT	The Fastest Growing Deep Water Seaport in Maine (Penobscot Bay)
	The Home of Old Sea Captains
	The Home of World Famous Sea Captains

SKOWHEGAN	The Friendliest Town in New England (on the Kennebec River, 1960 population 6,667)
SOUTH BERWICK	The Parish of Unity
WATERVILLE	The Elm City
WELLS	One of New England's Most Famous Coast Resorts
WISCASSET	The Modern Town Rich in History (historic homes built in the 1790's and early 1800's)
YARMOUTH	The Coastal Town of Charm and Beauty (on Casco Bay)

MARYLAND

ANNAPOLIS	Crabtown (crab fishing)
	The Ancient City (Capital of Maryland in 1694)
	The Capital City (1960 population 23,385)
	The City Where Land and Water Meet
	The Crabtown-on-the-Bay (crab fishing)
	The Gateway to the South
	The Heart of Maryland
	The Modern City With a Colonial Setting
	The Venice of America (many creeks and streams)
BALTIMORE	Maryland's Largest City (1960 population 939,024)
	The Convention City
	The Mobtown (lawless element which prevailed particularly during the Civil War)
	The Monumental City
	The National Anthem City (where the Star Spangled Banner was written)

CRISFIELD	The Seafood Capital of the World (on Tangier Sound, part of Chesapeake Bay)
CUMBERLAND	The Heart of the Potomac Highlands (eastern end of Georges Creek)
	The Queen City
EASTON	The Colonial Capital of the Eastern Shore (unofficial)
ELKTON	Gretna Green
	Gretna Green of Maryland
	Head of Elk

MASSACHUSETTS

AMESBURY	The Carriage Center of the World
ASHFIELD	The Little Switzerland
BEVERLY	The Birthplace of the American Navy (the schooner "Hannah" was armed, outfitted and commissioned by George Washington in 1775 as the first ship of the American Navy)
	The Garden City
	The Heart of the Famous North Shore (on the Atlantic Ocean)
BOSTON	Beantown
	Bostonia
	The American Athens
	The Athens
	The Athens of America
	The Athens of the New World
	The Athens of the United States
	The Athens of the West
	The Bay Horse
	The Bitches' Heaven
	The Capital City (1960 population 697,197)
	The Capital of New England

BOSTON (Cont'd)	The City of Baked Beans The City of Bean Eaters The City of Firsts The City of Kind Hearts The City of Notions The Classic City The Home of Baked Beans The Hub The Hub of New England The Hub of the Solar System (so called by Oliver Wendell Holmes) The Hub of the Universe The Hub Town The Literary Emporium The Metropolis of New England The Modern Athens The Mother City of America The Panhandler's Heaven The Puritan City The Trimountain City Tremont
BRAINTREE	The Future Industrial Capital of the South Shore
BROCKTON	The City of Shoes (shoe products)
BROOKLINE	The Richest Town in the World The Town of Millionaires (a residential suburb of Boston)
CAMBRIDGE	The Center of History, Education and Industry The Geographical Center of the Metropolitan Boston Area The Outstanding American City The University City (Harvard University, Radcliffe College, Massachusetts Institute of Technology, etc.)

CHATHAM	The First Stop of the East Wind (on Cape Cod)
	The Town Where Summer is Air-Conditioned (Atlantic Ocean on one side, Nantucket Sound on the other)
CHELSEA	The City of Transformations
CHICOPEE	The Future Minded City (1960 population 61,553)
CONCORD	The Cradle of Liberty (battle fought April 19, 1775)
	The Golden Age Haven
DEDHAM	The Sober-Minded (settled in 1636)
EVERETT	The Industrial Half-Sister
FALL RIVER	The Border City
	The City of Falling Water
	The Scholarship City (numerous scholarships offered)
	The Spindle City (cotton and textile mills)
FRAMINGHAM	The Diversified Manufacturing Community
GREENFIELD	The Dream-town
	The Well-balanced Community
HOLYOKE	The City of Diversified Industries
	The Industrial City
	The Paper City (better-grade writing paper produced)
LEXINGTON	The Birthplace of American Liberty
	The Cradle of Liberty (Minute Men resisted British troops, April 19, 1775)
LOWELL	The City of Magic
	The City of Spindles
	The Manchester of America (Manchester, England, cotton manufacturing city)
	The Modern American Athens (Lowell Technical Institute)

LOWELL (Cont'd)	The Spindle City (cotton and woolen mills)
LYNN	The City of Shoes
	The Machine City
	The Shoe City (manufacturing began 1635)
MALDEN	The Ideal City
MARBLEHEAD	The City Where Tradition Lingers
	The Greatest Town for fishing in New England (seacoast on Massachusetts Bay and Atlantic Ocean)
MARTHAS VINEYARD	One Hundred Square Miles of Picturesque Pleasure
	The Friendly Island (in Atlantic Ocean)
NANTUCKET	The Far Away Island (30 miles off the Massachusetts coast in the Atlantic Ocean)
	The Far Away Land (30 miles off the mainland in the Atlantic Ocean)
NEW BEDFORD	The Whaling City (at one time the greatest whaling port in the world)
NEWBURYPORT	The City of Captains' Houses
	The City of Industry
	The Yankee City
NEWTON	The Commuter's Haven (a suburb of Boston, Mass.)
	The Garden City
	The Tin Horn Village
NORTHAMPTON	The Heart of the Pioneer Valley
	The Meadow City
NORTON	The Typical New England City
ORANGE	The Home of Minute Tapioca
	The Sport Parachuting Center of the United States of America
PITTSFIELD	The Heart of the Berkshires (on the Housatonic River)

PLAINVILLE	The World's Largest Specialty Jewelry Manufacturing Center
PLYMOUTH	America's Home Town
	The First Town of America (December 1620, Pilgrims made first permanent settlement north of Virginia)
	The Land of the Pilgrims, Sun and Sand
	The Nation's Birthplace
PROVINCETOWN	The Tip of Cape Cod (projects into Cape Cod Bay and Atlantic Ocean, first landing place of Pilgrims, Nov. 11, 1920)
QUINCY	The Birthplace of Liberty
	The City of Presidents
	The Granite City
ROCKPORT	The City at the Tip of Cape Ann
SALEM	New England's Treasure House
	The Center of the Beautiful North Shore of Massachusetts
	The City of Peace
	The City of Witches (famous witchcraft trials in colonial days about 1692)
	The Most Historic City in the East
	The Paradise of New England
	The Witch City
	The Witchcraft City
SANDWICH	The Home of Sandwich Glass (manufactured from 1825 to 1887)
SCITUATE	The Vacation or Year Round Home City (on the Atlantic Ocean)
SOMERVILLE	The City of Hills
	The City of Homes

SOUTHBRIDGE	The Heart of New England
SPRINGFIELD	A Host Without Parallel
	One of the Most Accessible Cities in the Eastern States
	The Best Convention Point in the East
	The City of Homes
	The Crossroads of New England
	The Home of More Than 4,000 Commercial Travelers
	The Metropolis of Western Massachusetts
TAUNTON	The Cradle of American Liberty (A Liberty Pole was erected October 1774)
	The Largest City For Its Size (1960 population 41,132)
WALTHAM	The City of Five-Score Industries
WELLESLEY	The Town of Schools--And A College (Wellesley College for women, Babson Institute for men)
WESTFIELD	The Whip City (manufacturers of whips)
WEYMOUTH	An Aggregate of Villages
WILLIAMSTOWN	The Village Beautiful
WINCHENDON	The Toy Town (manufacturing center)
WOBURN	The Home of a Yankee Count
WOODS HOLE	America's Naples (on the southwestern tip of Cape Cod)
WORCESTER	The City of Prosperity
	The Faithful City
	The Heart of the Bay State
	The Heart of the Commonwealth

MICHIGAN

ADRIAN	The Maple City of Michigan (shade trees)

BATTLE CREEK	The Best Known City in the World (1960 population 44,169)
	The Best Known City of Its Size in the World (1960 population 44,169)
	The Breakfast Food City
	The Cereal Food Center of the World
	The Health City
	The Health Food City
BELDING	The Land of Chief Wabasis
BELLAIRE	America's "Bit O' Ireland" in County O' Antrim
BENTON HARBOR	Michigan's Most Famous Summer Resort
	The Heart of the Fruit Belt
	The Twin-Cities (with St. Joseph)
BLANEY PARK	The Playground of Paul Bunyon (Bunyon Museum)
BRONSON	The City the Depression Passed Up
CADILLAC	The Friendliest Area in Northern Lower Michigan
DEARBORN	Michigan's Dynamic City
	Michigan's Fastest Growing City
	Michigan's Fastest Growing Community
	The City of Advantages
DETROIT	Detroit the Beautiful
	Dynamic Detroit
	Fordtown (Ford Motor Company)
	The Auto City
	The Automobile Capital of the World
	The Automobile City
	The Automobile City of the World
	The City of Straits
	The City of the Straits

DETROIT (Cont'd)	The City of Twentieth Century America
	The Dynamic City
	The Most Beautiful City
	The Motor Capital of the World
	The Motor City
	The Overgrown Small Town
EATON RAPIDS	The Wool City
ELK RAPIDS	The City for a Vacation of a Lifetime
	The Entrance to the Chain-O-Lakes
FLINT	The Vehicle City (largest General Motors plant)
FRANKFORT	The Gateway to the Proposed Sleeping Bear National Park
GLADSTONE	The All Year Round Vacation Center
GRAND RAPIDS	The City in the Heart of 250 Sparkling Lakes and Streams
	The Furniture Capital of America
	The Furniture City
	The Gateway to the Water Wonderland
HAMTRAMCK	The Polish City (Polish community, a part of Detroit)
HOLLAND	The Clean, Colorful Tulip City on Scenic Lake Macatawa
	The Dutch City (settled in 1847 by the Dutch)
	The Tulip Center of America
	The Tulip City
HONOR	The Gateway to Sleeping Bear Dunes
HOUGHTON	America's First Mining Capital (site of Michigan College of Mining)
IRONWOOD	The Center of the Gogebic Iron Range (open pits and underground mines)

JACKSON	Jacksonopolis
	The Home of Illuminated Cascades (about 500 acres outside the city limits, illuminated cascades, winding canals and lagoons)
	The Prison City
	The Rose City
KALAMAZOO	The Celery City
LAKE CITY	The Center of a Marvelous Natural Playground
LANSING	The Capital City (1960 population 107,807)
MACKINAC ISLAND	The Summer Wonderland (state park, resort)
MACKINAW CITY	The Gateway to Mackinac Island and the Upper Peninsula of Michigan
MANISTEE	The Salt City (salt deposits)
MARQUETTE	The Queen City of Lake Superior
	The Queen City of the Northland
MEARS	The Gateway to the Sand Dune Mountains
MESICK	The Mushroom Capital
MORLEY	The Gateway to the Water Wonderland
MOUNT CLEMENS	America's Bath City (famous mineral springs)
MUNISING	The Gateway to Pictured Rocks (37 miles of cliffs and odd formations about 5 miles northeast)
	The Naples of America
MUSKEGON	The Gambling Queen
	The Lumber City of the World
	The Lumber Queen
	The Lumber Queen of the World
	The Red Light Queen
	The Saloon Queen
NEWAYGO	America's Little Switzerland

ROCKFORD	The Biggest Little City in Michigan (1960 population 2,074)
ROYAL OAK	The City of Homes (suburb of Detroit)
	The Gateway to Eastern Michigan
SAGINAW	The City of Opportunities
ST. JOSEPH	The Twin Cities (with Benton Harbor, Mich.)
SAULT STE. MARIE	Soo (Soo Locks, St. Mary's Falls Ship Canal)
	The Gateway of Lake Superior
SUTTONS BAY	The Alpine Village
TRAVERSE CITY	The Cherry Capital of the World
	The Cherry City
WHITE CLOUD	The City Where the North Begins and the Pure Waters Flow
WHITE ROCK	Michigan's Most Renowned Phantom City
WHITEHALL	The City For Every Vacation Pleasure

MINNESOTA

AITKIN	The Turkey Capital
AURORA	The City Down on the Mesabi (on eastern edge of the Mesabi iron range)
BARNUM	An Arrowhead Egg Basket (poultry raising industry)
BEAVER BAY	A North Shore Haven (at the mouth of the Beaver River)
BENA	The City Where the Partridge Finds a Refuge
BLACKDUCK	The Hunter's Rendezvous (on Blackduck Lake)
BRAINERD	Paul Bunyon's Capital (27-foot animated Bunyon statue)

BRAINERD (Cont'd)	The Capital of the Paul Bunyon Playground
	The Hub City
BUHL	The Springs of Health and Pits of Wealth (open pit mines)
CARLTON	The Birthplace of the Northern Pacific (where the first spike was driven)
CASS LAKE	The Capital of the Chippewa Nation (Indian tribe)
	The Permanent Home of the Pine
CLOQUET	The Modern Phoenix (built on the ashes of an earlier town)
COLERAINE	The Model Village (1960 population 1, 346)
COOK	The Home of the Christmas Tree Industry
CROSBY	The Cuyuna Capital (eastern end of the Cuyuna iron range)
DULUTH	The Air-Conditioned City
	The Air-Conditioned Duluth
	The Center of the Universe (1960 population 106,884)
	The City of Destiny
	The City Where the Prairie Meets the Sea (Lake Superior)
	The Coolest Summer City
	The Hay Fever Relief Haven of America
	The Metropolis of the Unsalted Seas
	The Old Maid City, Looking Under Her Bed Every Night for an Ocean
	The Popular Convention City
	The Recreational, Industrial City
	The Summer City
	The Year 'Round Playground
	The Zenith City

DULUTH (Cont'd)	The Zenith City of the Unsalted Seas
ELY	The Capital of the Vermilion Range (Vermilion iron range)
	The Gate to the Sportsman's Eden
	The Gateway to the Sportsman's Eden
EVELETH	The Hill Top City (altitude 1,574 feet)
	The Hockey Capital of the Nation
FARIBAULT	The Athens of the Northwest
	The Peony Center of the World (won peony prize at the Century of Progress Exposition 1933)
FERGUS FALLS	The City Beautiful in the Land O'Lakes
GILBERT	The Village of Destiny
GRAND MARAIS	The Place Where Lake Meets Forest (on Lake Superior)
GRAND PORTAGE	The Gateway to Isle Royale National Park
	The Oldest Settlement in Minnesota (central depot of the Northwest Company in 1792)
HIBBING	America's Iron Capital
	America's Mining Capital
	The Iron Ore Capital of the World (1960 population 17,731)
	The Richest Village on Earth
	The Town That Moved Overnight
HOVLAND	The Lake Trout Capital
INTERNATIONAL FALLS	The Trail's End (across the Rainy River from Fort Frances, Ontario, Canada)
MINNEAPOLIS	Milltown
	The City of Lakes

MINNEAPOLIS (Cont'd)	The Dual Cities (with St. Paul)
	The Flour City (extensive milling)
	The Gateway City
	The Sawdust City
	The Twin Cities (with St. Paul)
	The Twin City (with St.Paul)
	The Twins (with St. Paul)
MOOSE LAKE	The Southern Gateway (between Superior and St. Paul)
MOUNTAIN LAKE	The Birthplace of the Mesabi
NORTHFIELD	America's Holstein Capital
	The City of Cows, Colleges and Contentment (St. Olaf and Carleton College)
	The Holstein Capital of America
OWATONNA	The Butter Capital of the World
	The Typical American City
PROCTOR	The Hub
REDWOOD FALLS	The Scenic City of Southern Minnesota
ST. CLOUD	The Granite City (first quarry opened 1868)
ST. PAUL	Pig's Eye
	The Boston of the West
	The Capital City (1960 population 313,411)
	The City in the Land of Lakes
	The Dual Cities (with Minneapolis)
	The Gateway to the Northwest
	The Gem City
	The North Star City
	The Saintly City
	The Twin Cities (with Minneapolis)
	The Twin City (with Minneapolis)

ST. PAUL (Cont'd)	The Twins (with Minneapolis) The Winter Sport Capital of the Nation
VIRGINIA	The Queen City of the Iron Range The Queen City of the Range
WALKER	The Vacationer's Paradise (in the Chippewa National Forest)
WINONA	The Gate City (on Mississippi River)
WORTHINGTON	The Turkey Capital of Minnesota The Turkey Capital of the World

MISSISSIPPI

BILOXI	America's Riviera (27 mile sand beach) Heart of the Fabulous Gulf Coast Country Mississippi's Great Resort and Historic Center Nation's Seafood Center The Oldest French City in the United States The Year 'Round Resort and Convention Center
BROOKHAVEN	The Homeseeker's Paradise The Hospitality Capital of the New South The Industrial Paradise The Perfect Place for Growing Up
CANTON	The Historic Town of the Old South--Now a Progressive City
CLARKSDALE	The Golden Buckle on the Cotton Belt
COLUMBUS	The City Where Industrial and Agricultural Activities Are Blended With Dairying

COLUMBUS (Cont'd)	and Livestock Production
	The Friendly City
	The Town With The Most to Offer Industry
CORINTH	The City That Smiles Back
	The City Where Dixie Welcomes You
GREENVILLE	Mississippi's Largest River Port
	One of Mississippi's Fastest Growing Cities
	The Metropolis of the Mississippi Delta
GRENADA	The Heart of North Mississippi and Beautiful Grenada Lake
GULFPORT	America's Riviera (on Gulf of Mexico)
	The All Year Playground of the Old South
	The Hospitality City
JACKSON	A City of Rich Cultural and Residential Charm
	One of the Fastest Growing Cities in the Nation
	One of the South's Fastest Growing Cities
	The Agricultural Capital
	The Balanced Community of Opportunity and Happy Homes
	The Capital City (1960 population 144,422)
	The Capital of America's State of Opportunity
	The Center of Commerce and Agriculture
	The Center of Year 'Round Recreation
	The City of Fine Homes, Churches, and Schools
	The City Where a New South is in the Making

JACKSON (Cont'd)	The City Where the Old South and the New South Meet
	The Crossroads of the Old and the New South
	The Crossroads of the South
	The Educational Capital
	The Friendly City
	The Industrial Capital
	The Oil Capital
	The Oil Center for Mississippi
	The Vivid Capital of the Old South
LAUREL	Magnolia's Largest Industrial City
	Mississippi's Industrial City (canning, sweet potato, starch manufacturing, masonite)
	The Chemurgic City (pine lumber converted into masonite)
	The Magnolia's State Industrial City
	The Oil Capital of Mississippi
MC COMB	The Charm Circle of the South
	The City of Camellias
MERIDIAN	The Heart of the New South
NATCHEZ	The Bluff City (alluvial bluffs overlooking the Mississippi River)
	The City Where the Charm, Culture and Traditions of the Old South Blend in a Modern City
	The City Where the Old South Still Lives
	The Historic City of America (explored in 1682 by La Salle)

TUPELO — Mississippi's Best Example of the New South
Mississippi's Finest Example of the New South
The City Without City Limits
The Community Working Together for the Future
The First TVA City (first contract with the Tennessee Valley Authority to purchase electricity signed November 11, 1933)
The Former Capital of the Chickasaw Nation

VICKSBURG — The Gibraltar of America (on the Mississippi River, reputed to have been an impregnable fortification in the War of Secession, fell July 4, 1863 after seige of one year)
The Gibraltar of Louisiana
The Gibraltar of the Confederacy
The Gibraltar of the South
The Hill City (206 feet altitude)
The Key City

WEST POINT — The Point of Opportunity

YAZOO CITY — Mississippi's Thriving Industrial Center
The Gateway to the Delta (low flat on the Yazoo River)
The Oil Capital of Mississippi

MISSOURI

AURORA — The Tri-County Trading Center

BOLIVAR — The Largest Shopping Center in the Pomme de Terre Area

BUTLER — The West Gate to the Land-O-Lakes

CARTHAGE	The City at the Crossroads of Mid-America
	The Home of World Famous Carthage Marble
	The Ideal Place to Stay or Play
	The Pure Bred Jersey Capital of America
CASSVILLE	The City of Seven Valleys
	The Hub of the Scenic Ozarks (near Roaring River State Park)
	The Once Confederate Capital of America (1861)
COLUMBIA	The Athens of the Midwest (home of the University of Missouri)
CRANE	The Home of 'Old Hickory' Ham and Bacon
DE SOTO	The Fountain City (numerous artesian wells)
EL DORADO SPRINGS	The Land of Lakes Shopping Center
ELDON	The Gateway to Lake of the Ozarks (12 miles from Bagnell Dam)
FAYETTE	The Mother of Counties (organized January 13, 1816 from which 46 counties were formed, 36 in Missouri and 10 in Iowa)
FORSYTH	The Twin Lakes Capital of the Ozarks (Lake Tancycomo and Bull Shoals Lake)
GREENFIELD	The Headwaters of Stockton Lake
HANNIBAL	The Bluff City (Cardiff Hill and Lovers' Leap)
	The Boyhood Home of Mark Twain
	The Capital of Youth (Tom and Huck monument, Mark Twain's characters)

HANNIBAL (Cont'd)	The St. Petersburg of Tom Sawyer
INDEPENDENCE	The City Where the West Begins (starting place in 1849 of Santa Fe and Oregon Trails)
	The Gateway to the West
	The Queen City of the Trails
JEFFERSON CITY	Jeff City (named for Thomas Jefferson)
	The Capital City (1960 population 28,228)
	The Convention City
JOPLIN	The Crossroads of America
	The Town That "Jack" Built
KANSAS CITY	The City of the Future
	The Gateway to the West and the Southwest
	The Greatest Primary Winter Wheat Market
	The Heart of America
	The Heart of the United States of America
	The Home of the Athletics (baseball team)
	The Metropolis of the Missouri Valley
	The Mushroomopolis
	The Nation's Largest Winter Wheat Market
	The Overgrown Cow Town
	The Steak Center of the Nation (Kansas City Livestock Exchange and Stockyards)
KNOB NOSTER	The Gateway to the Whiteman Air Force Base
LAMAR	The Birthplace of Harry S. Truman
LINCOLN	Benton County's Fastest Growing City
MARCELINE	The Magic City

MARSHALL	The Center of a Lively Industrial and Agricultural Trade Area
	The City Beautiful
	The City With a Great Potential for Growth
	The Mother of the West
MEXICO	The Capital of Little Dixie
	The Fireclay Capital (manufactures clay products)
	The Fireclay Capital of the World
	The Saddle Horse Capital of the World
	The World's Saddle Horse Capital
MOBERLY	The Magic City
MONETT	The Big "M" of the Ozarks
	The Gateway to Outdoor Fishing and Hunting Activities
NEOSHO	The City of Springs
	The Flowerbox City
NEVADA	The Bushwacker's Capital (headquarters of several Confederate detachments in the War of Secession)
NOEL	The Christmas City
OSCEOLA	A Key Spot in the Future of Kaysinger Reservoir
PIERCE CITY	A Diversified Agricultural and Industrial Community
ST. CHARLES	The First Capital of Missouri (1821-1826)
	The Last Outpost of Civilization
ST. JOSEPH	The City Worth While
ST. LOUIS	America's Great Central Market and Tourist City
	America's Shoe Capital
	Paincourt
	The City of a Thousand Sights

ST. LOUIS (Cont'd)	The City of Culture and Entertainment
	The City of Learning
	The City of the French
	The Convention City
	The Family City
	The Future Great City of the World
	The Gateway Arch City
	The Gateway of the West
	The Gateway to the West
	The Great River City (on the Mississippi River)
	The Holiday City
	The Home of the World's Largest Brewery (Anheuser-Busch Brewery)
	The Hub of American Inland Navigation
	The Hub of the New High-Speed Interstate Highway System
	The Largest Metropolis in the Mississippi Valley
	The Memphis of the American Nile
	The Mound City
	The Parking Lot City
	The Pride of the Mississippi Valley
	The Queen City of the Mississippi
	The Showboat City
	The Solid City
	The Vacation City
	The Vatican City
SEDALIA	The Gateway to the Land O'Lakes
SENECA	The Northeastern Gateway to the Grand Lake Resort Area
SOUTH WEST CITY	The Busy Agricultural Community

SPRINGFIELD	The Gateway to Four Ozark Vacation Areas
	The Queen City of the Ozarks
STOCKTON	The Best Town in the State by a Damsite
TRENTON	The City With a Future
WINDSOR	The North Gateway to the Kaysinger Dam and Reservoir Area

MONTANA

ANACONDA	The City On The Top of the Rockies
	The Home of the Largest Copper Producing Smelter and Smokestack in the World (585 feet, Anaconda Mining Co.)
	The St. Moritz of the Rockies (winter sport resort)
	The Smelter City (one of the largest non-ferrous producing plants)
BILLINGS	A Great Intermountain Transportation Center
	America's Ideal Vacation Land
	Montana's Only Billion Dollar Market
	The Capital of the Midland Empire
	The City In the Heart of the Nation's Famous Dude Ranch Country
	The City in the Mountain Country
	The Civics Center of the Midland Empire
	The Commercial Center of the Midland Empire
	The Gateway to America's Wonderland

BILLINGS (Cont'd)	The Gateway to the West (on the west bank of the Yellowstone River)
	The Land of Shining Mountains
	The Magic City
	The Midland Empire City
	The Queen City of the Midland Empire
	The Silver Dollar City
BROADUS	The Biggest Little Town in the West (1960 population 628)
BUTTE	Heart of Montana's Magicland
	One of America's Most Unique Cities
	One of the Most Colorful Cities in America
	The Black Heart of Montana
	The Center of Montana's Wonderland
	The Copper City (numerous large copper mines)
	The Only Electric Lit Cemetery in the United States
	The Richest Hill on Earth (one of the world's greatest mining cities)
CUT BANK	Montana's Friendly Community
EUREKA	The Christmas Tree Capital of the World
FORSYTH	The City of Trees
GLENDIVE	The City with a Future to Share
	The Gateway to the Historic Northwest (seat of Dawson County)
GREAT FALLS	Montana's Largest and Friendliest City (55,357 population in 1960)

GREAT FALLS (Cont'd)	The Electric City (hydro-electric power plant on the Missouri River)
	The Niagara of the West (hydro electric plants on the Great Falls of the Missouri)
HELENA	The Capital City (20, 227 population in 1960)
	The Queen of the Mountains
JORDAN	The Lonesomest Town in the World (1960 population 557)
KALISPELL	The Center of a Land of Enchantment (the Swan Range on the east, the Whitefish Range to the north)
MISSOULA	The Garden City
SIDNEY	The Heart of the Yellowstone Valley

NEBRASKA

ALLIANCE	The Cattle Capital of Nebraska
BOYS TOWN	The City of Little Men (home for destitute boys)
FREMONT	A Good Place to Live, Work and Play
	The City Where Agriculture and Industry Meet
GOTHENBURG	The City in the Heart of the Irrigated Platte Valley
GRAND ISLAND	Nebraska's Third City
	A Good Place to Work and Live
	The Progressive City
HASTINGS	The City of Liquid Gold (abundant water supply)
	The Crossroads of the Nation
	The Fastest Growing City in the State
LINCOLN	The Capital City (1960 population 128, 521)

LINCOLN (Cont'd)	The City Worthy of a Noble Name
	The Hartford of the West (insurance companies)
	The Holy City
	The Lilac City
	The Loveliest Modern City in Mid-America
Mc COOK	The Center of a Fisherman's Paradise
	The Retail Center of Southwest Nebraska and Northeast Kansas
NEBRASKA CITY	The Town That Gave the World A Great Idea (Arbor Day)
NORFOLK	The Host City (Northeast Nebraska)
NORTH PLATTE	The Home of Buffalo Bill
OMAHA	The City of Recreation and Culture
	The Crossroads of the Nation
	The Gate City of the West
YORK	The City Where There Are No Strangers--Just New Friends

NEVADA

BEATTY	The Chicago of Nevada
	The Gateway to Death Valley
BOULDER CITY	The Gateway to the Lake Mead Recreational Area
CARSON CITY	The Capital City (territorial capital in 1861, state capital 1864)
	The Gateway to Lake Tahoe and Yosemite Valley
	The Smallest Capital in America (5,163 population in 1960)
ELKO	The Metropolis of Eastern Nevada (1960 population 6,298)

GENOA	The Oldest Town in Nevada (settled in 1845 by Mormon emigrants)
LAKE TAHOE	(see also Lake Tahoe, Calif.)
LAS VEGAS	The All-Season Convention-Vacation Location
	The Booming Convention City
	The Broadway of the Desert (lighted main street)
	The City of Destiny
	The City That Has Everything for Everyone--Anytime
	The City That Is Still a Frontier Town (used 1939)
	The City Without Clocks (book by Ed Reid)
	The Green Felt Jungle (book by Ed Reid and Ovid Demaris)
	The Metropolis of Southern Nevada
	The Town Blessed By An Ideal Year-Round Climate
	The Year-Round Center for Major Spectator Events
RENO	The Biggest Little City in the World (51,470 population in 1960)
VIRGINIA CITY	The City of Illusion (novel by Vardis Fisher)
	The City That Saved the Union (silver from the Comstock mines shipped to President Lincoln bolstered the buying power of the Union army)
	The Home of the Comstock Lode (one of the richest fissure vein deposits of gold and silver ever found)

NEW HAMPSHIRE

BERLIN	The Chemical City

BERLIN (Cont'd)	The City For the Full Life
	The City in the White Mountains
	The City That Trees Built
BETHLEHEM	The Heart of the White Mountains
CONCORD	The Capital City (28,991 population in 1960)
FRANKLIN	The Birthplace of Daniel Webster
GLEN	The City in the Center of the White Mountains
HAMPTON BEACH	The Favorite Family Seaside Resort (on the Atlantic Ocean)
HENNIKER	The Only Henniker on Earth
LACONIA	The City in the Heart of the Lakes Region
	The City of the Lakes
	The City on the Lakes (on Lake Winnipesaukee, overlooks four lakes)
MANCHESTER	The City of Opportunity
	The Manchester of America
	The Queen City
	The Queen City of New Hampshire
	The Queen City of the Merrimack Valley (on the Merrimack River)
MERRIMACK	The Fastest Growing Town in Hillsboro County
NASHUA	The Gate City (on the Nashua River)
NEWPORT	The Sunshine Town
NORTH CONWAY	The Year 'Round Vacation Town in the White Mountains
NORTH WALPOLE	Steamtown, U.S.A.
PORTSMOUTH	The Port City (New Hampshire's only seaport)
ROCHESTER	The City of Friendly People
	The City of Governors

RUMNEY	The Crutch Capital of the World (crutch manufacturing)
TILTON	The Boy's Town of New England (Spaulding Youth Center)
WINNIPESAUKEE	The Smile of the Great Spirit (name used by the Indians for Lake Winnipesaukee)
WOLFEBORO	The Oldest Summer Resort in America (founded 1759)

NEW JERSEY

ASBURY PARK	One of America's Foremost All Year Resorts
	The All Year Home Town
	The Beauty Spot of the North Jersey Coast (on the Atlantic Ocean)
	The Resort of Enjoyment
ATLANTIC CITY	America's Bagdad by the Sea (on the Atlantic Ocean)
	The Biggest Little City in America
	The Number One Host of the Jersey Coast
	The Playground of the World
	The Vacation Capital of the Nation
	The World's Playground
	The Year 'Round Vacation Playland
AVALON	The City Cooler By a Mile
	The Gem of the Jersey Coast
BAYONNE	The Oil City (refineries and tanks, pipeline to Longview, Texas)
BELMAR	The Fisherman's Paradise
	The Modern Little City
BRADLEY BEACH	The Friendly Resort City
CAMDEN	The Capital of Radio (home of the RCA-Victor Manufacturing Co.)

CAMDEN (Cont'd)	The Home of National Industries
CAPE MAY	The Nation's Oldest Seashore Resort (settled about 1664)
DOVER	The Business Heart of the Lakeland Area
	The Pittsburgh of New Jersey (industrial area)
ELIZABETH	Betsytown (humorous varient)
GARFIELD	The City of Industrial Peace
HAMMONTON	The Garden Spot of the Garden State
HARVEY CEDARS	America's Greatest Family Resort
HOBOKEN	The Mile Square City
JERSEY CITY	The City That Has Everything for Industry
KEARNY	The Heart of America's Industrial War Front
LONG BRANCH	America's First Seashore Resort (summer home of President Garfield)
MADISON	The Rose City (rose-growing center)
METUCHEN	The Brainy Borough
MILLVILLE	The Holly City of America
NEWARK	The City of Industry
OCEAN CITY	America's Greatest Family Resort (on island between Great Egg Harbor and Atlantic City)
PATERSON	The American Lyons (a mill town producing nylon, rayon, silk, wool and textile dyes)
	The Cotton Town of the U.S.A.
	The Lyons of America
	The Silk City (silk manufacturing)
PERTH AMBOY	The City by the Sea (on Raritan Bay)
PRINCETON	The Most Beautiful College Town in America (Princeton University)

STONE HARBOR	The Venice of America (seashore community, sheltered waterways)
TRENTON	The Capital City (1960 population 114,167)
VENTNOR CITY	The All-Year Residential Resort
WEST PORTAL	Little Switzerland
WILDWOOD	Five Miles of Health and Happiness
	The Tent City (popular summer resort, tents replaced by solid buildings)
	The World's Finest and Safest Bathing Beach (on Atlantic Ocean)

NEW MEXICO

ACOMA	The Sky City (steep cliffs)
ALAMOGORDO	The Rocket City (near site of first man-made atomic explosion of July 16, 1945 at White Sands Proving Ground)
ALBUQUERQUE	The Duke City (the Duke of Albuquerque created by Henry IV of Castile, brother of Queen Elizabeth)
	The Metropolis of New Mexico
CARLSBAD	The Cavern City (about 25 miles from Carlsbad Caverns National Park)
DULCE	The Home of the Jicarilla Apache Tribe
FARMINGTON	The Energy Capital of the West (producer of gas and oil, terminus of two natural gas pipelines)
GALLUP	The Indian Capital (site of the Intertribal Indian Ceremonial)

GRANTS	The Uranium Capital of the World (processing mills for uranium)
LOS ALAMOS	The Capital of the Atomic Age (Los Alamos Scientific Laboratory)
LOVINGTON	The City Where Oil and Water Mix (the Oil Patch area and fertile soil)
SANTA FE	The Capital City (1960 population 34,676)
	The Capital City Different
	The City Different
	The Center of Prehistoric, Historic and Scenic Interest
	The Oldest and Quaintest City in the United States (believed to have been settled by Indians in 1210 and by Europeans in 1610)

NEW YORK

ALBANY	The Capital City (1960 population 129,726)
	The City of Homes
	The Edinburgh of America
	The Governmental, Educational Recreational Center
	The Hub of the Empire State's Capital District
	The Oldest Chartered City in the United States (an exaggerated claim)
	The Oldest City in the United States Operating Under Its Original Charter
AMSTERDAM	The Carpet City of the World (the foremost manufacturing city for carpets and rugs)
	The Foot of the Adirondacks (on the Mohawk River and the New York Barge Canal)

AUBURN	The Cordage City (cord manufacturing)
AURIESVILLE	The Land of the Crosses
AUSAUBLE CHASM	The Grand Canyon of the East (scenic attraction)
BINGHAMTON	The Bran Town
	The Parlor City
BREWSTER	The Hub of the Harlem Valley
BROOKLYN	The Bedroom of New York (one of the boroughs of New York City, primarily a residential sector)
	The Church City
	The City of Churches
	The City of Homes
	The Dormitory of New York
	The Greatest City's Greatest Borough
BUFFALO	The Beautiful City of Homes, Diversified Business and Progressive Outlook
	The Bison City (the scientific name for buffalo)
	The Center of Industrial and Atomic Development
	The City of Flour (flour and feed milling)
	The City of Good Neighbors
	The City of Trees
	The Electric City of the Future
	The Flour City
	The Gateway City to Canada
	The Gateway to Picturesque Canada
	The Gateway to the Heartland of America
	The Metropolis in a Forest of Trees (more than 40,000 city-owned trees)
	The Queen City of the Great Lakes
	The Queen City of the Lakes

BUFFALO (Cont'd)	The Queen of the Lakes
	The Second Largest Railroad Center in the United States (12 freight terminals, 5 passenger terminals)
	The Transport Center of the Nation
	The Wonder City of America
COLD SPRING HARBOR	Bungtown
CONEY ISLAND	Sodom by the Sea (title of book by Oliver Pilat and Jo Ranson)
COOPERSTOWN	The Heart of the Leatherstocking Land
	The Home of Baseball (where Abner Doubleday introduced the game)
	The Home of James Fenimore Cooper
	The Village of Great Museums (the Baseball Museum, the Farmers Museum, etc.)
	The Village Where Nature Smiles
CORNING	The Crystal City (Steuben Glass Center and Steuben factory)
ELMIRA	The Glider Capital of the World
GOSHEN	The Cradle of the Trotter (two famous trotting tracks)
HANCOCK	The Switzerland of the Catskills
HARRIMAN	The Gateway to the Southern Catskills
HEMPSTEAD	The Hub of Nassau County
HYDE PARK	The Home of Franklin Delano Roosevelt (national shrine)
ISLIP	The Industrial Dynamo
	The Residential Haven
	The Town With a Split Personality

JOHNSON CITY	The Shoe City (site of Endicott-Johnson Corp., shoe factory)
KINGSTON	The Colonial City (first capital of New York State, 1777)
	The First Capital of New York
	The Gateway to the Catskills (Catskill Mountains)
	New York's First Capital
	New York State's First Capital
LAKE GEORGE	America's Family Playground
	Storytown, U.S.A.
LAKE LUZERNE	The Gateway to the Adirondacks (Adirondack Mountains)
LAKE PLACID	America's Switzerland (in the Adirondack Mountains on Mirror Lake)
	Nation's Finest Winter Sports Center
LONG BEACH	America's Healthiest City
	The City by the Sea (the Atlantic Ocean)
MIDDLETOWN	The Gateway to Upstate
NEWARK	The Rose Capital of America (rose cultivation, annual rose festival)
NEW ROCHELLE	The City of Huguenots (settled by the Huguenots in 1689)
	The Queen City of the Sound (Long Island Sound)
NEW YORK CITY	America's Leading Tourist Resort
	Father Knickerbocker (referring to the type of trousers worn by the early Dutch settlers)
	Gotham (name given to New York City by Washington Irving in the Salamagundi Papers, 1807)

NEW YORK CITY (Cont'd)

The Babylonian Bedlam (allusion to the confusion of tongues at Babel, described in Genesis XI)
The Bagdad of the Subway
The Bagdad on the Hudson
The Big Apple
The Big Burg
The Big City
The Big Town
The Burg
The Capital of the World
The City
The City of Islands (the borough of Manhattan and numerous other small islands within the city limits)
The City at the Crossroads of High Diplomacy
The City of Friendly People
The City of Orchestras (music center and "Tin Pan Alley")
The City of Skyscrapers (the tallest building in the world; the Empire State building, the Chrysler Building, 60 Wall Tower, etc.)
The City of Superlatives
The City of Towers
The Cleanest Big City in the World
The Coliseum City
The Commercial Emporium
The Cultural Center of the Nation
The Empire City
The Entertainment Capital of the World
The Financial Capital of the World
The First City of the World (the most populated city in

NEW YORK CITY (Cont'd)

the United States, approximately 8 million)
The Friendly City
The Frog and Toe
The Front Office of American Business
The Greatest All-Year Round Vacation City
The Host of the World
The Hub City of the World
The Mecca of Telephone Men
The Melting Pot (drama by Israel Zangwill, 1908)
The Metropolis
The Metropolis of America
The Metropolitan City
The Mighty Manhattan
The Modern Gomorrah (one of the cities of the plains destroyed by fire and brimstone because of wickedness, mentioned in the Old Testament)
The Money Town
The Most Colorful Exciting City in the World
The Nation's First City
The Nation's Largest Communications Center
The Nation's Largest Port
The Port of Many Ports
The Science City
The Seat of Empire (named in 1784 by George Washington)
The University of Telephony
The Vacation City
The Wonder City
The World's Capital City
The World's Fair City
The World's Financial Capital
The World's Metropolis

NEW YORK CITY (Cont'd)	The World's Most Exciting All Year Round Vacation Center
NIAGARA FALLS	America's Scenic Wonderland
	The Cataract City (descriptive)
	The City of Business
	The City of Fine Schools
	The City of Homes
	The City of Industry
	The City of Scenic Marvels
	The Honeymoon City (a favorite vacation spot for honeymoon couples)
	The Power City (hydroelectric stations)
	The Power City of Scenic Wonders
	The Quality City
NORTH POLE	Santa's Workshop (toy factory)
	Village of Breathtaking Beauty and Enchantment
	Village of Enchantment
ONEONTA	The City of Hills (west of the Catskill Mountain region)
OYSTER BAY	The Home of Theodore Roosevelt
RIPLEY	The Gretna Green (on Lake Erie)
ROCHESTER	The Aquaduct City
	The Camera City
	The City Built By Hands
	The City of Giant Industry
	The City of Great Industry
	The City of Homes
	The City of Many Industries
	The City of Quality Products
	The City of Varied Industries
	The Flour City
	The Flower City
	The Friendliest City
	The Home of One of the Nation's Largest Skilled Technical Work Forces

ROCHESTER (Cont'd)	The Kodak City
	The Photographic and Optical Center of the World
	The Power City
	The Quality City
ROME	The Copper City (about 10% of the copper factories of the U.S.)
RYE	America's Premier Playground
	The Border Town
SARATOGA SPRINGS	America's Most Wonderful Spa
	The Home of America's Greatest Spa
	The Home of Health, History and Horse
	The Inevitable Spa City
	The Queen of the Spas
SCHENECTADY	Dorp
	Old Dorp
	The City of Magic
	The City That Lights and Hauls the World
	The Electric City (site of the General Electric Co.)
	The Electrical City (site of the General Electric Co.)
	The Gateway to the West (on the Mohawk River)
	The Magic City
SCHROON LAKE	The Playground of the Adirondacks (summer resort)
SHARON SPRINGS	America's Mountain Spring (White sulphur spring four barrels a minute)
SHELTER ISLAND	The Vacationer's Paradise
SPECULATOR	The City in the Lake District of the Adirondacks
	The Land of Beautiful Lakes
	The Vacationland of Unlimited Enjoyment
SYRACUSE	The Central City
	The City of Conventions

SYRACUSE (Cont'd)	The City of Isms
	The City of Salt
	The City of the Plains
	The Crossroads of New York State
	The Electronics Capital of the World
	The Fair City
	The Heart of New York State
	The Hub of the Empire State
	The Salt City (salt springs and salt brine)
	The Telegraphic Hub
	The Venice of America
TROY	The Collar City (factories manufacturing Arrow shirts and collars)
	The Tide-Water City (at head of the Hudson River)
TRUMANSBURG	The City in the Heart of the Finger Lakes
UTICA	The Beautiful City of Homes in the Historic Mohawk Valley
	The City at the Crossroads of the Empire State
	The City of Successful Diversified Industry
	The Crossroads of New York
	The Gateway to the Adirondacks
	The Hub of the Empire State
	The Watering-Pot of America
WALTON	The Foothills of the Catskills
	The Heart and Hub of Delaware County
WARRENSBURG	The Queen Village of the Adirondacks
WELLS	A Truly Year 'Round Vacation Land
WHITE PLAINS	The Heart of Westchester (Westchester County)
WILLIAMSVILLE	The Gateway to Niagara Falls

YONKERS	The City of Graceful Living The Terrace City

NORTH CAROLINA

ASHEVILLE	One of the Leading Health and Tourist Resorts of the East The Capital City of the Land of the Sky The Land of the Sky (altitude 1,980 feet to 3,020 feet) The Popular Convention City The Preeminent Vacation Center
BREVARD	The Popular Summer Resort
CHARLOTTE	The Action City The City of Churches The Heart of the Piedmont The Home City The Hornets' Nest The Queen City The Spearhead of the New South
GOLDSBORO	The Community of Progress The Friendly City of Progress The Heart of Eastern North Carolina
HATTERAS	The Blue Marlin Capital of the World
HENDERSON	The Bird Sanctuary The City With a Future
HENDERSONVILLE	The City of Four Glorious Seasons The Dancingest Town in the United States (numerous street and other public dances) The Summer and Health Resort
HICKORY	The Best Balanced City
HIGH POINT	The Furniture City (about 90 furniture factories)

HIGHLANDS	The Highest Incorporated Town in Eastern America
KANNAPOLIS	The Cannon City (site of Cannon Mills)
LEXINGTON	The City Four-Dimensional
	The Winter Golf Capital of America
RALEIGH	The Capital City (1960 population 93,931)
	The City of Oaks
	The Oak City
SOUTHERN PINES	The Mid-South Resort
THOMASVILLE	The Chair Capital of the World
	The Chair City (furniture manufacturing since 1870)
TRYON	The Friendliest Town in America (in the Blue Ridge Mountains)
WAYNESVILLE	The Vacation and Health Resort
WHITE LAKE	The Nation's Safest Beach
WINSTON-SALEM	The Camel City (a brand cigarette manufactured by the American Tobacco Company)
	The City Founded Upon Co-operation
	The City of Culture, History, Industry
	The Twin Cities (Winston and Salem consolidated in 1913)
	The Twin City (Winston and Salem consolidated in 1913)

NORTH DAKOTA

BISMARCK	The Capital City (1960 population 27,670)
	The Capital of Opportunity
	The City Beside the Broad Missouri
	The Fastest Growing City in the Northwest

BISMARCK (Cont'd)	The Medical Center of North Dakota
DEVILS LAKE	The Satanic City (a synonym for devil)
DICKINSON	A Good Place to Visit, a Good Place to Live
	The Gateway of America's Scenic Wonderland
	The Gateway to the West
	The Queen City
	The Queen City of the Prairies
	The Threshold of Theodore Roosevelt National Memorial Park
FARGO	A Fine Residential Center
	An Important Livestock Center
	The Bread Basket of the World
	The Food Basket of the World
	The Gateway City
	The Gateway City to the Bread Basket of the World
	The Metropolis of North Dakota
	The Natural Location for Agricultural Industry
GRAND FORKS	The Heart of North Dakota
JAMESTOWN	Jimtown
	The City With a Future
MARMARTH	The City of Trees
MEDORA	The Cow Town
MINOT	The Magic City (referring to its fast growth)

OHIO

AKRON	The City of Opportunity
	The Heart of America's Workshop
	The Rubber Capital of the United States (numerous factories producing tires and other rubber products)

AKRON (Cont'd)	The Rubber Capital of the World The Rubber City The Summit City (950 feet altitude, highest point of old Ohio and Erie canal) The Tire City of the United States
BAINBRIDGE	The Cradle of Dental Education (school for dentists opened in 1826 by Dr. John Harris)
CADIZ	The Proudest Small Town in America (1960 population 3,259)
CEDAR POINT	The Atlantic City of the Middle West (resort area on Sandusky Bay)
CINCINNATI	America's Paris Pigopolis Porkopolis The Athens of the Middle West The Beautiful City The Birmingham of America The City of Personality The Conservative Cincinnati The Contented City The Crossroads of the Nation The Floral City The Paris of America The Queen City The Queen City of the Ohio The Queen City of the West The Queen of the Ohio (Ohio River) The Queen of the West The Ragtown (manufacture of cloaks and suits often referred to in the trade as "rags")
CLEVELAND	The Capital City of a Great Trade Empire The Forest City

CLEVELAND (Cont'd)	The Overgrown Country Town
	The Queen of Lake Erie
COLUMBUS	Ohio's Beautiful Capital
	The Capital City (1960 population 471, 316)
	The Heart of a Great State
CONNEAUT	The Plymouth of the Western Reserve (first settlers in Ohio, July 4, 1796)
DAYTON	The Birthplace of Aviation (Wright-Patterson Air Force Base)
	The Cash Register City (National Cash Register Co. factory)
	The City Beautiful
	The City of Beauty
	The City of Industry
	The City of Progress
	The Cradle of Aviation (Wright-Patterson Air Force Base)
	The Crossroads of Your National Market
	The Gem City
	The Gem City of Ohio
	The World Famous Manufacturing Center
DELPHOS	The Heart of Industrial America
DENNISON	The Clay Pipe Center of the World
DOVER	The Home of Warther Museum (world famous carvings)
EAST LIVERPOOL	The Ceramic City (leading pottery center)
ELYRIA	The City of Beauty and Unlimited Opportunities
	The City of Diversified Products
HAMILTON	The Postmark of Distinctive Trademarks (Gen. Arthur

HAMILTON (Cont'd)	St. Clair built Fort Hamilton in 1791)
HAYDENVILLE	The Ideal Town
LAKESIDE	The Chautauqua of the Great Lakes (summer conference grounds on the southern shore of Lake Erie)
LAKEWOOD	The City of Homes
LIMA	A City of Fine Homes and Streets
	The Hub of a $500,000 Trading Area
MARIETTA	A Town For Those in Love With Life
	Ohio's Oldest and Most Beautiful City (settled by 48 people in 1788)
	The City of Diversified Industries
	The City of Many Cultural Advantages
	The Most Historic City in the Northwest Territory (first civil government in the Northwest Territory when Arthur St. Clair took the oath of governor in 1788)
MARION	The Shovel City of the World
NILES	The Birthplace of Mc Kinley (President William Mc Kinley born Jan. 29, 1843)
PORTSMOUTH	The City Where Southern Hospitality Begins (on the Ohio River)
	The Steel City (iron and steel factory built 1872)
SABINA	The Eden of Ohio
SALEM	Ohio's City of Friends
	The Quaker City (founded in 1801 by Quakers)
SANDUSKY	The Gateway to Lake Erie
	The Gateway to the Ohio Lake Erie Islands (on Sandusky

SANDUSKY (Cont'd)	Bay of Lake Erie)
SPRINGFIELD	The Champion City The City of Progress The Flower City The Hub of Historic Ohio The Hub of Historical Ohio The Progressively Growing Well-Seasoned City
STEUBENVILLE	The Best Town Site on the Ohio (on the Ohio River, 1960 population 32,495)
SUGARCREEK	The Swiss Cheese Center of Ohio (numerous factories)
TOLEDO	One of America's Great Cities One of the Busiest Fresh-water Ports in the World (on the Maumee River flowing into Lake Erie) The Busiest Freshwater Port in the World The Central Gateway of the Great Lakes The City Where Coal and Iron Meet The City Where the Seaway Meets the Turnpike The Corn City The Glass Capital of the World (numerous glass factories) The Glass Center (factories of Owens-Illinois Glass Co., Ford Glass Co., Libby-Owens, etc.) The Mud Hen City The Pivot City of the Great Lakes (on Lake Erie) The World's Largest Coal-Shipping Port
UHRICHSVILLE	The Clay Pipe Center of the World

UPPER SANDUSKY	The Friendly Community of Beauty and Industry
	The Indian Village (home of Wyandot Indians)
WARREN	The Home of Little Steel (steel mills)
YOUNGSTOWN	The Capital City
	The Capital City of a Great Industrial Empire
	The Gateway to the Old Western Reserve
	The Land of Flowing Springs
	The Recreational, Educational and Cultural Center of Northeastern Ohio
ZANESVILLE	America's Typical City
	The Capital City (Ohio's capital from 1810-1812)
	The Pottery City (pottery, tile, glass manufacturing)
	The "Y" Bridge City (bridge built in the form of the letter "Y")

OKLAHOMA

ARDMORE	The Capital of South Central Oklahoma
BARTLESVILLE	The City With a Future
CHANDLER	The Largest Pecan Shipping Center in America
	The Pecan Capital of the World
CLAREMORE	The Best Known Little City in America (1960 population 6,639)
ENID	The Queen City of the Cherokee Strip
GROVE	The Friendly Community
	The Spot for a Home and Life of Joy
GUTHRIE	The Birthplace of Oklahoma (first state capital 1907)

GUTHRIE (Cont'd)	The Fraternal Capital of the Southwest (largest Scottish Rite Temple)
KETCHUM	The Home of the First Fully Automatic Non-Attended Dial Telephone Switchboard in the United States
LAWTON	The Post City (U.S. Army and Fort Lawton)
	The Rollicking, Hilarious Tent and Shack City
OKLAHOMA CITY	The Capital City (1960 population 324,253)
	The Capital of Soonerland
	The Central City of the Great Southwest
	The City of 1,000 Lakes (actually 1,514 lakes ranging from a few acres to 100,000 acre-foot Elm Creek Reservoir)
	The Hub of the Great Southwest
	The Industrial Frontier of America
	The Land of Perpetual Prosperity
	The Sedate Capital of the Bible Belt
	The Town Where Oil Derricks Loom In Almost Any Yard
	The Town Where the Office Ledger Has Replaced the Horse Pistol
OKMULGEE	The City Where Oil Flows, Gas Flows and Glass Glows
PONCA CITY	The City Built on Oil, Soil and Toil
PRYOR	The Gateway from South and West to Ozark Playgrounds
SALINA	The Oldest White Settlement in the State (founded by

SALINA (Cont'd) — Pierre Chouteaux, explorer, in 1796)

SEILING — The Little Louisville of the Southwest

TAHLEQUAH — The Former Capital of the Cherokee Indian Nation

TULSA — The City Beautiful
The Fair Little City
The Home of Diamond Products
The Home of the International Petroleum Exposition
The Magic City
The Oil Capital
The Oil Capital of the World

VINITA — The Ozark's Western Gateway (on the Texas Road, formerly the Osage Trace)
The Second Oldest Settlement in Oklahoma

OREGON

ALBANY — The Hole in the Ground (altitude 216 feet; the current washed away a section near the mouth of the Calapooya River)
The Hub City
The Hub of the Willamette Valley

ASHLAND — The American Carlsbad (mineral springs)
The City of Spas (lithia water mineral springs)
The Gateway
The Granite City (marble works 1865)
The Home Town of Southern Oregon

ASTORIA — The Salmon City (on the Columbia River)

AURORA	The Dutchtown (founded in 1857 by Dr. William Keil and German settlers)
BAKER	The Denver of Oregon The Friendly City on the Oregon Trail The Gold Coast of Oregon (gold discovered on Griffin Creek 1861)
COOS BAY	The Lumber Port of the World
COQUILLE	The Gem City of Cedar Empire (on the Coquille River)
CORNELIUS	The Corntown
CORVALLIS	The Heart of the Valley (Willamette Valley) The Ideal Community
ENTERPRISE	The Gateway to Wallowa National Forest
EUGENE	Skinner's Mudhole (Eugene F. Skinner established his land claim in 1846 near the Eugene and Willamette Rivers) The Spokane of Oregon
GARIBALDI	Little Holland (numerous dikes)
HILLSBORO	The Filbert Center of the United States
LA GRANDE	The Hub of Northeast Oregon (foot of Blue Mountains)
LAKEVIEW	The Tallest Town in Oregon (elevation 4,800 feet)
LANCASTER	The Fightin'est Town on the River
MC MINNVILLE	The Walnut City
MEDFORD	The Pear City (annual pear pack of the district about 4,000 carloads)
NEWBERG	The Quaker City (founded by Quakers)
NORTH BEND	The City of Progress (city government 1903)

ONTARIO	The Capital of Eastern Oregon
OREGON CITY	The City of Firsts
PENDLETON	The Round-Up City (Pendleton's first round-up, first 1912 big show)
PORTLAND	Little Stumptown (contempuously so-called in the early days by non-residents because there were so many stumps in the streets, sometimes painted white so they could be seen in the dark)
	The Beautiful City of Roses
	The Capital of the Land of Out-Doors
	The City of Homes
	The City of Roses
	The Convention City
	The Lumber Manufacturing Center of the Pacific Northwest
	The Lumber Industry's Capital
	The Metropolis of the State of Oregon
	The Rose City
	The Spinster City
	The Sub-Treasury of the Pacific Northwest
	The Summer Capital
PRINEVILLE	The Cowboy Capital of Oregon
REDMOND	The Hub of Central Oregon
ROGUE RIVER	Tailhold
ROSEBURG	The Lumber Capital of the Nation
SALEM	The Capital City (1960 population 49,142)
	The Capital City of Good Living, Commerce and Industry

SALEM (Cont'd)	The Cherry City
	The City of Diversified Industry
	The Heart of the Pacific Wonderland
	Oregon's Beautiful Capital City
SEASIDE	The Playground of the Northwest
STAYTON	The Green Bean Center
TILLAMOOK	The Land of Cheese, Trees and Ocean Breeze (on the Pacific Ocean)
WOODBURN	The Berry City

PENNSYLVANIA

ALLENTOWN	The Cement City
	The Queen City
	The Queen City of the Lehigh Valley (on the Lehigh River)
	The Scrapple City
ALTOONA	The Mountain City (altitude about 1,170 feet, east base of Allegheny Mountains)
	The Railroad City (shops and yards of Pennsylvania Railroad)
BEDFORD	The Mineral Springs City (resort area popular since 1795)
	The Resort and Convention Playground of the Alleghenies
BELLEFONTE	The City of Governors
	The City of the Belles
BERLIN	The Scenic City (in Brothers Valley)
BERWICK	The Car Shop City (American Car and Foundry plant)
BETHLEHEM	Allentown's Sister City
	America's Christmas City
	The Christmas City

BETHLEHEM (Cont'd)	The Historic Bethlehem
	The Hub of the Great Lehigh Valley
	The Star City With a Great Future
	The Steel City (Bethlehem Steel Co., plant and coke works)
BLOSSBURG	The Tannery City
BRADFORD	The Growing Industrial Center of Northwestern Pennsylvania
	The High Grade Oil Metropolis of the World
	The Metropolitan Center of McKean County
	The Natural Gas City
BUSHKILL	The Niagara of Pennsylvania (300-foot series of falls)
CARLISLE	The City of Molly Pitcher (grave of Molly Pitcher, heroine of Battle of Monmouth)
	The Crossroads of History
	The Crystal Center of the World (manufacturing of quartz crystals for radio sets, etc.)
CHESTER	The Ship-Building City (on the Delaware River)
CONNELLSVILLE	The Bituminous City
	The Iron Ore City
COUDERSPORT	The Ice Mine City (a vertical shaft 40 feet deep, 8 feet wide and 10 feet long containing ice formations during the spring, continuing through the summer and disappearing in the winter)
DOWNINGTOWN	The Gateway to the Pennsylvania Dutch Country
EASTON	The Transportation City

EBENSBURG	The Lookout City (altitude 2,022 feet)
ELKLAND	The Dairy City
ELLWOOD CITY	The City of Diversified Industry
ERIE	The Gem City of the Lakes
	The Harbor City (only lake port in Pennsylvania, located on Lake Erie)
GETTYSBURG	The Battlefield City (bloodiest battle of the War of Secession, July 1-3, 1863, loss 23,001 men)
GREENSBURG	The Tunnel City (bituminous coal mines)
HANOVER	The Shoe City
HARRISBURG	Pennsylvania's Capital City
	The Capital City (1960 population 79,697)
	The City That Puts Business on the Go
	The Courteous Capital City
	The Heart of the Commonwealth
	The Host City to Conventions
	The Hub of the Interstate and U.S. Highways
	The State City
	The Transportation King of the Mid-East
HERSHEY	Chocolate Town, U.S.A. (Hershey Chocolates)
	The Chocolate City
	The Chocolate Crossroads of the World
	The Chocolate Town
HOLLIDAYSBURG	The Canal City (in the 1830's a canal and railroad terminus)
	The Portage City (to Johnstown, Pa.)
HUMMELSTOWN	The Brownstone City

JERSEY SHORE	The Fair Play City (settled in 1785)
JOHNSONBURG	The Paper City (Castanea Paper Company)
JOHNSTOWN	The Cradle of the Steel Industry
	The Flood City (disastrous flood May 31, 1889)
	The Flood Free City
	The Friendly City
KANE	The Summit City (2,013 feet altitude)
	The Winter Sports City
LANCASTER	The Buying Center of a Quarter Million People
	The Heart of the Pennsylvania Dutch Country
	Pennsylvania's Above-Average Market of Industry and Agriculture
	The Pretzel City
	The Red Rose City
LEBANON	The Iron Mountain City (Cornall ore mines in operation since 1742, largest iron mines in eastern U.S.)
LEWISBURG	The College City (Bucknell University established 1846)
LOCK HAVEN	The Sawdust City (lumbering)
McKEESPORT	The Tube City (plant of National Tube Co.)
MANHEIM	The Rose City (on December 4, 1772 "Baron" von Stiegel, a trustee of the Manheim Lutheran Congregation deeded a plot of ground to them with the stipulation that "in the month of June forever hereafter the rent of one red rose if the same shall be lawfully demanded" shall be paid)

MAUCH CHUNK	The Switchback City (since 1827 site of first switchback railway)
NEW KENSINGTON	The Aluminum City (Aluminum Company of America plant)
NORRISTOWN	The Aqueduct City
OIL CITY	The Derrick City (site of derricks used since 1860 discovery of oil)
PHILADELPHIA	America's Great Convention City
	Philly
	The Birthplace of American Liberty (Declaration of Independence signed July 4, 1776)
	The Birthplace of the Nation
	The City of Brotherly Love
	The City of Churches
	The City of Firsts
	The City of Homes
	The City of Penn (William Penn settled in 1682)
	The Cradle of Liberty
	The Modern City of Great Historical Interest
	The Quaker City (settled by William Penn and Quaker colony)
	The Quakertown
	The Rebel Capital
	The Sleepy Town
	The World's Greatest Workshop
PITTSBURGH	The Big Smoke
	The Big Smoky
	The Birmingham of America
	The Center of Eastern Steel Making
	The City of Bridges (Liberty Bridge, Smithfield St. Bridge, Ft. Pitt Bridge, etc.)

PITTSBURGH (Cont'd)	The City of Steel (U.S. Steel Corp.) The City of the Unexpected The Coal City The Gateway to the West The Iron City The Most Bridged City in the World The Smoky City The Steel Capital of the World The Steel City The World's Workshop
POTTSVILLE	The Coal City (southern gateway to the anthracite region)
READING	Penn's Town (founded in 1748 by Thomas and Richard Penn, sons of William Penn) The Brewing City The Capital of Pennsylvania German Land The Center of the World's Best Market The City of Progress The Industrial Metropolis The Pretzel City (J. T. Adams Pretzel Bakery, established 1873) The Textile City
SCRANTON	America's Year 'Round Playground The Anthracite Capital of the World (coal mines) The Anthracite City The City of Black Diamonds (coal) The Electric City (first electric streetcar line on which fares were collected, 1886) The Friendly City

SCRANTON (Cont'd)	The Wonderful Convention City
	The World's Largest Anthracite Coal Mining City
SMETHPORT	The Bucktail City (Bucktail Regiment organized in 1861 by Gen. Thomas L. Kane)
SOMERSET	The Frosty City
	The Roof Garden of Pennsylvania (Mt. Davis, altitude 3,240 feet)
STATE COLLEGE	The Penn State City (site of Pennsylvania State College)
STROUDSBURG	The Gateway to the Poconos (about fourteen miles from the heart of the Pocono Mountains)
TITUSVILLE	The Town That Outlives and Outgrew the Oil Boom (first successful oil well drilled 1859, Drake well)
UNIONTOWN	The City of Coal Kings
	The Coke City
WARREN	The City of Industrial Opportunity
WAYNESBURG	The Catacomb City
WELLSBORO	The Canyon City (Pine Creek Gorge, the Grand Canyon of Pennsylvania)
	The Pennsylvania Athens
WILKES-BARRE	The Black Diamond City (coal)
	The Diamond City
	The Heart of the Valley That Warms a Nation (Wyoming Valley)
WILKINSBURG	The City of Churches
WILLIAMSPORT	The Lumber City
	The Queen City
	The Scenic Capital of Central Pennsylvania (on the west branch of the Susquehanna River)

YORK	The Castle City The City of Diversified Industry and Civic Achievement The Plough-Share City The White Rose City

RHODE ISLAND

CENTRAL FALLS	The Twin Cities (with Pawtucket, R.I.)
CUMBERLAND	The Mineral Pocket of New England (iron, copper and other minerals have been found within its borders)
EAST GREENWICH	The Heart of Rhode Island
JAMESTOWN	A Safe Place for Children The City Where the Breezes Blow (on Conanicut Island)
JOHNSTON	The Friendly City The Friendly Town
LINCOLN	Historic and Scenic Lincoln
MIDDLETOWN	The Woods (on Aquidneck Island between Newport and Portsmouth)
NEW SHOREHAM	America's Bermuda (on Block Island) The Fisherman's Paradise of the North Atlantic
NEWPORT	America's Oldest Summer Resort America's Society Capital Rhode Island's Most Historic Town The Capital of Vacation Land The City By the Sea The Historic Showplace of America The Naval Center The Queen of Summer Resorts The Summer Capital of Society

NEWPORT (Cont'd)	The Summer Resort
PAWTUCKET	The Birthplace of the American Cotton Industry (Samuel Slater established his mill in 1790)
	The Twin Cities (with Central Falls, R.I.)
PORTSMOUTH	The Home for Your Business
	The Home for Your Family
	The Vacation Center
PROVIDENCE	The Bee-hive of Industry
	The Capital City (1960 population 207,498)
	The First City of America's First Vacationland
	The Gateway of Southern New England
	The Perry Davis' Pain Killer City
	The Roger Williams City (founded in 1636 by Roger Williams)
	The Southern Gateway of New England
WICKFORD	The Art Center of Rhode Island
	The Venice of America (on Narragansett Bay)

SOUTH CAROLINA

ABBEVILLE	The Cradle and the Grave of the Confederacy (secession movement originated Nov. 22, 1860, last cabinet meeting of President Jefferson Davis May 2, 1865)
AIKEN	One of the Most Fashionable Winter Resorts of the South
	One of the Most Favorable Winter Resorts of the South
	The Polo Capital of the South

AIKEN (Cont'd)	The Sports Center of the South (steeplechase and horse show annual events)
BEAUFORT	The Capital of the Sea Islands
	The City in the Heart of the Coastal Sea Islands
	The Newport of the South
CHARLESTON	America's Most Historic City
	The Air Capital of the Carolinas
	The Capital of the Carolinas
	The Capital of the Coastal Empire of South Carolina
	The Capital of the Plantations
	The City by the Sea
	The City of Churches
	The City of History and Romance
	The City of Secession (first ordnance of secession, 1860)
	The Cradle of Secession
	The Earthquake City
	The Holy City
	The Palmetto City
	The Plumb Line Port to Panama
	The Queen City of the Sea
	The Queen City of the South
COLUMBIA	South Carolina's Capital City
	The Capital City (1960 population 97,433)
	The Gateway to the South
	The Golden Rule City
ELLENTON	The H-Bomb's Home Town
FLORENCE	The Magic City
GREENVILLE	The Textile Center of the World (textile finishing and garment production)
HARTSVILLE	The City of Lovely Gardens
NEWBERRY	The City of Friendly Folks
SPARTANBURG	The Crossroads of the New South

SPARTANBURG (Cont'd)	The Hub City of the Southeast
	The South's Largest Producer of Cotton Cloth
SUMMERVILLE	The Flower Town in the Pines
SUMTER	The Gamecock City (named for General Thomas Sumter "the gamecock of the Revolution")

SOUTH DAKOTA

ABERDEEN	A Good Place to Live
	The Convention Hub of the Dakotas
	The Hub City (in the James River Valley)
	The Hub City of the Dakotas (four railroads in the area resemble the spokes of a wheel)
BELLE FOURCHE	The Northern Gateway to the Black Hills
BROOKINGS	The Home City
	The Home of South Dakota State College
DEADWOOD	The Historic City of the Black Hills (gold discoveries about 1876)
	The Twin Cities of the Northern Black Hills of South Dakota
HOT SPRINGS	The City in a Valley Where Recuperation, Rehabilitation, Rest and Relaxation With Recreation and Scenic Beauty Abound
	The City of Healing Waters (mineral springs)
HURON	The Center of the World's Largest Irrigation Power Navigation Flood Control Project

HURON (Cont'd)	The City With Future Unlimited
	The Fair City (site of the South Dakota State Fair)
	The Natural City (geographically nearest both the center of population of the entire state and population center of that portion of the state lying east of the Missouri River)
	The Pheasant Capital of the World
LAKE ANDES	The Fish City (site of state fish hatchery)
LEAD	The Mile High City
	The Twin Cities of the Northern Black Hills of South Dakota
MADISON	The City That Says "Welcome Neighbor"
	The Water City (Lake Madison and Lake Herman)
MARTIN	The Metropolis of the Pine Ridge Reservation Country
MILBANK	The Granite City (Milbank granite quarries)
MITCHELL	A Pleasant Place to Visit
	A Wonderful Place to Live
	South Dakota's City of Opportunity
PIERRE	A Real Western City
	The Center of Great Wealth
	The Center of the Sunshine State
	The Capital City (1960 population 10,088)
	The City in the Center of Hunting Lands
	The City in the Heart of Western Ranch Land
	The Coming City of the Great North West

PIERRE (Cont'd)	The Future Great City
	The Home of Friendly People
	The Home of the Giant Oahe Dam
	The Site of the Oahe Dam
RAPID CITY	The Denver of South Dakota
	The Eastern Gateway to the Black Hills
	The Eastern Gateway to the Mountainous Black Hills Where East Meets West and the Friendly Hospitality
	The Gate City
	The Gateway City of the Hills
	The Gateway to the Black Hills
SIOUX FALLS	The Crossroads of the Nation
	The Gateway to the Dakotas
	The Gateway to the West
	The Growing City
	The Pheasant Capital of the World
	The Progressive City
	The Queen City
SPEARFISH	The Queen City
	The Queen City of the Hills (the Black Hills)
SPENCER	The Granite City
VERMILLION	The Home of the University of South Dakota
	The University City (University of South Dakota)
WALL	The Gateway to the Badlands National Park
WEBSTER	The Gateway to the Lake Region
YANKTON	The City Where Your Dream Vacation Can Become A Reality
	The Gateway to South Dakota's Vacation Wonderland
	The Mother City

YANKTON (Cont'd)	The Mother City of the Dakotas (oldest city in Dakota territory, territorial capital 1861)

TENNESSEE

ATHENS	The City Where Business and Industry Thrive and People Enjoy a Wide Variety of Year Around Recreation
	The Progressive City
BRISTOL	The City in the Heart of Eastern America (see also Virginia)
	The Outdoorman's Paradise
	The Shopping Center of the Appalachians (see also Virginia)
CHATTANOOGA	One of America's Most Interesting Cities
	The Dynamo of Dixie
	The Gate City
	The Mountain City
	The Scenic Center of the South
GATLINBURG	The Convention Center of the Great Smokies
	The Convention City of the Great Smokies
	The Gateway to the Great Smokies (the Great Smoky Mountains National Park)
GLEASON	Taterville
	The Tater Town
KINGSPORT	The City of Diversified Industry (planned 1916)
KNOXVILLE	The City of the Great Smokies
	The Marble City
	The Metropolis of East Tennessee

KNOXVILLE (Cont'd)	The Queen City of the Mountains
MEMPHIS	Babylon on the Bluff
	Big Shelby
	Crumptown
	Homocide Headquarters
	Queen of the American Nile
	Sodom of the South
	The Bluff City
	The City at the Crossroads of the South
	The City Beautiful
	The City of Hospitality
	The City of Opportunity
	The City of Tradition
	The Commercial Metropolis of West Tennessee
	The Crossroads of the Mid-South
	The First City
	The Murder Capital of America
	The Place of Good Abode
	The Progressive City
MORRISTOWN	The City Always Expanding
	The Cleanest City in the United States
	The Vacation Wonderland
NASHVILLE	Music City, U.S.A. (recordings)
	Tennessee's Beauty Spot
	The Athens of the South (Nashville contains a replica of the Parthenon)
	The Capital City (1960 population 170,874)
	The Capital City of Industrial Progress
	The Capital City of Tennessee
	The City Beautiful
	The City of Diversified Interests

NASHVILLE (Cont'd)	The City of Opportunity
	The City of Rocks
	The Dimple of the Universe
	The Gateway of the South
	The Iris City
	The Rock City
	The Wall Street of the South
OAK RIDGE	The Atomic Capital of the World
	The Atomic Energy City (manufacture of atomic bomb)
TULLAHOMA	The Thermopylae of Middle Tennessee (winter headquarters of Gen. Braxton Bragg fell to Union General Rosecrans on July 3, 1863)

TEXAS

ABILENE	The Athens of the West (Hardin-Simmons University, McMurray and Abilene Christian colleges)
ALPINE	The Roof Garden of Texas (altitude 4,484 feet)
	The Roof Garden Resort of Texas (altitude 4,484 feet)
AMARILLO	The Queen City of the Panhandle
AUSTIN	The Big Heart of Texas
	The Boom Town Without Oil
	The Capital City (1960 population 186,545)
	The City of the Violet Crown
BAY CITY	The Deep South of Texas (on Bay Prairie)
BEAUMONT	The City Where Great East Texas Meets the Sea
	The Queen of the Neches (on the Sabine-Neches waterway)
BROWNSVILLE	The City Where Mexico Meets Uncle Sam (across the river

BROWNSVILLE (Cont'd)	is Matamoras, Mexico)
	The Metropolis of the Magic Valley
CARRIZO SPRINGS	The Hub of the Winter Garden (in Dimmit County)
CHILDRESS	The City of the Plains (county seat of Childress County)
CORPUS CHRISTI	The City Where Texas Meets the Sea (on Corpus Christi Bay)
	The Fastest Growing City in Texas (1960 population 167,690)
CRYSTAL CITY	The Spinach Capital of the World
	The World's Spinach Capital (a statue of Popeye stands in Popeye Park)
DALLAS	Athens of the Southwest
	Big "D"
	The All-American Town
	The Bright Spot
	The City of Homes
	The City of Opportunity
	The City of the Hour
	The Metropolis of North Texas
	The Metropolis of the Southwest
	The Murder Capital of the World (so-called after the assassination of President John Fitzgerald Kennedy)
DENISON	The Gate City (in northeastern Grayson County)
EL PASO	The Crossroads of America
	The Crossroads of the Americas
	The Host City of the Sunland Empire
	The Hub of the International Southwest

FORT WORTH	The Arsenal of Democracy
	The Chicago of the Southwest
	The City of Beautiful Heights
	The City of Delight
	The City of Lakes
	The City of Western Charm and Hospitality
	The City Where The West Begins
	The Cow Town (largest livestock marketing and processing center south of Kansas City)
	The Fort Town
	The Friendly City
	The Fun Spot of the Southwest
	The Gateway to the West
	The Gateway to West Texas
	The Hub of Banking and Insurance Interests
	The Medical Center (17 hospitals and 85 private clinics)
	The Panther City
	The Queen City of the Plains
	The Queen City of the Prairies
	The Second Largest Aircraft Production Center in the Country
	The Stage Coach Town
	The World's Greatest Storehouse of Raw Material
GALVESTON	The Oleander City
	The Oleander City by the Sea
	The Oleander City of Texas
	The Port and Playground of the Southwest (on Gulf of Mexico)
	The Port of the Southwest
	The Treasure Island of the Southwest

GONZALES	A Great Place to Live The City Where the Fight for Texas Liberty Began The Lexington of Texas The Mecca for History Lovers The Opportunity for History The Playground for Vacationers
GRAND PRAIRIE	The Center of the Aircraft Industry
HEREFORD	The City Without a Toothache (low dental decay rate)
HOUSTON	The Bayou City The City That Built Its Seaport The First City in Texas The First Cotton Port The Land of the Big Inch (oil pipe line) The Largest City in the South The Largest City in the Southwest The Leading Industrial City of the Southwest The Leading Spot Cotton Market The Magnolia City The Metropolis of the West The Murder Capital of the World The Oil Center of the World
HUNTSVILLE	The Mount Vernon of Texas (last home and burial place of Sam Houston)
LAREDO	The Gate City (on the Rio Grande River which separates it from Nuevo Laredo, Texas)
LUBBOCK	The Home of Texas Tech (Texas Technological College)

LUBBOCK (Cont'd)	The Hub of the Plains (county seat of Lubbock County)
MC ALLEN	The City of Palms
MC KINNEY	The Home of Prosperous Agriculture Business and Industry
ODESSA	A City Where Growth Has Become a Habit
	America's Newest Industrial Frontier
	The City of Dreams
	The New Industrial Frontier of the Southwest
	The Oil City of the Southwest (Penn field opened 1929, Crowden field 1930)
PALESTINE	The Homesteader's Paradise (in the center of Anderson County)
PANNA MARIA	The Polish City in Texas (established 1854 by Catholic Poles)
PHARR	The City of Palms
	The Industrial Frontier of the Magic Lower Rio Grande Valley of Texas
PORT ARTHUR	The City of Homes
RANGER	The City of Flowing Gold (oil wells)
SAN ANGELO	The City of Angels
SAN ANTONIO	The Alamo City (March 6, 1837 Alamo siege climaxed)
	The City of Contrast and Romance
	The City of Contrasts
	The City of Flaming Adventure
	The City of Missions
	The City Where Life Is Different
	The Cradle of Texas Liberty
	The Free State of Bexar
	The Gateway to Mexico

SAN ANTONIO (Cont'd)	The Mission City The Old Garrison The Venice of the Prairie (canals winding through the streets) The Winter Playground of America St. Anthony's Town (mission authorized 1716) Unsainted Anthony
STONEWALL	The Home of LBJ (President Lyndon Baines Johnson) The Peach Capital of Texas
TEXARKANA	The Twin Cities (with Texarkana, Ark.; twin cities on the Arkansas-Texas border)
TYLER	The Rose Capital The Rose Capital of the World
UVALDE	The City Beautiful The Honey Capital of the United States The Honey Capital of the World The Town of Many Opportunities
WACO	The Athens of Texas (home of Baylor University) The Hub of Texas The Queen of the Brazos (on the Brazos River) The Target of Opportunity
WEST COLUMBIA	The Birthplace of a Republic (the first congress of the Republic of Texas assembled on October 3, 1836 at Columbia) The First Capital of the Republic of Texas
YOAKUM	A City of Homes, Schools and Churches The City by Accident

YOAKUM (Cont'd)	The Hub City of South Texas (in western Lavaca County)
	The Tomato Capital of South Central Texas

UTAH

BRIGHAM CITY	The City of Peaches (peach production)
	The Gateway to the Bear River Migratory Bird Refuge
CORINNE	The Burg on the Bear (Bear River)
	The Gentile City
PRICE	The Gateway to the Canyonlands and Highlands of Southeastern Utah
	The Heart of a Hunter's Paradise
PROVO	The City of Beauty, Progress and Culture
	The Gateway to Vacation-Land
	The Host to the West's Scenic Wonder-Ways
SALT LAKE CITY	Deseret
	The Capital City (1960 population 189,454)
	The Center of Scenic America
	The City by the Great Salt Lake
	The City of the Saints (home of the Church of Jesus Christ of Latter-Day Saints)
	The Crossroads of the West
	The Great Salt Lake City
	The Mormon City
	The Mormon's Mecca
	The New Jerusalem
	The Utah Zion
	Zion
SALTAIR	The Coney Island of the West

VERMONT

BARRE	The Granite Center of the World (granite quarries)
BENNINGTON	Vermont's Most Historic Town (British expedition defeated August 16, 1777 by General John Stark)
BRATTLEBORO	The City Where Vermont Begins (on the Connecticut River)
BURLINGTON	The City of Homes and Parks
	The Queen City of Vermont
	The Year 'Round Vacationland
MONTPELIER	The Capital City (1960 population 8,782)
	The Green Mountain City
PLYMOUTH	The Birthplace of Calvin Coolidge (July 4, 1872)
PROCTOR	The Marble Capital of the United States (home of Vermont Marble Company)
RUTLAND	The Community on the Move
	The Heart of the Green Mountains
	The Marble City (large marble quarries)
ST. ALBANS	The Railroad City (yards and shops of the Central Vermont Railway)
ST. JOHNSBURY	The Maple Center of the World
	The Maple Sugar Center of the World
SPRINGFIELD	The Cradle of Industry
STOWE	The Gateway to Smuggler's Notch (between Mt. Mansfield and the Sterling Mountains)
	The Ski Capital of the East (a single and two double chair lifts, three T-bar lifts, etc.)

VIRGINIA

ALBERTA	The Land of the Pines
ALEXANDRIA	The Heart of the Nation's Heritage
	The Historic Home Town of General George Washington
	The Home Town of George Washington
APPALACHIA	The Center of the Coal Fields
ARLINGTON	The City of the Slain (Arlington National Cemetery)
	The Resting Place of the Unknown American Hero (in Arlington National Cemetery)
ASHLAND	The Slash Town (1848 health resort Slash Cottage)
BEDFORD	The Mineral Springs City (limestone, sulphur, iron and sweet water springs) (see also Pa.)
BERRYVILLE	Battletown (name applied to local tavern where fights were frequent)
BLACKSBURG	A Good Place to Live and Work
	The City Where Industry and Education Meet (home of Virginia Polytechnic Institute)
BLACKSTONE	The Heart of the Old Dominion
	The Lunchstone
BLUEFIELD	Nature's Air-Conditioned City (adjoining Bluefield, W. Va.)
BOYKINS	Tarrara City
BRISTOL	The City in the Heart of Eastern America (see also Tennessee)
	The Shopping Center of the Appalachians (see also Tennessee)

CHARLOTTESVILLE	The Home of the Albemarle Pippin (extensive peach and apple orchards)
CHASE CITY	Christiansville
CHINCOTEAGUE	The Sportsman's Paradise (on the eastern shore of Chincoteague Bay)
CHRISTIANSBURG	The Gateway to the Southwest (on the Blue Ridge Plateau)
CLARKSVILLE	The Old Mart (tobacco market)
CLINCHPORT	The Frog Level
COLONIAL BEACH	Las Vegas on the Potomac (river resort on Potomac River)
CULPEPER	A Beautiful Community in Beautiful Virginia
DAMASCUS	The Gateway to Three Local Slogan States: Virginia, Tennessee, North Carolina
DANVILLE	The Capital City of South Side Virginia
	The Capital City of Southern Virginia
	The City on the Dan (Dan River)
	The Home of the World's Largest Single-Unit Textile Mill
	The Last Capital of the Confederacy (April 3-10, 1865 occupied by Jefferson Davis and his cabinet after the evacuation of Richmond)
	The World's Best Tobacco Market
DRAKES BRANCH	Ducks' Puddle
DUNGANNON	Bumgannon
FREDERICKSBURG	America's Most Historic City (numerous battles between 1861-1865)
	George Washington's Boyhood Home

FREDERICKSBURG (Cont'd)	The Boyhood Home of George Washington
	The Cockpit of the Civil War
	The Gateway to Historyland
GRETNA	The Junction
HAMILTON	Harmony
HAMPTON	Crab Town (oyster and fishing industry)
	The Oldest Continuous English Speaking Settlement in America (settled in 1610)
HAMPTON ROADS	The World's Greatest Harbor (the James, Nansemund and Elizabeth Rivers flow into Chesapeake Bay)
HARRISONBURG	The City With the Planned Future
	Virginia's Biggest Little City (1960 population 11,916)
HILLSVILLE	The Hill Town
HOLLAND	Holland's Corner
HOPEWELL	The Wonder City (on the James River)
INDEPENDENCE	Pinhook
JAMESTOWN	The Birthplace of the Nation (English colony, permanent settlement in 1607)
LEXINGTON	The Athens of Virginia (home of Washington and Lee University)
	The Shrine of the South (home of Virginia Military Institute, burial place of Stonewall Jackson, etc.)
LYNCHBURG	Lunchburg (humorous)
	The Center of Old Virginia
	The City of Charming Houses
	The City of Friendliness, Culture and Traditions
	The City of Hills (overlooking the James River)
	The City of Industry and Opportunity

LYNCHBURG (Cont'd)	The Community of Culture and Traditions
	The Friendly City
	The Hill City
MARTINSVILLE	The Furniture City (numerous furniture factories)
	The Sweatshirt Capital of the World
NEWPORT NEWS	The City of Ships and Shipbuilding
	The World's Greatest Harbor (James River)
NORFOLK	The Capital of the Most Historic Resort Area in America
	The City That Does Things
PENNINGTON GAP	The Gap (in Cumberland Mountains)
PETERSBURG	America's Most Historic City
	The Cockade City (Captain Richard Mc Roe and his company of volunteers wore a cockade)
PORTSMOUTH	The Navy's First City of the Sea (Norfolk Naval Shipyard)
PULASKI	The Gem City
RICHMOND	America's Fastest Growing Industrial City
	Byrd Town (foundation laid in 1733 by William Byrd II)
	The Capital City (1960 population 219,958)
	The Capital of the Confederacy
	The Capital of the Old South
	The City of Monuments
	The City of Seven Hills
	The Cockade City
	The Confederate Capital
	The Modern Rome
	The Monument City
	The Nine Hills

RICHMOND (Cont'd)	The Queen City of the South
	The Queen on the James (James River)
	The Tobacco Capital of the World
ROANOKE	The Magic City
	The Magic City of Virginia
	The Star City of the South
RODA	The Happy Hollow
SINGERS GLEN	The Glen
STAUNTON	The Queen City of the Shenandoah Valley
SUFFOLK	The Peanut City (processing plant of Planters Peanuts)
TOMS BROOK	The Brook
VIRGINIA BEACH	The City Where the Pines Meet the Sea
	The Garden Spot for Golf
	Virginia's Atlantic City
WILLIAMSBURG	The Capital of Colonial Virginia
	The Colonial Capital of Virginia
	The Historic City
	The Restored Colonial City (a project supported by John D. Rockefeller, Jr.)
	Virginia Colony's Elegant Old Capital
WINCHESTER	The Apple Capital
	The City in the Heart of the Shenandoah Valley of Virginia
	The Home of the Apple Blossom Festival
	The Northern Gateway to the Shenandoah Valley
YORKTOWN	The Waterloo of the Revolution (October 19, 1781 General Cornwallis surrendered)

WASHINGTON

ABERDEEN	The Plank Island
	The Twin Cities (with Hoquiam, Grays Harbor)
ANACORTES	The Magic City (on Fidalgo Island)
	The Ship Harbor
	The Squaw Harbor
AUBURN	The Slaughter House (named for Lt. W.A. Slaughter, renamed Auburn in 1893)
BANGOR	The Three Spits
BELLINGHAM	The Tulip City (tulip cultivation)
BREMERTON	The Home of the Pacific Fleet (Puget Sound Navy Yard)
	The String Town
BUCKLEY	The City of Good Water (on the White River)
BURLEY	The Circle City
CAMAS	The City of Paper (Crown-Zellerbach mills)
CARBONADO	The Model Mining Community (ceased operations about 1920)
CARNATION	The Home of the Contented Cows (Carnation Milk Products Company Farms)
CASHMERE	The Home of Aplets, the Confection of the Fairies (apple juice flavored enriched by walnuts and spices)
CENTRALIA	The Hub City (junction of the Chehalis and Skookumchuck Rivers)
	The Hub City of Southwestern Washington
CHEHALIS	The Friendly City
CHELAN	The Deep Water (Lake Chelan, bottom 400 feet

CHELAN (Cont'd)	below sea level)
CHENEY	The Depot Springs
CLARKSTON	Jawbone Flats (original name, changed in 1900 to Clarkston)
COLBY	The Coal Bay
CONCONULLY	The Money Hole (a mountain recess settled in 1886 by prospectors)
COULEE CITY	The Engineers' Town (junction point of the railroad and stage lines)
COUPEVILLE	The Port of Sea Captains (first of whom was Captain Thomas Coupe who settled in 1852)
COYLE	The Fisherman's Harbor
DAYTON	The City of Shady Walks and Pleasant Lawns
EDMONDS	The Princess City of Puget Sound (between Seattle and Everett)
ELLENSBURG	The Robbers' Roost (original name in 1867)
	The Rodeo City (rodeo held on Labor Day weekend)
ENUMCLAW	The Home of the Evil Spirits
EVERETT	The City of Smokestacks
FALL CITY	The Falls (on the Snoqualmie River)
	The Landing (original name)
FERNDALE	The Gem of the Nooksack Valley (on the Nooksack River)
FRUITLAND	The Robbers' Roost (early rendezvous for cattle thieves and desperadoes)
GRANITE FALLS	The Portage (the Stillaquamish River and the Pilchuck River)
HILLYARD	The Horse Plains

HOQUIAM	The Twin Cities (with Aberdeen, the Grays Harbor Cities)
	The Board Foot (saw mills)
INDEX	The Tourist's Paradise (near Snoqualmie National Forest)
KAHLOTUS	The Hole-in-the-Ground (Indian word, town on Washtucna Lake)
KALAMA	The City Where Rail Meets Water (Northern Pacific Railroad at confluence of Columbia and Kalama Rivers)
KENNEWICK	The Grassy Place (irrigated farmlands)
KITTITAS	The Land of Bread
LA CONNER	The Venice of Puget Sound (sloughs and marshes)
LATAH	The Hangman Creek
LONGVIEW	The City Practical That Vision Built (first planned city in the northwest, dedicated 1923)
MANETTE	The String Town
MASON CITY	The All-Electric Community (pre-fabricated)
MAZAMA	Goat Creek
MESA	The Table-Land
MONROE	Park Place
	The Model Municipality
MONTESANO	Mount Zion
MUKILTEO	Good Camping Ground
OCOSTA	Ocasta by the Sea (on Grays Harbor)
OLYMPIA	The Bear's Place (domicile of the brown bear)
	The Capital City (1960 population 18,273)
	The Capital of the Evergreen State
ORONDO	The Town Which Held the Key

PAHA	The Big Water
PALISADES	The Beulah Land
PALOUSE	The Grass Lands
PATAHA	Favorsburg (town site plotted in 1882 by "Vine" Favor)
	Waterstown (former name)
POMONA	The Roman Goddess of Fruit Trees (whose name was Pomona)
PORT ANGELES	Our Lady of the Angels
PORT GAMBLE	Boston
	The Brightness of the Noon-Day Sun
PORT MADISON	The Oleman House
PORT TOWNSEND	The Key City (a key city on Port Townsend Bay in the sailing boat era)
	The Port of Entry (on the Olympic Peninsula where the Straight of Juan de Fuca joins Puget Sound)
PULLMAN	The Home of State College of Washington
	The Three Forks
PUYALLUP	The Generous People
QUILCENE	The Salt Water People
RICHLAND	The Town the Atom Built (Hanford Engineer Works)
RUBY	The Babylon of Washington Territory (a lawless wide open town when formed)
SEATTLE	The Cannery City
	The City of Eternal Views (vistas of lakes, mountains and sound waters)
	The City of Homes
	The City of Seven Hills
	The Evergreen Playground
	The Gateway to Alaska
	The Gateway to the Orient
	The Little Portage (between Puget Sound and Lake Washington)

SEATTLE (Cont'd)	The Metropolis of the Pacific Northwest
	The Most Scenic City on the Continent
	The Nation's Most Beautiful City
	The Queen City
	The Queen City of the Sound
	The World Port
SEQUIM	The Smooth Water
	The Still Water
SHELTON	Christmas Town, U.S.A. (famous for its Christmas tree crop)
	The Strong Water
SKAMOKAWA	Little Venice (on Skamokawa Creek)
	The Smoke on the Water
SNOHOMISH	The Hub (at the confluence of the Pilchuck and Snohomish Rivers)
SPOKANE	The Friendly City
	The Heart of the Inland Empire
	The Home of the Mining Barons
	The Metropolis of the Inland Empire
	The Minneapolis of the West
SPRINGDALE	The Squire City
SUNNYSIDE	The Holy City (Christian Co-operative Movement settlement in 1898)
TACOMA	The Center of Industry
	The City of Destiny
	The City of Fine Hotels
	The Commencement City
	The Evergreen Playground
	The Forest Products Capital of America
	The Gateway to Mount Ranier
	The Lumber Capital

TACOMA (Cont'd)	The Lumber Capital of America
	The Lumber Capital of the World
	The Nearest Metropolitan Center to All Five Gateways of Ranier National Park
TOUCHET	The White Stallion (original name designated by Lewis and Clark)
TUKWILA	The Land of Hazel Nuts
TUMWATER	The Falls (on the Deschutes River)
	The New Market
	The Waterfalls
UNION	Another Clyde City
	The Venice of the Pacific
UTSALADDY	The Land of Berries
VANCOUVER	Columbia City (on the Columbia River)
VASHON	The Metropolis of Vashon Island (midway between Seattle and Tacoma)
WALLA WALLA	The Cradle of Pacific Northwest History
	The Place of Many Waters
WATERVILLE	The Jumper's Flats (claim jumping)
	The Sour Dough Flats
WENATCHEE	The Apple Capital of the World
	The Gateway to the Valley of Perfect Apples
WILBUR	The Goosetown (in 1888 Samuel Wilbur Condit shot a tame gander believing it was a wild goose)
WILLAPA	The Venice of the Northwest (on the Willapa River)
WISHRAM	The Food Emporium
YAKIMA	The Eastern Gateway to Mt. Ranier National Park
	The Fruit Bowl of the Nation

WEST VIRGINIA

BECKLEY	The Smokeless Coal Capital of the World (center of coal mining and natural gas region)
BLUEFIELD	The Air Conditioned City (adjoining Bluefield, Va.)
CHARLESTON	The Capital City (1960 population 85,796)
	The Chemical City (produces calcium chlorine, iodine, etc.)
ELKINS	The Vacation Capital of the Appalachian Highlands (on the Tygarts Valley River)
HUNTINGTON	The Gateway City (southwestern section of W. Va.)
MARTINSBURG	The Chief Industrial City of the Eastern Panhandle
MIDDLEWAY	The Wizard's Clip
MORGANTOWN	The Home of West Virginia University (founded 1867)
SHEPHERDSTOWN	The Oldest Town in West Virginia (established 1732)
SOUTH CHARLESTON	The Chemical Center of the World
WELCH	Little New York (closely built congested area)
WHEELING	The Chief City of West Virginia (1960 population 53,500) (3rd in pop.)
	The City of Beautiful Parks (Oglebay Park, largest in W. Va.)
	The City of Historic Lore (first visitor, Captain de Bienville, 1749)
	The City of Magnificent Stores
	The City of Thriving Industries
	The Nail City

WISCONSIN

APPLETON	The Crescent City
BELOIT	A Metropolitan Community of Opportunity
	One of Wisconsin's Fastest Growing Cities
COLBY	The Midget City
CRIVITZ	The Gateway to the Lakes and Streams of the Thunder Mountain Region (on the Peshtigo River)
EAU CLAIRE	The City of the Green Light
FOND DU LAC	The Fountain City
GREEN BAY	The Home of the Packers (stadium and playing field of the professional football team known as the Green Bay Packers)
	The Packers Town
IRON RIVER	The Blueberry Capital of the Nation
LA CROSSE	The Gateway City (on the Mississippi River at the confluence of the Black and La Crosse Rivers)
LAKE GENEVA	The Newport of Chicago Society (a summer residential colony which received its impetus in 1871 as a result of the Chicago fire)
MADISON	The Capital City (1960 population 126,706)
	The City Built on an Isthmus (between Lakes Monona and Mendota)
	The City of Beautiful Homes and Thriving Industry
	The City of Parks
	The Cultural Center
	The Four Lake City

MADISON (Cont'd)	The Four Lakes City (Lakes Mendota, Monona, Waubesa and Kegonsa)
	The Home of the University of Wisconsin
	The Ideal Convention and Vacation City
	The Key Shopping and Manufacturing Center
	The Lake City
	The Most Beautiful Little City in America (1960 population 126,706)
	The Recreational Center
MANITOWOC	The Clipper City (a shipbuilding center where clipper ships were built from 1860 to 1880)
MARSHFIELD	The Crossroads of Wisconsin
MENASHA	The Twin Cities (with Neenah, Wis.)
MILWAUKEE	Milwaukee the Beautiful
	The American Munich
	The Beer Capital of America (numerous breweries)
	The Beer City
	The Blonde Beauty of the Lakes
	The Brewing Capital of the World (Blatz Brewery, Pabst Brewery, etc.)
	The Bright Spot
	The City Beautiful
	The City of Homes
	The Cream City
	The Cream White City of the Unsalted Seas
	The Deutsch-Athens (German immigrants)
	The Fair White City
	The Foam City
	The Friendly City

MILWAUKEE (Cont'd)	The German Athens (German immigrants)
	The Industrial City
	The Middlewest Center for Diversified Manufacture
	Wisconsin's Beautiful Capitol City
MINERAL POINT	The Shake-Rag City (Shake Rag Street where women waved rags and dishcloths to summon miners on an opposite hill to return for dinner)
MONROE	America's Swiss Cheese Capital (about 300 factories)
	The Swiss Cheese Capital of the United States (numerous factories)
NEENAH	The Paper City (numerous paper mills)
	The Twin Cities (with Menasha, Wis.)
ORFORDVILLE	The Grass Roots of America
OSHKOSH	The Sawdust City
PARK FALLS	The City in the Center of the Beautiful North Woods
	The City in the Heart of the Chequamegon National Forest
	The Fun Town (popular recreation area)
	The Vacationland of Northern Wisconsin
PORT WING	The Hub of Lake Superior's Beautiful South Shore Drive
PRAIRIE DU CHIEN	America's Wild Life Preserver
	The Gateway to the Winneshiek (Winneshiek Bluff)
	The Historical City (seen in 1673 by Joliet and Marquette)

PRENTICE	The Friendly Village (1960 population 427)
RACINE	Kringleville (after the Dane's favorite pastry)
	The Belle City
	The Belle City of the Lakes (on Lake Michigan)
	The City of Advantages
	The Czech Bethlehem (Bohemian settlement)
	The Danish Capital of the United States (one-third of its population of Danish descent)
	Wisconsin's Second City (actually now third city in population in 1960, population 89,144)
RHINELANDER	The Capital of the Heart O' the Lakes (trading center for hunters, campers, fishermen)
RIPON	The Birthplace of the Republican Party (organized Feb. 28, 1854)
	The City of the Twin Spires (the spires on College Hill of the Grace Lutheran and Congregational Churches)
SHEBOYGAN	The Bratwurst Capital of the World (German settlement)
	The Chair City (industry declined about 1918)
	The City of Cheese, Chairs, Children and Churches (seldom used after 1940)
	The Evergreen City
STURGEON BAY	The Canal City (canal connecting Green Bay with Lake Michigan)
SUPERIOR	America's Second Port (on Lake Superior)

SUPERIOR (Cont'd)	The City of One Hundred Lakes and Streams
	The City of the Northland
	The Consumer Cooperative Center of the United States
	The Hub of North America
	The Playground of Presidents
	The Summer Capital of America (on Lake Superior)
	The Transportation Center of North America (grain center and shipping terminus for copper and iron)
WAUKESHA	The Saratoga of the West (medicinal springs)
	The Spring City (medicinal springs)
WAUSAU	The Forest City
WISCONSIN DELLS	America's Scenic Wonderland (on the Wisconsin River, lined by rock formations)
WISCONSIN RAPIDS	The Geographic Heart of the State (on the Wisconsin River)

WYOMING

AFTON	The Switzerland of America (6,134 feet altitude)
BASIN	Bean Town (marketing center for the bean crop)
	The Garden City (a tree and shrub planting campaign was instituted in 1910)
CASPER	The Convention City
	The Growing City
	The Hub
	The Hub City (seat of Natrona County)
	The Magic City of the Plains

CASPER (Cont'd)	The Oil Capital of the Rockies (oil fields, 3 major oil refineries, 400 oil affiliated concerns)
	The Oil City
	The Progress City of the Rockies
CHEYENNE	Hell on Wheels (formerly used)
	The Capital City (1960 population 43,505)
	The Home of Frontier Days
	The Magic City of the Plains
	The Magic City of the West
DOUGLAS	The Tent Town (name conferred in 1886 when the town was founded)
EVANSTON	The Most Typical Western City in Wyoming
GLENROCK	The Oil City (oil refinery)
LANDER	The Apple City
	The City Where the Rails and the Trails Begin (western terminus of the Chicago and Northwestern Railway)
	The Push Root City
LARAMIE	The Athens of Wyoming (home of the University of Wyoming)
	The Gem City
SHERIDAN	The Center of the Dude Ranch Industry
	The City in the Shadow of the Big Horn
	The City Where the West Remains
	The Headquarters of the Big Horn National Forest
	The Optimist City
THERMOPOLIS	The City of Heat (thermal springs)

THERMOPOLIS (Cont'd)	The World's Largest Mineral Hot Springs (13,000 gallons flow per minute) Wyoming's Year 'Round Health and Scenic Center

Nicknames Index
Cities

A

ACTION CITY	Charlotte, N. C.
AGGREGATE OF VILLAGES	Weymouth, Mass.
AGRICULTURAL AND INDUSTRIAL CENTER OF NORTHWEST ARKANSAS	Springdale, Ark.
AGRICULTURAL AND TIMBER EMPIRE	Blountstown, Fla.
AGRICULTURAL CAPITAL	Jackson, Miss.
AIR CAPITAL OF AMERICA	Wichita, Kans.
AIR CAPITAL OF THE CAROLINAS	Charleston, S. C.
AIR CAPITAL OF THE WEST	San Diego, Calif.
AIR CAPITAL OF THE WORLD	Miami, Fla.
AIR CAPITAL OF THE WORLD	Wichita, Kans.
AIR-CONDITIONED CITY	Bluefield, W. Va.
AIR-CONDITIONED CITY	Duluth, Minn.
AIR-CONDITIONED DULUTH	Duluth, Minn.
AIR CROSSROADS OF AMERICA	Evansville, Ind.
AIR CROSSROADS OF THE WORLD	Anchorage, Alaska
AIRWAYS OF AMERICA	Valdosta, Ga.
AIR HUB OF THE AMERICAS	New Orleans, La.
ALAMO CITY	San Antonio, Texas
ALASKA'S CAPITAL CITY	Juneau, Alaska
ALASKA'S LITTLE NORWAY	Petersburg, Alaska
ALEX CITY	Alexander City, Ala.
ALEXANDRIA OF AMERICA	New Orleans, La.

ALL-AMERICAN CITY

While the term "All-American City" is often referred to as a nickname, it is an award sponsored by the National Municipal League and Look Magazine. Its use is authorized for one year only. The cities so honored and the years in which the awards were made are listed at the conclusion of this general index beginning with page 309.

AMERICA'S FAVORITE SUN AND FUN VACATIONLAND	Phoenix, Ariz.
AMERICA'S FIRST CITY OF SUNSHINE	Tucson, Ariz.
AMERICA'S FIRST MINING CAPITAL	Houghton, Mich.
AMERICA'S FIRST SEASHORE RESORT	Long Branch, N.J.
AMERICA'S FOREMOST DESERT RESORT	Palm Beach, Calif.
AMERICA'S FOREMOST YEAR 'ROUND SPORTS CENTER	Sun Valley, Idaho
AMERICA'S GREAT CENTRAL MARKET AND TOURIST CITY	St. Louis, Mo.
AMERICA'S GREAT CONVENTION CITY	Philadelphia, Pa.
AMERICA'S GREATEST FAMILY RESORT	Harvey Cedars, N.J.
AMERICA'S GREATEST FAMILY RESORT	Ocean City, N.J.
AMERICA'S GREATEST HEALTH AND PLEASURE RESORT	French Lick, Ind.
AMERICA'S GREATEST HEALTH AND RESORT CENTER	Hot Springs, Ark.
AMERICA'S GREATEST HEALTH AND REST CENTER	Hot Springs, Ark.
AMERICA'S GREATEST INLAND CITY	Indianapolis, Ind.
AMERICA'S HEALTHIEST CITY	Long Beach, N. Y.
AMERICA'S HOLSTEIN CAPITAL	Northfield, Minn.
AMERICA'S HOME TOWN	Plymouth, Mass.
AMERICA'S IDEAL VACATION LAND	Billings, Mont.
AMERICA'S INDUSTRIAL CITY	Fort Smith, Ark.
AMERICA'S IRON CAPITAL	Hibbing, Minn.
AMERICA'S LEADING TOURIST RESORT	New York, N.Y.
AMERICA'S LITTLE SWITZERLAND	Eureka Springs, Ark.
AMERICA'S LITTLE SWITZERLAND	Fayetteville, Ark.
AMERICA'S LITTLE SWITZERLAND	Newaygo, Mich.

AMERICA'S LOW SPOT	Death Valley, Calif.
AMERICA'S MILK CENTER	Harvard, Ill.
AMERICA'S MINING CAPITAL	Hibbing, Minn.
AMERICA'S MOST BEAUTIFUL CITY	Savannah, Ga.
AMERICA'S MOST HISTORIC CITY	Charleston, S. C.
AMERICA'S MOST HISTORIC CITY	Fredericksburg, Va.
AMERICA'S MOST HISTORIC CITY	Petersburg, Va.
AMERICA'S MOST INTEREST-ING CITY	New Orleans, La.
AMERICA'S MOST WONDER-FUL SPA	Saratoga Springs, N. Y.
AMERICA'S MOUNTAIN SPRING	Sharon Springs, N. Y.
AMERICA'S NAPLES	Woods Hole, Mass.
AMERICA'S NEWEST INDUS-TRIAL CENTER	Paducah, Ky.
AMERICA'S NEWEST INDUS-TRIAL FRONTIER	Odessa, Texas
AMERICA'S NO. 1 CONTRARY CITY	Chicago, Ill.
AMERICA'S OLDEST CITY	St. Augustine, Fla.
AMERICA'S OLDEST SUMMER RESORT	Newport, R. I.
AMERICA'S OWN SPA	Hot Springs, Ark.
AMERICA'S PARIS	Cincinnati, Ohio
AMERICA'S PREMIER PLAY-GROUND	Rye, N. Y.
AMERICA'S RIVIERA	Biloxi, Minn.
AMERICA'S RIVIERA	Chicago, Ill.
AMERICA'S RIVIERA	Gulfport, Miss.
AMERICA'S SCENIC WONDER-LAND	Niagara Falls, N. Y.
AMERICA'S SCENIC WONDER-LAND	Wisconsin Dells, Wis.
AMERICA'S SECOND PORT	Superior, Wis.
AMERICA'S SHOE CAPITAL	St. Louis, Mo.
AMERICA'S SINGAPORE	Key West, Fla.
AMERICA'S SOCIETY CAPITAL	Newport, R. I.
AMERICA'S SOUTHERNMOST CITY	Key West, Fla.

AMERICA'S SPORTS MECCA	French Lick, Ind.
AMERICA'S SUGAR BOWL	Brush, Colo.
AMERICA'S SUNRISE GATEWAY	Portland, Me.
AMERICA'S SWEETEST TOWN	Clewiston, Fla.
AMERICA'S SWEETHEART CITY	Loveland, Colo.
AMERICA'S SWISS CHEESE CAPITAL	Monroe, Wis.
AMERICA'S SWITZERLAND	Lake Placid, N. Y.
AMERICA'S TYPICAL CITY	Zanesville, Ohio
AMERICA'S WILD LIFE PRESERVER	Prairie du Chien, Wis.
AMERICA'S YEAR 'ROUND HOLIDAY ISLAND	Jekyll Island, Ga.
AMERICA'S YEAR 'ROUND PLAYGROUND	Miami Beach, Fla.
AMERICA'S YEAR 'ROUND PLAYGROUND	Scranton, Pa.
AMERICAN ATHENS	Boston, Mass.
AMERICAN CARLSBAD	Ashland, Ore.
AMERICAN LYONS	Paterson, N. J.
AMERICAN MUNICH	Milwaukee, Wis.
ANCIENT AND HONORABLE PUEBLO	Tucson, Ariz.
ANCIENT CITY	Annapolis, Md.
ANCIENT CITY	St. Augustine, Fla.
ANGEL CITY	Los Angeles, Calif.
ANNAPOLIS OF THE AIR	Pensacola, Fla.
ANNIE'S TOWN	Anniston, Ala.
ANOTHER CLYDE CITY	Union, Wash.
ANTHRACITE CAPITAL OF THE WORLD	Scranton, Pa.
ANTHRACITE CITY	Scranton, Pa.
APPLE CAPITAL	Winchester, Va.
APPLE CAPITAL OF THE WORLD	Wenatchee, Wash.
APPLE CITY	Lander, Wyo.
AQUEDUCT CITY	Norristown, Pa.
AQUEDUCT CITY	Rochester, N. Y.
AREA OF OPPORTUNITY	Ruskin, Fla.
ARIZONA'S COPPER CAPITAL	Bisbee, Ariz.
ARIZONA'S FIRST CAPITAL	Prescott, Ariz.

ARIZONA'S SECOND LARGEST CITY	Tucson, Ariz.
ARK CITY	Arkansas City, Ark.
ARKANSAS' INDUSTRIAL CENTER	Fort Smith, Ark.
ARKANSAS' LARGEST HEALTH AND PLEASURE RESORT	Hot Springs, Ark.
ARKANSAS' ONLY SEAPORT	Helena, Ark.
ARKOPOLIS	Little Rock, Ark.
ARROWHEAD EGG BASKET	Barnum, Minn.
ARSENAL OF DEMOCRACY	Fort Worth, Texas
ART CENTER OF RHODE ISLAND	Wickford, R. I.
ARTESIAN CITY	Albany, Ga.
ARTESIAN CITY	Martinsville, Ind.
ASPARAGUS CAPITAL OF THE WORLD	Isleton, Calif.
ATHENS	Boston, Mass.
ATHENS OF ALABAMA	Tuscaloosa, Ala.
ATHENS OF AMERICA	Boston, Mass.
ATHENS OF AMERICA	Iowa City, Iowa
ATHENS OF AMERICA	New Harmony, Ind.
ATHENS OF ARKANSAS	Fayetteville, Ark.
ATHENS OF CALIFORNIA	Benicia, Calif.
ATHENS OF FLORIDA	De Land, Fla.
ATHENS OF INDIANA	Crawfordsville, Ind.
ATHENS OF INDIANA	Roanoke, Ind.
ATHENS OF IOWA	Iowa City, Iowa
ATHENS OF TEXAS	Waco, Texas
ATHENS OF THE MIDDLE WEST	Cincinnati, Ohio
ATHENS OF THE MIDWEST	Columbia, Mo.
ATHENS OF THE NEW WORLD	Boston, Mass.
ATHENS OF THE NORTHWEST	Faribault, Minn.
ATHENS OF THE SOUTH	Nashville, Tenn.
ATHENS OF THE SOUTHWEST	Dallas, Texas
ATHENS OF THE UNITED STATES	Boston, Mass.
ATHENS OF THE WEST	Abilene, Texas
ATHENS OF THE WEST	Berkeley, Calif.
ATHENS OF THE WEST	Boston, Mass.
ATHENS OF THE WEST	Lexington, Ky.
ATHENS OF VIRGINIA	Lexington, Va.

ATHENS OF WYOMING	Laramie, Wyo.
ATHENS YOU WILL WANT TO SEE	Athens, Ga.
ATLANTIC CITY OF THE MIDDLE WEST	Cedar Point, Ohio
ATOMIC CAPITAL OF THE WORLD	Oak Ridge, Tenn.
ATOMIC ENERGY CITY	Oak Ridge, Tenn.
AUTO CITY	Detroit, Mich.
AUTOMOBILE CAPITAL OF THE WORLD	Detroit, Mich.
AUTOMOBILE CITY	Detroit, Mich.
AUTOMOBILE CITY OF THE WORLD	Detroit, Mich.
AZALIA TRAIL CITY	Lafayette, La.

B

BABYLON OF WASHINGTON TERRITORY	Ruby, Wash.
BABYLON ON THE BLUFF	Memphis, Tenn.
BABYLONIAN BEDLAM	New York, N. Y.
BAD BIRMINGHAM	Birmingham, Ala.
BAGDAD BY THE BAY	San Francisco, Calif.
BAGDAD OF THE SUBWAY	New York, N. Y.
BAGDAD ON THE HUDSON	New York, N. Y.
BALANCED CITY	Berkeley, Calif.
BALANCED COMMUNITY OF OPPORTUNITY AND HAPPY HOMES	Jackson, Miss.
BANANA BELT CITY	Lewiston, Idaho
BARBED WIRE CAPITAL OF THE WORLD	De Kalb, Ill.
BATTLEFIELD CITY	Gettysburg, Pa.
BATTLEFIELD OF THE REVOLUTION	Augusta, Ga.
BATTLETOWN	Berryville, Va.
BAY CITY	San Francisco, Calif.
BAY HORSE	Boston, Mass.
BAYOU CITY	Houston, Texas
BEAN TOWN	Basin, Wyo.
BEANTOWN	Boston, Mass.
BEAR'S PLACE	Olympia, Wash.

BEAUTIFUL CITY	Cincinnati, Ohio
BEAUTIFUL CITY BY A BEAUTIFUL LAKE	Coeur d'Alene, Idaho
BEAUTIFUL CITY BY THE SEA	Portland, Me.
BEAUTIFUL CITY OF HOMES, DIVERSIFIED BUSINESS AND PROGRESSIVE OUTLOOK	Buffalo, N. Y.
BEAUTIFUL CITY OF HOMES IN THE HISTORIC MOHAWK VALLEY	Utica, N. Y.
BEAUTIFUL CITY OF ROSES	Portland, Ore.
BEAUTIFUL PLACE BY THE SEA	Ogunquit, Me.
BEAUTIFUL COMMUNITY IN BEAUTIFUL VIRGINIA	Culpeper, Va.
BEAUTIFUL TOWN THAT IS SEATED BY THE SEA	Portland, Me.
BEAUTY SPOT OF THE NORTH JERSEY COAST	Asbury Park, N. J.
BEDROOM OF NEW YORK	Brooklyn, N. Y.
BEE-HIVE OF INDUSTRY	Providence, R. I.
BEER CAPITAL OF AMERICA	Milwaukee, Wis.
BEER CITY	Milwaukee, Wis.
BELL TOWN	East Hampton, Conn.
BELL TOWN OF AMERICA	East Hampton, Conn.
BELLE CITY	Racine, Wis.
BELLE CITY OF THE BLUEGRASS REGIONS	Lexington, Ky.
BELLE CITY OF THE LAKES	Racine, Wis.
BENTON COUNTY'S FASTEST GROWING CITY	Lincoln, Mo.
BERRY CITY	Woodburn, Ore.
BEST BALANCED CITY	Hickory, N. C.
BEST CONVENTION POINT IN THE EAST	Springfield, Mass.
BEST KNOWN CITY IN THE WORLD	Battle Creek, Mich.
BEST KNOWN CITY OF ITS SIZE IN THE WORLD	Battle Creek, Mich.

BEST KNOWN LITTLE CITY IN AMERICA	Claremore, Okla.
BEST LIGHTED TOWN IN THE WEST	Burley, Idaho
BEST PECAN PRODUCING AREA IN THE SOUTH	Fort Valley, Ga.
BEST TOWN IN THE STATE BY A DAMSITE	Stockton, Mo.
BEST TOWN SITE ON THE OHIO	Steubenville, Ohio
BETSYTOWN	Elizabeth, N. J.
BEULAH LAND	Palisades, Wash.
BIG APPLE	New York, N. Y.
BIG BURG	New York, N. Y.
BIG CITY	New York, N. Y.
BIG "D"	Dallas, Texas
BIG HEART OF TEXAS	Austin, Texas
BIG "M" OF THE OZARKS	Monett, Mo.
BIG SHELBY	Memphis, Tenn.
BIG SMOKE	Pittsburgh, Pa.
BIG SMOKY	Pittsburgh, Pa.
BIG TOWN	Chicago, Ill.
BIG TOWN	New York, N. Y.
BIG WATER	Paha, Wash.
BIGGEST LITTLE CITY	Abilene, Kans.
BIGGEST LITTLE CITY IN AMERICA	Atlantic City, N. J.
BIGGEST LITTLE CITY IN MICHIGAN	Rockford, Mich.
BIGGEST LITTLE CITY IN THE U.S.A.	Dodge City, Kans.
BIGGEST LITTLE CITY IN THE WORLD	Reno, Nev.
BIGGEST LITTLE TOWN IN THE WEST	Broadus, Mont.
BIG-HEADED BURG	Hollywood, Calif.
BILLTOWN	Williamstown, Kans.
BIRD SANCTUARY	Henderson, N. C.
BIRMINGHAM OF AMERICA	Cincinnati, Ohio
BIRMINGHAM OF AMERICA	Pittsburgh, Pa.
BIRTHPLACE OF A REPUBLIC	West Columbia, Tex.
BIRTHPLACE OF THE AMERICAN COTTON INDUSTRY	Pawtucket, R. I.

BIRTHPLACE OF AMERICAN LIBERTY	Lexington, Mass.
BIRTHPLACE OF AMERICAN LIBERTY	Philadelphia, Pa.
BIRTHPLACE OF AVIATION	Dayton, Ohio
BIRTHPLACE OF CALIFORNIA	San Diego, Calif.
BIRTHPLACE OF CALVIN COOLIDGE	Plymouth, Vt.
BIRTHPLACE OF DANIEL WEBSTER	Franklin, N. H.
BIRTHPLACE OF DIXIE	Montgomery, Ala.
BIRTHPLACE OF HARRY S. TRUMAN	Lamar, Mo.
BIRTHPLACE OF LIBERTY	Quincy, Mass.
BIRTHPLACE OF MC KINLEY	Niles, Ohio
BIRTHPLACE OF MAINE	Freeport, Me.
BIRTHPLACE OF OKLAHOMA	Guthrie, Okla.
BIRTHPLACE OF RADIO	Murray, Ky.
BIRTHPLACE OF SPEED	Ormond Beach, Fla.
BIRTHPLACE OF THE AMERICAN NAVY	Beverly, Mass.
BIRTHPLACE OF THE MESABI	Mountain Lake, Minn.
BIRTHPLACE OF THE NATION	Jamestown, Va.
BIRTHPLACE OF THE NATION	Philadelphia, Pa.
BIRTHPLACE OF THE NORTHERN PACIFIC	Carlton, Minn.
BIRTHPLACE OF THE REPUBLICAN PARTY	Ripon, Wis.
BIRTHPLACE OF U. S. NAVAL AVIATION	Pensacola, Fla.
BISON CITY	Buffalo, N. Y.
BIT OF NEW ENGLAND WITH A SOMBRERO ON IT	Claremont, Calif.
BIT OF THE OLD WEST TRANSPLANTED IN THE TWENTIETH CENTURY	Wickenburg, Ariz.
BITCHES HEAVEN	Boston, Mass.
BITUMINOUS CITY	Connellsville, Pa.
BLACK DIAMOND CITY	Wilkes-Barre, Pa.
BLACK HEART OF MONTANA	Butte, Mont.

BLONDE BEAUTY OF THE LAKES	Milwaukee, Wis.
BLUE MARLIN CAPITAL OF THE WORLD	Hatteras, N. C.
BLUEBERRY CAPITAL OF THE NATION	Iron River, Wis.
BLUEGRASS CAPITAL	Frankfort, Ky.
BLUEGRASS CAPITAL	Lexington, Ky.
BLUFF CITY	Eufaula, Ala.
BLUFF CITY	Hannibal, Mo.
BLUFF CITY	Memphis, Tenn.
BLUFF CITY	Natchez, Miss.
BOARD FOOT	Hoquiam, Wash.
BOOM TOWN WITHOUT OIL	Austin, Texas
BOOMING CONVENTION CITY	Las Vegas, Nev.
BORDER CITY	Fall River, Mass.
BORDER TOWN	Rye, N. Y.
BOSTON	Port Gamble, Wash.
BOSTON OF THE WEST	St. Paul, Minn.
BOSTONIA	Boston, Mass.
BOYHOOD HOME OF GEORGE WASHINGTON	Fredericksburg, Va.
BOYHOOD HOME OF MARK TWAIN	Hannibal, Mo.
BOY'S TOWN OF NEW ENGLAND	Tilton, N. H.
BRAINY BOROUGH	Metuchen, N. J.
BRAN TOWN	Binghampton, N. Y.
BRASS CITY	Waterbury, Conn.
BRATWURST CAPITAL OF THE WORLD	Sheboygan, Wis.
BREAD BASKET OF THE WORLD	Fargo, N. D.
BREAKFAST FOOD CITY	Battle Creek, Mich.
BREEZY TOWN	Chicago, Ill.
BREWING CAPITAL OF THE WORLD	Milwaukee, Wis.
BREWING CITY	Reading, Pa.
BRIDE OF THE MOUNTAINS	Talladega, Ala.
BRIGHT SPOT	Dallas, Texas
BRIGHT SPOT	Milwaukee, Wis.
BRIGHT SPOT OF AMERICA	Peoria, Ill.

BRIGHTNESS OF THE NOON-DAY SUN	Port Gamble, Wash.
BRIGHTON'S FUTURE IS BRIGHT	Brighton, Colo.
BROADWAY COLONY IN THE HEART OF MAINE	Lakewood, Me.
BROADWAY OF THE DESERT	Las Vegas, Nev.
BROILER CAPITAL OF MAINE	Belfast, Me.
BROOK	Toms Brook, Va.
BROOKLYN OF THE SOUTH	Anniston, Ala.
BROWNSTONE CITY	Hummelstown, Pa.
BUCCANEER CITY	Fernandina Beach, Fla.
BUCKLE ON THE KANSAS WHEAT BELT	Dodge City, Kans.
BUCKTAIL CITY	Smethport, Pa.
BUMGANNON	Dungannon, Va.
BUNGTOWN	Cold Spring Harbor, N. Y.
BURG	New York, N. Y.
BURG ON THE BEAR	Corinne, Utah
BUSHWACKERS' CAPITAL	Nevada, Mo.
BUSIEST FRESHWATER PORT IN THE WORLD	Toledo, Ohio
BUSINESS HEART OF THE LAKELAND AREA	Dover, N. J.
BUSTLING CENTER OF INDUSTRY, AGRICULTURE, WHOLESALE TRADE AND SHIPPING	Fresno, Calif.
BUSY AGRICULTURAL COMMUNITY	Southwest City, Mo.
BUTTER CAPITAL OF THE WORLD	Owatonna, Minn.
BUTTER CITY	Manteca, Calif.
BUYING CENTER OF A QUARTER MILLION PEOPLE	Lancaster, Pa.
BYRD TOWN	Richmond, Va.

C

CALADIUM CAPITAL OF THE WORLD	Lake Placid, Fla.

CALIFORNIA'S INLAND HARBOR	Stockton, Calif.
CALIFORNIA'S WORLD-FAMOUS ALL-YEAR RESORT	Santa Barbara, Calif.
CAMEL CITY	Winston-Salem, N.C.
CAMELLIA CITY	Greenville, Ala.
CAMERA CITY	Rochester, N. Y.
CANAL CITY	Hollidaysburg, Pa.
CANAL CITY	Sturgeon Bay, Wis.
CANNERY CITY	Seattle, Wash.
CANNON CITY	Kannapolis, N. C.
CANOE CITY	Old Town, Me.
CANYON CITY	Wellsboro, Pa.
CAPITAL CITY	Albany, N. Y.
CAPITAL CITY	Annapolis, Md.
CAPITAL CITY	Atlanta, Ga.
CAPITAL CITY	Augusta, Me.
CAPITAL CITY	Austin, Texas
CAPITAL CITY	Baton Rouge, La.
CAPITAL CITY	Bismarck, N. D.
CAPITAL CITY	Boise, Idaho
CAPITAL CITY	Boston, Mass.
CAPITAL CITY	Carson City, Nev.
CAPITAL CITY	Charleston, W. Va.
CAPITAL CITY	Cheyenne, Wyo.
CAPITAL CITY	Columbia, S. C.
CAPITAL CITY	Columbus, Ohio
CAPITAL CITY	Concord, N. H.
CAPITAL CITY	Denver, Colo.
CAPITAL CITY	Des Moines, Iowa
CAPITAL CITY	Dover, Del.
CAPITAL CITY	Frankfort, Ky.
CAPITAL CITY	Harrisburg, Pa.
CAPITAL CITY	Hartford, Conn.
CAPITAL CITY	Helena, Mont.
CAPITAL CITY	Honolulu, Hawaii
CAPITAL CITY	Indianapolis, Ind.
CAPITAL CITY	Jackson, Miss.
CAPITAL CITY	Jefferson City, Mo.
CAPITAL CITY	Juneau, Alaska
CAPITAL CITY	Lansing, Mich.
CAPITAL CITY	Lincoln, Neb.
CAPITAL CITY	Little Rock, Ark.

CAPITAL CITY	Madison, Wis.
CAPITAL CITY	Montgomery, Ala.
CAPITAL CITY	Montpelier, Vt.
CAPITAL CITY	Nashville, Tenn.
CAPITAL CITY	Oklahoma City, Okla.
CAPITAL CITY	Olympia, Wash.
CAPITAL CITY	Phoenix, Ariz.
CAPITAL CITY	Pierre, S. D.
CAPITAL CITY	Providence, R. I.
CAPITAL CITY	Raleigh, N. C.
CAPITAL CITY	Richmond, Va.
CAPITAL CITY	Sacramento, Calif.
CAPITAL CITY	St. Paul, Minn.
CAPITAL CITY	Salem, Ore.
CAPITAL CITY	Salt Lake City, Utah
CAPITAL CITY	Santa Fe, N. M.
CAPITAL CITY	Springfield, Ill.
CAPITAL CITY	Tallahassee, Fla.
CAPITAL CITY	Topeka, Kans.
CAPITAL CITY	Trenton, N. J.
CAPITAL CITY	Washington, D. C.
CAPITAL CITY	Youngstown, Ohio
CAPITAL CITY	Zanesville, Ohio
CAPITAL CITY DIFFERENT	Santa Fe, N. M.
CAPITAL CITY OF A GREAT INDUSTRIAL EMPIRE	Youngstown, Ohio
CAPITAL CITY OF A GREAT NATION	Washington, D. C.
CAPITAL CITY OF A GREAT TRADE EMPIRE	Cleveland, Ohio
CAPITAL CITY OF ARIZONA	Phoenix, Ariz.
CAPITAL CITY OF FABULOUS FLORIDA	Tallahassee, Fla.
CAPITAL CITY OF GOOD LIVING, COMMERCE AND INDUSTRY	Salem, Ore.
CAPITAL CITY OF INDUSTRIAL PROGRESS	Nashville, Tenn.
CAPITAL CITY OF SOUTHERN VIRGINIA	Danville, Va.
CAPITAL CITY OF SOUTHSIDE VIRGINIA	Danville, Va.
CAPITAL CITY OF TENNESSEE	Nashville, Tenn.

CAPITAL CITY OF THE COUNTRY WITH A COPPER BOTTOM	Globe, Ariz.
CAPITAL CITY OF THE LAND OF ARK-LA-TEX	Shreveport, La.
CAPITAL CITY OF THE LAND OF THE SKY	Asheville, N. C.
CAPITAL OF AMERICA	Washington, D. C.
CAPITAL OF AMERICA'S STATE OF OPPORTUNITY	Jackson, Miss.
CAPITAL OF AN EMPIRE	Juneau, Alaska
CAPITAL OF COLONIAL VIRGINIA	Williamsburg, Va.
CAPITAL OF CRACKPOTS	Los Angeles, Calif.
CAPITAL OF DUNELAND	Michigan City, Ind.
CAPITAL OF EASTERN OREGON	Ontario, Ore.
CAPITAL OF LITTLE DIXIE	Mexico, Mo.
CAPITAL OF MISERABLE HUTS	Washington, D. C.
CAPITAL OF NEW ENGLAND	Boston, Mass.
CAPITAL OF OLD CALIFORNIA	Monterey, Calif.
CAPITAL OF OPPORTUNITY	Bismarck, N. D.
CAPITAL OF PENNSYLVANIA GERMAN-LAND	Reading, Pa.
CAPITAL OF RADIO	Camden, N. J.
CAPITAL OF SOONERLAND	Oklahoma City, Okla.
CAPITAL OF SOUTH CENTRAL OKLAHOMA	Ardmore, Okla.
CAPITAL OF THE ATOMIC AGE	Los Alamos, N.M.
CAPITAL OF THE BIG LAKE	Bull Shoals, Ark.
CAPITAL OF THE BLUE-GRASS REGION	Lexington, Ky.
CAPITAL OF THE CAROLINAS	Charleston, S. C.
CAPITAL OF THE CHIPPEWA NATION	Cass Lake, Minn.
CAPITAL OF THE COASTAL EMPIRE OF SOUTH CAROLINA	Charleston, S. C.
CAPITAL OF THE CONFED-ERACY	Richmond, Va.
CAPITAL OF THE EVERGREEN CLUB	Olympia, Wash.

CAPITAL OF THE FIRST STATE	Dover, Del.
CAPITAL OF THE HEART O' THE LAKES	Rhinelander, Wis.
CAPITAL OF THE LAND OF OUT-DOORS	Portland, Ore.
CAPITAL OF THE MIDLAND EMPIRE	Billings, Mont.
CAPITAL OF THE MOST HISTORIC RESORT AREA IN AMERICA	Norfolk, Va.
CAPITAL OF THE OLD SOUTH	Richmond, Va.
CAPITAL OF THE PAUL BUNYAN PLAYGROUND	Brainerd, Mich.
CAPITAL OF THE PLANTA-TIONS	Charleston, S. C.
CAPITAL OF THE ROCKY MOUNTAIN EMPIRE	Denver, Colo.
CAPITAL OF THE SEA ISLANDS	Beaufort, S. C.
CAPITAL OF THE VAST REPUBLIC	Washington, D. C.
CAPITAL OF THE VERMILION RANGE	Ely, Minn.
CAPITAL OF THE WORLD	New York, N.Y.
CAPITAL OF VACATION-LAND	Newport, R. I.
CAPITAL OF WESTERN KENTUCKY	Paducah, Ky.
CAPITAL OF YOUTH	Hannibal, Mo.
CAPITAL RESORT OF THE OZARKS	Eureka Springs, Ark.
CAR SHOP CITY	Berwick, Pa.
CARLSBAD OF AMERICA	French Lick, Ind.
CARPET CITY OF THE WORLD	Amsterdam, N. Y.
CARRIAGE CENTER OF THE WORLD	Amesbury, Mass.
CASH REGISTER CITY	Dayton, Ohio
CASTLE CITY	York, Pa.
CATACOMB CITY	Waynesburg, Pa.
CATARACT CITY	Niagara Falls, N.Y.

CATHEDRAL OF THE PLAINS	Victoria, Kans.
CATTLE CAPITAL AND AGRICULTURAL CENTER OF THE GREAT SOUTHWEST	Willcox, Ariz.
CATTLE CAPITAL OF NEBRASKA	Alliance, Neb.
CATTLE CAPITAL OF THE NATION	Willcox, Ariz.
CATTLE CAPITAL OF THE WORLD	Willcox, Ariz.
CAVERN CITY	Carlsbad, N. M.
CELERY CITY	Kalamazoo, Mich.
CELERY CITY	Sanford, Fla.
CELESTIAL CITY	Pekin, Ill.
CELLULOID CITY	Hollywood, Calif.
CEMENT CITY	Allentown, Pa.
CENTER CITY	Fort Smith, Ark.
CENTER CITY OF SOUTHERN GEORGIA	Waycross, Ga.
CENTER OF A FISHERMAN'S PARADISE	McCook, Neb.
CENTER OF A LAND OF ENCHANTMENT	Kalispell, Mont.
CENTER OF A LIVELY INDUSTRIAL AND AGRICULTURAL TRADE AREA	Marshall, Mo.
CENTER OF A MARVELOUS NATURAL PLAYGROUND	Lake City, Mich.
CENTER OF A RICH AND HIGHLY DIVERSIFIED AGRICULTURAL EMPIRE	Augusta, Ga.
CENTER OF A SPORTSMAN'S PARADISE	Palm Beach, Fla.
CENTER OF ALL VACATION FUN	Indio, Calif.
CENTER OF CALIFORNIA	Stockton, Calif.
CENTER OF CENTRAL FLORIDA	Astatula, Fla.
CENTER OF COMMERCE AND CULTURE	Jackson, Miss.
CENTER OF EASTERN STEEL MAKING	Pittsburgh, Pa.

CENTER OF EVERYTHING IN NORTHERN ARIZONA	Flagstaff, Ariz.
CENTER OF GOODING COUNTY	Wendell, Idaho
CENTER OF GREAT WEALTH	Pierre, S. D.
CENTER OF HISTORY, EDUCATION AND INDUSTRY	Cambridge, Mass.
CENTER OF HISTORY IN THE MAKING	Washington, D. C.
CENTER OF INDUSTRIAL AND ATOMIC DEVELOPMENT	Buffalo, N. Y.
CENTER OF INDUSTRY	Gary, Ind.
CENTER OF INDUSTRY	Tacoma, Wash.
CENTER OF MONTANA'S WONDERLAND	Butte, Mont.
CENTER OF NORTHERN ARIZONA'S SCENIC BEAUTY	Winslow, Ariz.
CENTER OF OLD VIRGINIA	Lynchburg, Va.
CENTER OF OUR NATION'S PLAYGROUND	Eustis, Fla.
CENTER OF PREHISTORIC, HISTORIC AND SCENIC INTEREST	Santa Fe, N. M.
CENTER OF PROGRESS IN MAINE	Pittsfield, Me.
CENTER OF SCENIC AMERICA	Salt Lake City, Utah
CENTER OF THE AIRCRAFT INDUSTRY	Grand Prairie, Texas
CENTER OF THE BEAUTIFUL NORTH SHORE OF MASSACHUSETTS	Salem, Mass.
CENTER OF THE COAL FIELDS	Appalachia, Va.
CENTER OF THE DUDE RANCH INDUSTRY	Sheridan, Wyo.
CENTER OF THE GOGEBIC IRON RANGE	Ironwood, Mich.
CENTER OF THE MIDWEST AND THE COUNTRY	Des Moines, Iowa
CENTER OF THE MOST POPULAR RESORT SECTION IN THE OZARKS	Mountain Home, Ark.

CENTER OF THE NATION'S GREATEST CONCENTRATION OF VARIED NATURAL ATTRACTIONS	Prescott, Ariz.
CENTER OF THE PALM BEACHES	Riviera Beach, Fla.
CENTER OF THE SUNSHINE STATE	Pierre, S. D.
CENTER OF THE UNIVERSE	Duluth, Minn.
CENTER OF THE WORLD'S BEST MARKET	Reading, Pa.
CENTER OF THE WORLD'S LARGEST IRRIGATION, POWER NAVIGATION FLOOD CONTROL PROJECT	Huron, S. D.
CENTER OF YAVAPAI	Prescott, Ariz.
CENTER OF YEAR 'ROUND RECREATION	Jackson, Miss.
CENTRAL CITY	Syracuse, N. Y.
CENTRAL CITY OF THE GREAT SOUTHWEST	Oklahoma City, Okla.
CENTRAL GATEWAY OF THE GREAT LAKES	Toledo, Ohio
CERAMIC CITY	East Liverpool, Ohio
CEREAL FOOD CENTER OF THE WORLD	Battle Creek, Mich.
CESSPOOL FOR GAMBLING JOINTS	Lake Tahoe, Calif.
CHAIR CAPITAL OF THE WORLD	Thomasville, N. C.
CHAIR CITY	Sheboygan, Wis.
CHAIR CITY	Thomasville, N. C.
CHAMPION CITY	Springfield, Ohio
CHARM CIRCLE OF THE SOUTH	McComb, Miss.
CHARM SPOT OF THE DEEP SOUTH	Mobile, Ala.
CHARTER OAK CITY	Hartford, Conn.
CHAUTAUQUA OF THE GREAT LAKES	Lakeside, Ohio
CHEMICAL CAPITAL OF THE WORLD	Wilmington, Del.

CHEMICAL CENTER OF THE WORLD	South Charleston, W. Va.
CHEMICAL CITY	Berlin, N. H.
CHEMICAL CITY	Charleston, W. Va.
CHEMURGIC CITY	Laurel, Miss.
CHERRY CAPITAL OF THE WORLD	Traverse City, Mich.
CHERRY CITY	Salem, Ore.
CHERRY CITY	Traverse City, Mich.
CHERRY CITY OF CALIFORNIA	San Leandro, Calif.
CHI	Chicago, Ill.
CHICAGO OF NEVADA	Beatty, Nev.
CHICAGO OF THE NORTH	Anchorage, Alaska
CHICAGO OF THE SOUTH	Okeechobee, Fla.
CHICAGO OF THE SOUTHWEST	Fort Worth, Texas
CHIEF CITY OF THE BLUE-GRASS REGION	Lexington, Ky.
CHIEF CITY OF WEST VIRGINIA	Wheeling, W. Va.
CHIEF INDUSTRIAL CITY OF THE EASTERN PANHANDLE	Martinsburg, W. Va.
CHOCOLATE CITY	Hershey, Pa.
CHOCOLATE CROSSROADS OF THE WORLD	Hershey, Pa.
CHOCOLATE TOWN	Hershey, Pa.
CHOCOLATE TOWN, U.S.A.	Hershey, Pa.
CHOICEST SPOT IN ALL FLORIDA	Anna Maria, Fla.
CHRISTIANSVILLE	Chase City, Va.
CHRISTMAS CITY	Bethlehem, Pa.
CHRISTMAS CITY	Noel, Mo.
CHRISTMAS TOWN, U.S.A.	Shelton, Wash.
CHRISTMAS TREE CAPITAL OF THE WORLD	Eureka, Mont.
CHURCH CITY	Brooklyn, N. Y.
CIGAR CAPITAL OF THE WORLD	Key West, Fla.
CIGAR CITY	Tampa, Fla.
CINEMA CAPITAL	Hollywood, Calif.
CINEMALAND	Hollywood, Calif.
CINEMATOWN	Hollywood, Calif.

CINEMA VILLAGE	Hollywood, Calif.
CIRCLE CITY	Corona, Calif.
CIRCLE CITY	Hollywood, Calif.
CIRCUS CITY	Burley, Wash.
CIRCUS CITY	Peru, Ind.
CIRCUS CITY OF THE WORLD	Peru, Ind.
CIRCUS WITHOUT A TENT	Los Angeles, Calif.
CITADEL OF THE CONFEDERACY	Atlanta, Ga.
CITADEL OF THE OLD NORTHWEST	Vincennes, Ind.
CITRUS CENTER	Cocoa, Fla.
CITRUS METROPOLIS	Los Angeles, Calif.
CITRUS CENTER OF THE WORLD	Winter Haven, Fla.
CITY	New York, N. Y.
CITY ALWAYS EXPANDING	Morristown, Tenn.
CITY AT THE CROSSROADS DOWN EAST	Ellsworth, Me.
CITY AT THE CROSSROADS OF HIGH DIPLOMACY	New York, N. Y.
CITY AT THE CROSSROADS OF MID-AMERICA	Carthage, Mo.
CITY AT THE CROSSROADS OF THE EMPIRE STATE	Utica, N. Y.
CITY AT THE CROSSROADS OF THE SOUTH	Memphis, Tenn.
CITY AT THE CROSSROADS OF TRANS-AMERICA'S HIGHWAY AND THE NAVAJO TRAIL	Alamosa, Colo.
CITY AT THE TIP OF CAPE ANN	Rockport, Mass.
CITY ATOP THE NATION'S ROOF GARDEN	Salida, Colo.
CITY BEAUTIFUL	Birmingham, Ala.
CITY BEAUTIFUL	Chicago, Ill.
CITY BEAUTIFUL	Coral Gables, Fla.
CITY BEAUTIFUL	Dayton, Ohio
CITY BEAUTIFUL	Hartford, Conn.
CITY BEAUTIFUL	Marshall, Mo.
CITY BEAUTIFUL	Memphis, Tenn.
CITY BEAUTIFUL	Milwaukee, Wis.

CITY BEAUTIFUL	Nashville, Tenn.
CITY BEAUTIFUL	Nauvoo, Ill.
CITY BEAUTIFUL	Orlando, Fla.
CITY BEAUTIFUL	San Francisco, Calif.
CITY BEAUTIFUL	Tavares, Fla.
CITY BEAUTIFUL	Tulsa, Okla.
CITY BEAUTIFUL	Uvalde, Texas
CITY BEAUTIFUL	Washington, D. C.
CITY BEAUTIFUL IN THE LAND O'LAKES	Fergus Falls, Minn.
CITY BESIDE THE BROAD MISSOURI	Bismarck, N. D.
CITY BETWEEN THE MOUNTAINS AND THE SEA	Montebello, Calif.
CITY BUILT ON OIL, SOIL AND TOIL	Ponca City, Okla.
CITY BUILT ON SAND	Los Angeles, Calif.
CITY BUILT BY HANDS	Rochester, N. Y.
CITY BUILT ON A ISTHMUS	Madison, Wis.
CITY BY ACCIDENT	Yoakum, Texas
CITY BY THE FALLS	Louisville, Ky.
CITY BY THE GOLDEN GATE	San Francisco, Calif.
CITY BY THE GREAT SALT LAKE	Salt Lake City, Utah
CITY BY THE LAKE	Chicago, Ill.
CITY BY THE LAKE	Coeur d'Alene, Idaho
CITY BY THE SEA	Charleston, S. C.
CITY BY THE SEA	Long Beach, N. Y.
CITY BY THE SEA	Newport, R. I.
CITY BY THE SEA	Perth Amboy, N. J.
CITY CARE FORGOT	New Orleans, La.
CITY COOLER BY A MILE	Avalon, N. J.
CITY COSMOPOLITAN	San Francisco, Calif.
CITY DIFFERENT	Santa Fe, N. M.
CITY DOWN ON THE MESABI	Aurora, Minn.
CITY FOR A VACATION ON A LIFETIME	Elk Rapids, Mich.
CITY FOR EVERY VACATION PLEASURE	Whitehall, Mich.
CITY FOR THE FULL LIFE	Berlin, N. H.
CITY FOUNDED UPON CO-OPERATION	Winston-Salem, N. C.
CITY FOUR DIMENSIONAL	Lexington, N. C.

CITY IN A FOREST	Washington, D. C.
CITY IN A VALLEY WHERE RECUPERATION, REHABILITATION, REST AND RELAXATION WITH RECREATION AND SCENIC BEAUTY ABOUND	Hot Springs, S. D.
CITY IN ARIZONA'S VALLEY OF THE SUN	Phoenix, Ariz.
CITY IN BEAUTIFUL BAY COUNTY	Panama City, Fla.
CITY IN CENTRAL CALIFORNIA CONVENIENT TO EVERYTHING	Oakdale, Calif.
CITY IN THE CENTER OF HUNTING LANDS	Pierre, S. D.
CITY IN THE CENTER OF THE BEAUTIFUL NORTH WOODS	Park Falls, Wis.
CITY IN THE CENTER OF THE WHITE MOUNTAINS	Glen, N. H.
CITY IN THE COUNTRY	Danbury, Conn.
CITY IN THE HEART OF ARIZONA VACATIONLAND	Mesa, Ariz.
CITY IN THE HEART OF COLORFUL NAPA VALLEY	St. Helena, Calif.
CITY IN THE HEART OF EASTERN AMERICA	Bristol, Tenn.-Va.
CITY IN THE HEART OF SOUTH CENTRAL LOUISIANA	Lafayette, La.
CITY IN THE HEART OF THE CHEQUAMEGON NATIONAL FOREST	Park Falls, Wis.
CITY IN THE HEART OF THE CITRUS BELT AND HOLIDAY HIGHLANDS	Auburndale, Fla.
CITY IN THE HEART OF THE COASTAL SEA ISLANDS	Beaufort, S. C.
CITY IN THE HEART OF THE FINGER LAKES	Trumansburg, N. Y.
CITY IN THE HEART OF THE IRRIGATED PLATTE VALLEY	Gothenburg, Neb.

CITY IN THE HEART OF THE LAKES REGION	Laconia, N. H.
CITY IN THE HEART OF THE NATION'S FAMOUS DUDE RANCH COUNTRY	Billings, Mont.
CITY IN THE HEART OF THE NATION'S SUNNIEST STATE	Winslow, Ariz.
CITY IN THE HEART OF THE SHENANDOAH VALLEY OF VIRGINIA	Winchester, Va.
CITY IN THE HEART OF THE SOUTHWEST WONDERLAND	Willcox, Ariz.
CITY IN THE HEART OF TWO HUNDRED AND FIFTY SPARKLING LAKES AND STREAMS	Grand Rapids, Mich.
CITY IN THE LAKE DISTRICT OF THE ADIRONDACKS	Speculator, N. Y.
CITY IN THE HEART OF WESTERN RANCH LAND	Pierre, S. D.
CITY IN THE LAND OF CHIEF WABASIS	Belding, Mich.
CITY IN THE LAND OF LAKES	St. Paul, Minn.
CITY IN THE MOUNTAIN COUNTRY	Billings, Mont.
CITY IN THE PINES	Flagstaff, Ariz.
CITY IN THE SHADOW OF THE BIG HORN	Sheridan, Wyo.
CITY IN THE VALLEY OF THE ARKANSAS	Salida, Colo.
CITY IN THE VALLEY OF OPPORTUNITY	Evansville, Ind.
CITY IN THE VALLEY OF PROMISE	Mishawaka, Ind.
CITY IN THE VALLEY OF THE SUN	Glendale, Ariz.
CITY IN THE WHITE MOUNTAINS	Berlin, N. H.
CITY METROPOLIS	Los Angeles, Calif.
CITY MOST CONVENIENT TO ALL FLORIDA	Plant City, Fla.

CITY 'NEATH THE HILLS	Madison, Ind.
CITY OF A HUNDRED HILLS	San Francisco, Calif.
CITY OF A THOUSAND SIGHTS	St. Louis, Mo.
CITY OF A THOUSAND THRILLS	Washington, D. C.
CITY OF ACHIEVEMENT	Decatur, Ala.
CITY OF ADVANTAGES	Dearborn, Mich.
CITY OF ADVANTAGES	Racine, Wis.
CITY OF ANGELS	Los Angeles, Calif.
CITY OF ANGELS	San Angelo, Texas
CITY OF BAKED BEANS	Boston, Mass.
CITY OF BALANCE	Fort Smith, Ark.
CITY OF BEAN EATERS	Boston, Mass.
CITY OF BEAUTIFUL CHURCHES	Augusta, Ga.
CITY OF BEAUTIFUL CHURCHES	Louisville, Ky.
CITY OF BEAUTIFUL CHURCHES, HOMES AND BUILDINGS	Florence, Ala.
CITY OF BEAUTIFUL HEIGHTS	Fort Worth, Texas
CITY OF BEAUTIFUL HOMES	Augusta, Ga.
CITY OF BEAUTIFUL HOMES	Boise, Idaho
CITY OF BEAUTIFUL HOMES	Rockford, Ill.
CITY OF BEAUTIFUL HOMES AND THRIVING INDUSTRY	Madison, Wis.
CITY OF BEAUTIFUL PARKS	Fort Collins, Colo.
CITY OF BEAUTIFUL PARKS	Wheeling, W. Va.
CITY OF BEAUTY	Davenport, Iowa
CITY OF BEAUTY	Dayton, Ohio
CITY OF BEAUTY	Montgomery, Ala.
CITY OF BEAUTY AND UN-LIMITED OPPORTUNITIES	Elyria, Ohio
CITY OF BEAUTY, PROGRESS AND CULTURE	Provo, Utah
CITY OF BLACK DIAMONDS	Scranton, Pa.
CITY OF BRICK	Pullman, Ill.
CITY OF BRIDGES	Logansport, Ind.
CITY OF BRIDGES	Pittsburgh, Pa.
CITY OF BRIDGES	San Francisco, Calif.
CITY OF BROTHERLY LOVE	Philadelphia, Pa.
CITY OF BUSINESS	Niagara Falls, N.Y.
CITY OF CAMELLIAS	McComb, Miss.

CITY OF CAMELLIAS	Pensacola, Fla.
CITY OF CAPTAINS' HOUSES	Newburyport, Mass.
CITY OF CERTAINTIES	Des Moines, Iowa
CITY OF CHARM	New Orleans, La.
CITY OF CHARMING HOUSES	Lynchburg, Va.
CITY OF CHEESE, CHAIRS, CHILDREN AND CHURCHES	Sheboygan, Wis.
CITY OF CHILDHOOD	Mooseheart, Ill.
CITY OF CHURCHES	Anniston, Ala.
CITY OF CHURCHES	Blytheville, Ark.
CITY OF CHURCHES	Brooklyn, N. Y.
CITY OF CHURCHES	Charleston, S. C.
CITY OF CHURCHES	Charlotte, N. C.
CITY OF CHURCHES	Philadelphia, Pa.
CITY OF CHURCHES	Wilkinsburg, Pa.
CITY OF COAL KINGS	Uniontown, Pa.
CITY OF CONTRAST AND ROMANCE	San Antonio, Texas
CITY OF CONTRASTS	Huntsville, Ala.
CITY OF CONTRASTS	New Orleans, La.
CITY OF CONTRASTS	San Antonio, Texas
CITY OF CONVENTIONS	Syracuse, N. Y.
CITY OF CONVERSATION	Washington, D. C.
CITY OF COWS, COLLEGES AND CONTENTMENT	Northfield, Minn.
CITY OF CULTURE AND ENTERTAINMENT	St. Louis, Mo.
CITY OF CULTURE, HISTORY, INDUSTRY	Winston-Salem, N.C.
CITY OF DELIGHT	Fort Worth, Texas
CITY OF DESTINY	Duluth, Minn.
CITY OF DESTINY	Las Vegas, Nev.
CITY OF DESTINY	Tacoma, Wash.
CITY OF DIVERSIFIED INDUSTRIES	Holyoke, Mass.
CITY OF DIVERSIFIED INDUSTRIES	Marietta, Ohio
CITY OF DIVERSIFIED INDUSTRIES AND CIVIC ACHIEVEMENT	York, Pa.
CITY OF DIVERSIFIED INDUSTRY	Ellwood City, Pa.

CITY OF DIVERSIFIED INDUSTRY	Kingsport, Tenn.
CITY OF DIVERSIFIED INDUSTRY	Salem, Ore.
CITY OF DIVERSIFIED INTERESTS	Nashville, Tenn.
CITY OF DIVERSIFIED PRODUCTS	Elyria, Ohio
CITY OF DIVERSITY	Tampa, Fla.
CITY OF DREADFUL JOY	Los Angeles, Calif.
CITY OF DREAMS	Odessa, Texas
CITY OF DREAMS	Salida, Colo.
CITY OF ELMS	New Haven, Conn.
CITY OF ETERNAL VIEWS	Seattle, Wash.
CITY OF EXCEPTIONAL BEAUTY	Riverside, Calif.
CITY OF EXECUTIVES	Birmingham, Ala.
CITY OF EXPANDING INDUSTRY	Nampa, Idaho
CITY OF EXTREMES	Chicago, Ill.
CITY OF FALLING WATER	Fall River, Mass.
CITY OF FINE EDUCATIONAL INSTITUTIONS	Rome, Ga.
CITY OF FINE HOMES AND STREETS	Lima, Ohio
CITY OF FINE HOMES, CHURCHES AND SCHOOLS	Jackson, Miss.
CITY OF FINE HOTELS	Tacoma, Wash.
CITY OF FINE SCHOOLS	Niagara Falls, N.Y.
CITY OF FIRSTS	Boston, Mass.
CITY OF FIRSTS	Oregon City, Ore.
CITY OF FIRSTS	Philadelphia, Pa.
CITY OF FIRSTS	San Francisco, Calif.
CITY OF FIVE FLAGS	Mobile, Ala.
CITY OF FIVE-SCORE INDUSTRIES	Waltham, Mass.
CITY OF FLAMING ADVENTURE	San Antonio, Texas
CITY OF FLOUR	Buffalo, N. Y.
CITY OF FLOWERS	Los Angeles, Calif.
CITY OF FLOWERS	Montebello, Calif.
CITY OF FLOWERS	Springfield, Ill.
CITY OF FLOWING GOLD	Ranger, Texas

CITY OF FLOWERS AND SUNSHINE	Los Angeles, Calif.
CITY OF FOUR GLORIOUS SEASONS	Hendersonville, N.C.
CITY OF FRIENDLINESS AND BEAUTY	Riverside, Calif.
CITY OF FRIENDLINESS, CULTURE AND TRADITIONS	Lynchburg, Va.
CITY OF FRIENDLY FOLKS	Newberry, S. C.
CITY OF FRIENDLY PEOPLE	New York, N. Y.
CITY OF FRIENDLY PEOPLE	Rochester, N. H.
CITY OF GALLOPING TIN-TYPES	Hollywood, Calif.
CITY OF GARDENS	Montebello, Calif.
CITY OF GIANT INDUSTRY	Rochester, N. Y.
CITY OF GIGANTIC INDUSTRIES, UNPARALLELED SCHOOLS	Pine Bluff, Ark.
CITY OF GOOD LIVING	Anaheim, Calif.
CITY OF GOOD LIVING	St. Petersburg, Fla.
CITY OF GOOD NEIGHBORS	Buffalo, N. Y.
CITY OF GOOD WATER	Buckley, Wash.
CITY OF GOVERNORS	Bellefonte, Pa.
CITY OF GOVERNORS	Huntsville, Ala.
CITY OF GOVERNORS	Rochester, N. H.
CITY OF GRACIOUS LIVING	Huntsville, Ala.
CITY OF GRACIOUS LIVING	Yonkers, N. Y.
CITY OF GREAT INDUSTRY	Rochester, N. Y.
CITY OF HEALING WATERS	Hot Springs, S. D.
CITY OF HEALTH, HISTORY, HOSPITALITY	Tombstone, Ariz.
CITY OF HEAT	Thermopolis, Wyo.
CITY OF HILLS	Lynchburg, Va.
CITY OF HILLS	Oneonta, N. Y.
CITY OF HILLS	Somerville, Mass.
CITY OF HISTORIC LORE	Wheeling, W. Va.
CITY OF HISTORICAL CHARM	Savannah, Ga.
CITY OF HISTORY AND ROMANCE	Charleston, S. C.
CITY OF HISTORY AND ROMANCE	Monterey, Calif.
CITY OF HOMES	Albany, Calif.
CITY OF HOMES	Albany, Ga.

CITY OF HOMES	Atlanta, Ga.
CITY OF HOMES	Auburn, Me.
CITY OF HOMES	Brooklyn, N. Y.
CITY OF HOMES	Dallas, Texas
CITY OF HOMES	Fort Myers, Fla.
CITY OF HOMES	Lakewood, Ohio
CITY OF HOMES	Louisville, Ky.
CITY OF HOMES	Milwaukee, Wis.
CITY OF HOMES	Montebello, Calif.
CITY OF HOMES	Newnan, Ga.
CITY OF HOMES	Niagara Falls, N. Y.
CITY OF HOMES	Philadelphia, Pa
CITY OF HOMES	Port Arthur, Texas
CITY OF HOMES	Portland, Ore.
CITY OF HOMES	Rochester, N. Y.
CITY OF HOMES	Royal Oak, Mich.
CITY OF HOMES	St. Petersburg, Fla.
CITY OF HOMES	Seattle, Wash.
CITY OF HOMES	Somerville, Mass.
CITY OF HOMES	Springfield, Mass.
CITY OF HOMES	Vero Beach, Fla.
CITY OF HOMES	Winter Haven, Fla.
CITY OF HOMES	Winter Park, Fla.
CITY OF HOMES AND INDUSTRY	East Point, Ga.
CITY OF HOMES AND INDUSTRY	Pueblo, Colo.
CITY OF HOMES AND PARKS	Burlington, Vt.
CITY OF HOMES, CHURCHES AND FINE SCHOOLS	Moscow, Idaho
CITY OF HOMES, SCHOOLS AND CHURCHES	Yoakum, Texas
CITY OF HOSPITALITY	Decatur, Ala.
CITY OF HOSPITALITY	Memphis, Tenn.
CITY OF HOUSES WITHOUT STREETS	Washington, D. C.
CITY OF HUGUENOTS	New Rochelle, N. Y.
CITY OF HUNDRED LAKES	Winter Haven, Fla.
CITY OF ILLUSION	Virginia City, Nev.
CITY OF INDIVIDUALITY AND CHARM	Riverside, Calif.
CITY OF INDUSTRIAL OPPORTUNITY	Benicia, Calif.

CITY OF INDUSTRIAL OPPORTUNITY	Helena, Ark.
CITY OF INDUSTRIAL OPPORTUNITY	Warren, Pa.
CITY OF INDUSTRIAL PEACE	Garfield, N. J.
CITY OF INDUSTRY	Dayton, Ohio
CITY OF INDUSTRY	Montebello, Calif.
CITY OF INDUSTRY	Newark, N. J.
CITY OF INDUSTRY	Newburyport, Mass.
CITY OF INDUSTRY	Niagara Falls, N.Y.
CITY OF INDUSTRY AND OPPORTUNITY	Lynchburg, Va.
CITY OF ISLANDS	New York, N. Y.
CITY OF ISMS	Syracuse, N. Y.
CITY OF KIND HEARTS	Boston, Mass.
CITY OF LAKES	Fort Worth, Texas
CITY OF LAKES	Lakeland, Fla.
CITY OF LAKES	Minneapolis, Minn.
CITY OF LEARNING	St. Louis, Mo.
CITY OF LIQUID GOLD	Hastings, Neb.
CITY OF LIQUID SUNSHINE	Los Angeles, Calif.
CITY OF LIVING AND LEARNING	Claremont, Calif.
CITY OF LITTLE MEN	Boys Town, Neb.
CITY OF LOST FOOTSTEPS	Washington, D. C.
CITY OF LOVELY GARDENS	Hartsville, S.C.
CITY OF MAGIC	Lowell, Mass.
CITY OF MAGIC	Schenectady, N.Y.
CITY OF MAGNIFICENT CHURCHES, BEAUTIFUL HOMES	Pine Bluff, Ark.
CITY OF MAGNIFICENT DISTANCES	Washington, D. C.
CITY OF MAGNIFICENT MOUNTAINS	Fort Collins, Colo.
CITY OF MAGNIFICENT STORES	Wheeling, W. Va.
CITY OF MANY ADVENTURES	San Francisco, Calif.
CITY OF MANY CULTURAL ADVANTAGES	Marietta, Ohio
CITY OF MANY INDUSTRIES	Rochester, N. Y.
CITY OF MISSIONS	San Antonio, Texas

CITY OF MOLLY PITCHER	Carlisle, Pa.
CITY OF MONUMENTS	Richmond, Va.
CITY OF NOTIONS	Boston, Mass.
CITY OF OAKS	Bartow, Fla.
CITY OF OAKS	Raleigh, N. C.
CITY OF OAKS	Tuscaloosa, Ala.
CITY OF OAKS AND AZALEAS	Bartow, Fla.
CITY OF ONE HUNDRED HILLS	San Francisco, Calif.
CITY OF ONE HUNDRED LAKES	Winter Haven, Fla.
CITY OF ONE HUNDRED LAKES AND STREAMS	Superior, Wis.
CITY OF ONE THOUSAND LAKES	Oklahoma City, Okla.
CITY OF OPPORTUNITIES	Brunswick, Ga.
CITY OF OPPORTUNITIES	Miami, Fla.
CITY OF OPPORTUNITIES	Saginaw, Mich.
CITY OF OPPORTUNITY	Akron, Ohio
CITY OF OPPORTUNITY	Conway, Ark.
CITY OF OPPORTUNITY	Dallas, Texas
CITY OF OPPORTUNITY	Evansville, Ind.
CITY OF OPPORTUNITY	Manchester, N. H.
CITY OF OPPORTUNITY	Memphis, Tenn.
CITY OF OPPORTUNITY	Montgomery, Ala.
CITY OF OPPORTUNITY	Nashville, Tenn.
CITY OF ORCHARDS	Hilo, Hawaii
CITY OF ORCHESTRAS	New York, N. Y.
CITY OF OUTSTANDING EDUCATIONAL ADVANTAGES	Florence, Ala.
CITY OF PALMS	Fort Myers, Fla.
CITY OF PALMS	McAllen, Texas
CITY OF PALMS	Pharr, Texas
CITY OF PANORAMIC BOULEVARDS	Fort Collins, Colo.
CITY OF PAPER	Camas, Wash.
CITY OF PARKS	Madison, Wis.
CITY OF PEACE	Salem, Mass.
CITY OF PEACE AND PLENTY	Pine Bluff, Ark.
CITY OF PEACHES	Brigham City, Utah
CITY OF PENN	Philadelphia, Pa.

CITY OF PEOPLE	Demopolis, Ala.
CITY OF PERSONALITY	Cincinnati, Ohio
CITY OF PLEASANT LIVING	Pensacola, Fla.
CITY OF PLEASANT MEMORIES	Jacksonville, Fla.
CITY OF PLENTIFUL PLAINS	Fort Collins, Colo.
CITY OF PRESIDENTS	Quincy, Mass.
CITY OF PROGRESS	Dayton, Ohio
CITY OF PROGRESS	Dubuque, Iowa
CITY OF PROGRESS	Edgewater, Fla.
CITY OF PROGRESS	North Bend, Ore.
CITY OF PROGRESS	Reading, Pa.
CITY OF PROGRESS	Springfield, Ohio
CITY OF PROGRESS AND OPPORTUNITY	Phenix City, Ala.
CITY OF PROGRESS AND PROSPERITY	Oakland, Calif.
CITY OF PROSPERITY	Worcester, Mass.
CITY OF QUALITY PRODUCTS	Rochester, N. Y.
CITY OF RECEPTIONS	Washington, D. C.
CITY OF RECREATION AND CULTURE	Omaha, Neb.
CITY OF RICH CULTURAL AND RESIDENTIAL CHARM	Jackson, Miss.
CITY OF ROCKS	Nashville, Tenn.
CITY OF ROSES	Little Rock, Ark.
CITY OF ROSES	New Castle, Ind.
CITY OF ROSES	Paramount, Calif.
CITY OF ROSES	Pasadena, Calif.
CITY OF ROSES	Portland, Ore.
CITY OF ROSES	Thomasville, Ga.
CITY OF SALT	Syracuse, N. Y.
CITY OF SCENIC MARVELS	Niagara Falls, N.Y.
CITY OF SECESSION	Charleston, S. C.
CITY OF SERENE LIVING	Laguna Beach, Calif.
CITY OF SEVEN HILLS	Richmond, Va.
CITY OF SEVEN HILLS	Seattle, Wash.
CITY OF SEVEN VALLEYS	Cassville, Mo.
CITY OF SHADY WALKS AND PLEASANT LAWNS	Dayton, Wash.

CITY OF SHIPS AND SHIP-BUILDING	Newport News, Va.
CITY OF SHOES	Brockton, Mass.
CITY OF SHOES	Lynn, Mass.
CITY OF SIX FLAGS	Mobile, Ala.
CITY OF SKYSCRAPERS	New York, N. Y.
CITY OF SMOKESTACKS	Everett, Wash.
CITY OF SPAS	Ashland, Ore.
CITY OF SPINDLES	Lowell, Mass.
CITY OF SPRINGS	Neosho, Mo.
CITY OF STEEL	Pittsburgh, Pa.
CITY OF STRAITS	Detroit, Mich.
CITY OF STREETS WITHOUT HOUSES	Washington, D. C.
CITY OF SUCCESSFUL DIVERSIFIED INDUSTRY	Utica, N. Y.
CITY OF SUNSHINE	Colorado Springs, Colo.
CITY OF SUNSHINE	Los Angeles, Calif.
CITY OF SUNSHINE	Tucson, Ariz.
CITY OF SUNSHINE AND SILVER	Tombstone, Ariz.
CITY OF SUPERLATIVES	New York, N. Y.
CITY OF THE BELLES	Bellefonte, Pa.
CITY OF THE BIG SHOULDERS	Chicago, Ill.
CITY OF THE CARILLON	Lake Wales, Fla.
CITY OF THE FALLS	Louisville, Ky.
CITY OF THE FRENCH	St. Louis, Mo.
CITY OF THE FRIENDLY PEOPLE	Apalachicola, Fla.
CITY OF THE FUTURE	Cape Coral, Fla.
CITY OF THE FUTURE	Kansas City, Mo.
CITY OF THE FUTURE	New Haven, Conn.
CITY OF THE GOLDEN GATE	San Francisco, Calif.
CITY OF THE GREAT SMOKIES	Knoxville, Tenn.
CITY OF THE GREEN LIGHT	Eau Claire, Wis.
CITY OF THE HOUR	Dallas, Texas
CITY OF THE LAKES	Chicago, Ill.
CITY OF THE LAKES	Laconia, N. H.
CITY OF THE LAKES AND PRAIRIES	Chicago, Ill.
CITY OF THE NORTHLAND	Superior, Wis.

CITY OF THE PEOPLE	Demopolis, Ala.
CITY OF THE PLAINS	Abilene, Kans.
CITY OF THE PLAINS	Childress, Texas
CITY OF THE PLAINS	Denver, Colo.
CITY OF THE PLAINS	Sacramento, Calif.
CITY OF THE PLAINS	Syracuse, N. Y.
CITY OF THE SAINTS	Salt Lake City, Utah
CITY OF THE SEVEN HILLS	Rome, Ga.
CITY OF THE SLAIN	Arlington, Va.
CITY OF THE STRAITS	Detroit, Mich.
CITY OF THE TWIN SPIRES	Ripon, Wis.
CITY OF THE UNEXPECTED	Pittsburgh, Pa.
CITY OF THE VIOLET CROWN	Austin, Texas
CITY OF THREE CAPITALS	Little Rock, Ark.
CITY OF THRIVING INDUSTRIES	Wheeling, W. Va.
CITY OF TOWERS	New York, N. Y.
CITY OF TRADITION	Memphis, Tenn.
CITY OF TRANSFORMATIONS	Chelsea, Mass.
CITY OF TREES	Boise, Idaho
CITY OF TREES	Buffalo, N. Y.
CITY OF TREES	Forsyth, Mont.
CITY OF TREES	Marmarth, N. D.
CITY OF TREES	Sacramento, Calif.
CITY OF TREES WITHOUT HOUSES	Washington, D. C.
CITY OF TWENTIETH CENTURY AMERICA	Detroit, Mich.
CITY OF VARIED INDUSTRIES	Rochester, N. Y.
CITY OF WASHINGTON	Washington, D. C.
CITY OF WESTERN CHARM AND HOSPITALITY	Fort Worth, Texas
CITY OF WINDS	Chicago, Ill.
CITY OF WITCHES	Salem, Mass.
CITY OF YOUR FUTURE	Fort Smith, Ark.
CITY ON THE COOL GULF COAST	Panama City, Fla.
CITY ON THE DAN	Danville, Va.
CITY ON THE GULF	Naples, Fla.
CITY ON THE GULF OF MEXICO	St. Petersburg Beach, Fla.

CITY ON THE HIGHWAY TO HEAVEN	Salida, Colo.
CITY ON THE HILL	Paris, Me.
CITY ON THE LAKES	Laconia, N. H.
CITY ON THE TOP OF THE ROCKIES	Anaconda, Mont.
CITY PRACTICAL THAT VISION BUILT	Longview, Wash.
CITY READY FOR TOMORROW	Jonesboro, Ark.
CITY SET ON A HILL	Angwin, Calif.
CITY SUBSTANTIAL	Frankfort, Ind.
CITY THAT BUILT ITS SEAPORT	Houston, Texas
CITY THAT CAME BACK	Alton, Ill.
CITY THAT DOES THINGS	Norfolk, Va.
CITY THAT HAS EVERYTHING FOR ENJOYABLE LIVING	Tavares, Fla.
CITY THAT HAS EVERYTHING FOR EVERYONE--ANYTIME	Las Vegas, Nev.
CITY THAT HAS EVERYTHING FOR INDUSTRY	Jersey City, N.J.
CITY THAT HAS SOMETHING FOR YOU	Stockton, Calif.
CITY THAT HAS THE RESOURCES TO FIT YOUR BUSINESS NEEDS	Indianapolis, Ind.
CITY THAT IS ONLY TWO HOURS TO THE SIERRAS OR THE SEA	Modesto, Calif.
CITY THAT IS STILL A FRONTIER TOWN	Las Vegas, Nev.
CITY THAT LIGHTS AND HAULS THE WORLD	Schenectady, N. Y.
CITY THAT PROGRESS BUILT	Fayetteville, Ark.
CITY THAT PUTS BUSINESS ON THE GO	Harrisburg, Pa.
CITY THAT SAVED THE UNION	Virginia City, Nev.
CITY THAT SAYS WELCOME NEIGHBOR	Madison, S. D.
CITY THAT SMILES BACK	Corinth, Miss.
CITY THAT STARTED WITH A PLAN	Margate, Fla.

CITY THAT TREES BUILT	Berlin, N. H.
CITY THE DEPRESSION PASSED UP	Bronson, Mich.
CITY TIME FORGOT	Galena, Ill.
CITY WAY DOWN UPON THE SUWANNEE RIVER	Cross City, Fla.
CITY WHERE A NEW SOUTH IS IN THE MAKING	Jackson, Miss.
CITY WHERE AGRICULTURE AND INDUSTRY MEET	Fremont, Neb.
CITY WHERE AMERICA BEGAN IN THE WEST	Monterey, Calif.
CITY WHERE BUSINESS AND INDUSTRY THRIVE AND PEOPLE ENJOY A WIDE VARIETY OF YEAR AROUND RECREATION	Athens, Tenn.
CITY WHERE CALIFORNIA AND MEXICO MEET THE BLUE PACIFIC	San Diego, Calif.
CITY WHERE CALIFORNIA BEGAN	Sacramento, Calif.
CITY WHERE CALIFORNIA BEGAN	San Diego, Calif.
CITY WHERE COAL AND IRON MEET	Toledo, Ohio
CITY WHERE COAL MEETS IRON	Ashland, Ky.
CITY WHERE DIXIE WELCOMES YOU	Corinth, Miss.
CITY WHERE GREAT EAST TEXAS MEETS THE SEA	Beaumont, Texas
CITY WHERE GROWTH HAS BECOME A HABIT	Odessa, Texas
CITY WHERE HISTORIC YESTERDAY GREETS DYNAMIC TOMORROW	Bingham, Me.
CITY WHERE HISTORIC YESTERDAY GREETS DYNAMIC TOMORROW	Moscow, Me.
CITY WHERE HOSPITALITY IS A TRADITION	Santa Barbara, Calif.

CITY WHERE INDUSTRIAL AND AGRICULTURAL ACTIVITIES ARE BLENDED WITH DAIRYING AND LIVESTOCK PRODUCTION	Columbus, Miss.
CITY WHERE INDUSTRY AND EDUCATION MEET	Blacksburg, Va.
CITY WHERE INDUSTRY AND RECREATION MEET	Palatka, Fla.
CITY WHERE INDUSTRY PROFITS	Atmore, Ala.
CITY WHERE IT'S JUNE IN JANUARY ALONG THE ROMANTIC APACHE TRAIL	Mesa, Ariz.
CITY WHERE LAND AND WATER MEET	Annapolis, Md.
CITY WHERE LIFE IS DIFFERENT	Biddeford, Me.
CITY WHERE LIFE IS DIFFERENT	Saco, Me.
CITY WHERE LIFE IS DIFFERENT	San Antonio, Texas
CITY WHERE LIFE IS LIVED EVERY DAY OF THE YEAR	Englewood, Fla.
CITY WHERE LIFE IS WORTH LIVING	Dania, Fla.
CITY WHERE MEXICO MEETS UNCLE SAM	Brownsville, Texas
CITY WHERE MOUNTAINS AND PLAINS MEET	Boulder, Colo.
CITY WHERE NATURE SMILES THE YEAR 'ROUND	Fortuna, Calif.
CITY WHERE OIL AND WATER MIX	Lovington, N. M.
CITY WHERE OIL FLOWS, GAS BLOWS AND GLASS GLOWS	Okmulgee, Okla.
CITY WHERE PEOPLE ARE HAPPY AND INDUSTRY FLOURISHES	East Point, Ga.

CITY WHERE PEOPLE LIKE TO LIVE	Homer, Alaska
CITY WHERE PLEASURE BEGINS	West Palm Beach,Fla.
CITY WHERE PROGRESS AND PLEASURES ARE PARTNERS	Douglas, Ariz.
CITY WHERE RAIL MEETS WATER	Kalama, Wash.
CITY WHERE RIVER, AIR, RAIL AND HIGHWAY MEET	Decatur, Ill.
CITY WHERE SHE DANCED	Salome, Ariz.
CITY WHERE SOUTHERN HOSPITALITY BEGINS	Portsmouth, Ohio
CITY WHERE SUMMER WINTERS	Chandler, Ariz.
CITY WHERE SUMMER WINTERS	Phoenix, Ariz.
CITY WHERE TEXAS MEETS THE SEA	Corpus Christi, Tex.
CITY WHERE THE AMERICAN TROPICS BEGIN	Fort Myers, Fla.
CITY WHERE THE BREEZES BLOW	Jamestown, R. I.
CITY WHERE THE CHARM, CULTURE AND TRADITION OF THE OLD SOUTH BLEND IN A MODERN CITY	Natchez, Miss.
CITY WHERE THE FIGHT FOR TEXAS LIBERTY BEGINS	Gonzales, Texas
CITY WHERE THE HISTORY OF THE WEST BEGINS	Fort Leavenworth, Kans.
CITY WHERE THE INDUSTRIAL EAST MEETS THE AGRICULTURAL WEST	Sioux City, Iowa
CITY WHERE THE MIGHTY SMITHY STANDS	Birmingham, Ala.
CITY WHERE THE MOUNTAIN MEETS THE SEA	Santa Monica, Calif.
CITY WHERE THE MOUNTAINS MEET THE SEA	Camden, Me.

CITY WHERE THE NORTH BEGINS AND THE PURE WATERS FLOW	White Cloud, Mich.
CITY WHERE THE OLD SOUTH AND THE NEW SOUTH MEET	Jackson, Miss.
CITY WHERE THE OLD SOUTH STILL LIVES	Natchez, Miss.
CITY WHERE THE PALMS MEET THE SEA	Miami Beach, Fla.
CITY WHERE THE PART-RIDGE FINDS A REFUGE	Bena, Minn.
CITY WHERE THE PINES MEET THE SEA	Virginia Beach, Va.
CITY WHERE THE PRAIRIE MEETS THE SEA	Duluth, Minn.
CITY WHERE THE RAILS AND THE TRAILS BEGIN	Lander, Wyo.
CITY WHERE THE SEAWAY MEETS THE TURNPIKE	Toledo, Ohio
CITY WHERE THE TROPICS BEGIN	Lake Worth, Fla.
CITY WHERE THE WEST BEGINS	Fort Worth, Texas
CITY WHERE THE WEST BEGINS	Independence, Mo.
CITY WHERE THE WEST REMAINS	Sheridan, Wyo.
CITY WHERE THE WORLD BATHES AND PLAYS	Hot Springs, Ark.
CITY WHERE THERE ARE NO STRANGERS..JUST NEW FRIENDS	York, Neb.
CITY WHERE TRADITION LINGERS	Marblehead, Mass.
CITY WHERE VERMONT BEGINS	Brattleboro, Vt.
CITY WHERE WORK AND PLAY ARE ONLY MINUTES AWAY	Palatka, Fla.
CITY WHERE YOU CAN WORK, LIVE, PLAY, THE WESTERN WAY	Yuma, Ariz.

CITY WHERE YOUR DREAM VACATION CAN BECOME A REALITY	Yankton, S. D.
CITY WITH A BIG FUTURE	Chowchilla, Calif.
CITY WITH A FUTURE	Bartlesville, Okla.
CITY WITH A FUTURE	Cape Coral, Fla.
CITY WITH A FUTURE	Henderson, N. C.
CITY WITH A FUTURE	Jamestown, N. D.
CITY WITH A FUTURE	Port St. Joe, Fla.
CITY WITH A FUTURE	San Bruno, Calif.
CITY WITH A FUTURE	Trenton, Mo.
CITY WITH A FUTURE TO SHARE	Glendive, Mont.
CITY WITH A GREAT CIVIC PRIDE AND A SOUND BUSINESS CLIMATE	Alexander City, Ala.
CITY WITH A GREAT POTENTIAL FOR GROWTH	Marshall, Mo.
CITY WITH A HEART IN THE HEART OF DIXIE	Birmingham, Ala.
CITY WITH A HOLE IN THE MIDDLE	Lake Tahoe, Calif.
CITY WITH A MILLION AMBASSADORS	St. Petersburg, Fla.
CITY WITH A SPARKLE	Clearwater, Fla.
CITY WITH FUTURE UNLIMITED	Huron, S. D.
CITY WITH OPPORTUNITY FOR ALL	Decatur, Ala.
CITY WITH ROOM TO STRETCH AND GROW IN	Atmore, Ala.
CITY WITH SMALL TOWN HOSPITALITY	Trussville, Ala.
CITY WITH THE PLANNED FUTURE	Harrisonburg, Va.
CITY WITH TWO FACES	Chicago, Ill.
CITY WITHOUT A TOOTH-ACHE	Hereford, Texas
CITY WITHOUT CITY LIMITS	Tupelo, Miss.
CITY WITHOUT CLOCKS	Las Vegas, Nev.
CITY WORTH WHILE	St. Joseph, Mo.

CITY WORTHY OF A NOBLE NAME	Lincoln, Neb.
CITY YOU CAN BE PROUD TO LIVE AND WORK IN	East Point, Ga.
CIVICS CENTER OF THE MIDLAND EMPIRE	Billings, Mont.
CLAM TOWN	Norwalk, Conn.
CLAREMONT, THE BEAUTIFUL	Claremont, Calif.
CLASSIC CITY	Boston, Mass.
CLASSIC CITY OF THE SOUTH	Athens, Ga.
CLAY CITY	Brazil, Ind.
CLAY PIPE CENTER OF THE WORLD	Dennison, Ohio
CLAY PIPE CENTER OF THE WORLD	Uhrichsville, Ohio
CLEAN COLORFUL TULIP CITY ON SCENIC LAKE MACATAWA	Holland, Mich.
CLEANEST BEACH IN THE WORLD	Old Orchard Beach, Me.
CLEANEST BIG CITY IN THE WORLD	New York, N. Y.
CLEANEST CITY IN THE UNITED STATES	Morristown, Tenn.
CLIPPER CITY	Manitowoc, Wis.
CLOCK CITY	Thomaston, Conn.
CLOCK CENTER OF THE WORLD	Bristol, Conn.
CLOSEST STATE TO HEAVEN	Salida, Colo.
CLOUD CITY	Leadville, Colo.
COAL BAY	Colby, Wash.
COAL CITY	Pittsburgh, Pa.
COAL CITY	Pottsville, Pa.
COASTAL TOWN OF CHARM AND BEAUTY	Yarmouth, Me.
COCKADE CITY	Petersburg, Va.
COCKADE CITY	Richmond, Va.
COCKPIT OF THE CIVIL WAR	Fredericksburg, Va.

COKE CITY	Uniontown, Pa.
COLISEUM CITY	New York, N.Y.
COLLAR CITY	Troy, N.Y.
COLLEGE CITY	Galesburg, Ill.
COLLEGE CITY	Lewisburg, Pa.
COLONIAL CAPITAL OF THE EASTERN SHORE	Easton, Md.
COLONIAL CAPITAL OF VIRGINIA	Williamsburg, Va.
COLONIAL CITY	Kingston, N.Y.
COLONY CITY	Fitzgerald, Ga.
COLORADO'S SECOND CITY	Pueblo, Colo.
COLORFUL KEY CENTER FOR DEFENSE ACTIVITIES	Jacksonville, Fla.
COLUMBIA CITY	Vancouver, Wash.
COMING CITY OF THE GREAT NORTHWEST	Pierre, S.D.
COMING VEGAS	Lake Tahoe, Calif.
COMMENCEMENT CITY	Tacoma, Wash.
COMMERCIAL CENTER OF IRRIGATED IDAHO	Gooding, Idaho
COMMERCIAL CENTER OF THE MIDLAND EMPIRE	Billings, Mont.
COMMERCIAL EMPIRE OF THE UNITED STATES	Washington, D.C.
COMMERCIAL EMPORIUM	New York, N.Y.
COMMERCIAL METROPOLIS OF WEST TENNESSEE	Memphis, Tenn.
COMMUNICATION CENTER OF FLORIDA	Jacksonville, Fla.
COMMUNITY OF CULTURE AND TRADITIONS	Lynchburg, Va.
COMMUNITY OF FRIENDLY PEOPLE	Decatur, Ark.
COMMUNITY OF PROGRESS	Goldsboro, N.C.
COMMUNITY ON THE MOVE	Rutland, Vt.
COMMUNITY WELL PLANNED, WELL DEVELOPED, WELL EQUIPPED FOR COMMERCE, INDUSTRY AND FAMILY LIFE	East Point, Ga.
COMMUNITY WITH A HEART IN THE HEART OF FABULOUS FLORIDA	Leesburg, Fla.

COMMUNITY WORKING TOGETHER FOR THE FUTURE	Tupelo, Miss.
COMMUTER'S HAVEN	Newton, Mass.
CONCENTRATOR CITY	Miami, Ariz.
CONEY ISLAND OF THE WEST	Saltair, Utah
CONFEDERATE CAPITAL	Richmond, Va.
CONSERVATIVE CINCINNATI	Cincinnati, Ohio
CONSTITUTION CITY	Port St. Joe, Fla.
CONSUMER COOPERATIVE CENTER OF THE UNITED STATES	Superior, Wis.
CONTENTED CITY	Cincinnati, Ohio
CONVENTION CENTER OF THE GREAT SMOKIES	Gatlinburg, Tenn.
CONVENTION CITY	Baltimore, Md.
CONVENTION CITY	Casper, Wyo.
CONVENTION CITY	Denver, Colo.
CONVENTION CITY	Jefferson City, Mo.
CONVENTION CITY	Juneau, Alaska
CONVENTION CITY	Louisville, Ky.
CONVENTION CITY	Portland, Ore.
CONVENTION CITY	St. Louis, Mo.
CONVENTION CITY OF THE EAST	Hartford, Conn.
CONVENTION CITY OF THE GREAT SMOKIES	Gatlinburg, Tenn.
CONVENTION HUB OF THE DAKOTAS	Duluth, Minn.
COOLEST SUMMER CITY	Aberdeen, S. D.
COPPER CITY	Butte, Mont.
COPPER CITY	Rome, N. Y.
CORDAGE CITY	Auburn, N. Y.
CORN CITY	Toledo, Ohio
CORNOPOLIS	Chicago, Ill.
CORNTOWN	Cornelius, Ore.
COSMOPOLITAN CITY	San Francisco, Calif.
COSMOPOLITAN SAN FRANCISCO	San Francisco, Calif.
COTTON TOWN OF THE U.S.A.	Paterson, N. J.
COTTONWOOD CITY	Leavenworth, Kans.

COUNTRY'S GREATEST RAIL CENTER	Chicago, Ill.
COURT CITY OF A NATION	Washington, D. C.
COURTEOUS CAPITAL CITY	Harrisburg, Pa.
COW CAPITAL	Wichita, Kans.
COW TOWN	Coffeyville, Kans.
COW TOWN	Fort Worth, Texas
COW TOWN	Medora, N. D.
COW TOWN OF THE SOUTH	Montgomery, Ala.
COWBOY BOOT CAPITAL	Olathe, Kans.
COWBOY CAPITAL	Dodge City, Kans.
COWBOY CAPITAL	Prescott, Ariz.
COWBOY CAPITAL OF OREGON	Prineville, Ore.
CRAB TOWN	Hampton, Va.
CRABTOWN	Annapolis, Md.
CRABTOWN-ON-THE-BAY	Annapolis, Md.
CRADLE AND THE GRAVE OF THE CONFEDERACY	Abbeville, S. C.
CRADLE OF AMERICAN LIBERTY	Taunton, Mass.
CRADLE OF AVIATION	Dayton, Ohio
CRADLE OF DENTAL EDUCATION	Bainbridge, Ohio
CRADLE OF GEORGIA	Savannah, Ga.
CRADLE OF INDUSTRY	Springfield, Vt.
CRADLE OF LIBERTY	Concord, Mass.
CRADLE OF LIBERTY	Lexington, Mass.
CRADLE OF LIBERTY	Philadelphia, Pa.
CRADLE OF NAVAL AVIATION	Pensacola, Fla.
CRADLE OF PACIFIC NORTHWEST HISTORY	Walla Walla, Wash.
CRADLE OF SECESSION	Charleston, S. C.
CRADLE OF SQUARE RIGGERS	Mystic, Conn.
CRADLE OF TEXAS LIBERTY	San Antonio, Texas
CRADLE OF THE CONFEDERACY	Montgomery, Ala.
CRADLE OF THE MEXICAN WAR	Fort Jessup, La.

CRADLE OF THE REVOLUTION	Midway, Ga.
CRADLE OF THE STEEL INDUSTRY	Johnstown, Pa.
CRADLE OF THE TROTTER	Goshen, N. Y.
CRAWFISH CAPITAL OF THE WORLD	Breaux Bridge, La.
CRAWFISH TOWN	New Orleans, La.
CREAM CITY	Milwaukee, Wis.
CREAM WHITE CITY OF THE UNSALTED SEAS	Milwaukee, Wis.
CRESCENT CITY	Appleton, Wis.
CRESCENT CITY	Hilo, Hawaii
CRESCENT CITY	New Orleans, La.
CRESCENT CITY OF THE NORTHWEST	Galena, Ill.
CRIME CAPITAL	Chicago, Ill.
CROSSROADS FOR NORTH-SOUTH EAST-WEST TRAFFIC	Alma, Ark.
CROSSROADS OF AMERICA	El Paso, Texas
CROSSROADS OF AMERICA	Indianapolis, Ind.
CROSSROADS OF AMERICA	Joplin, Mo.
CROSSROADS OF AMERICA	Seymour, Ind.
CROSSROADS OF HISTORY	Carlisle, Pa.
CROSSROADS OF LOUISIANA	Alexandria, La.
CROSSROADS OF LOUISIANA	Pineville, La.
CROSSROADS OF NEW ENGLAND	Springfield, Mass.
CROSSROADS OF NEW YORK	Utica, N.Y.
CROSSROADS OF NEW YORK STATE	Syracuse, N.Y.
CROSSROADS OF SOUTHERN INDIANA	Paoli, Ind.
CROSSROADS OF THE CONTINENT	Carbondale, Ill.
CROSSROADS OF THE AMERICAS	El Paso, Texas
CROSSROADS OF THE MID-SOUTH	Memphis, Tenn.
CROSSROADS OF THE MIDDLE WEST	Rockford, Ill.

CROSSROADS OF THE NATION	Cincinnati, Ohio
CROSSROADS OF THE NATION	Hastings, Neb.
CROSSROADS OF THE NATION	Omaha, Neb.
CROSSROADS OF THE NATION	Sioux Falls, S.D.
CROSSROADS OF THE NEW SOUTH	Spartanburg, S.C.
CROSSROADS OF THE OLD AND THE NEW SOUTH	Jackson, Miss.
CROSSROADS OF THE SOUTH	Jackson, Miss.
CROSSROADS OF THE WEST	Salt Lake City, Utah
CROSSROADS OF THE WORLD	Anchorage, Alaska
CROSSROADS OF THE WORLD	Washington, D. C.
CROSSROADS OF WISCONSIN	Marshfield, Wis.
CROSSROADS OF YOUR NATIONAL MARKET	Dayton, Ohio
CROSSROADS TO THE UNIVERSE	Melbourne, Fla.
CROSSROADS TO WONDER-LAND	Salida, Colo.
CROWN CITY	Pasadena, Calif.
CROWN CITY OF THE VALLEY	Pasadena, Calif.
CRUMPTOWN	Memphis, Tenn.
CRUTCH CAPITAL OF THE WORLD	Rumney, N. H.
CRYSTAL CENTER OF THE WORLD	Carlisle, Pa.
CRYSTAL CITY	Corning, N. Y.
CULTURAL CENTER	Madison, Wis.
CULTURAL CENTER OF THE NATION	New York, N. Y.
CUYUNA CAPITAL	Crosby, Minn.
CZECH BETHLEHEM	Racine, Wis.

D

DAIRY CITY	Elkland, Pa.
DANCINGEST TOWN IN THE UNITED STATES	Hendersonville, N.C.
DANISH CAPITAL OF THE UNITED STATES	Racine, Wis.
DATE CAPITAL OF THE UNITED STATES	Indio, Calif.
DEEP SOUTH OF TEXAS	Bay City, Texas
DEEP WATER	Chelan, Wash.
DEEP WATER PORT	Jacksonville, Fla.
DELAWARE'S SUMMER CAPITAL	Rehoboth Beach, Del.
DENVER OF OREGON	Baker, Ore.
DENVER OF SOUTH DAKOTA	Rapid City, S.D.
DEPOT SPRINGS	Cheney, Wash.
DERRICK CITY	Oil City, Pa.
DESERET	Salt Lake City, Utah
DESERT WONDERLAND	Indio, Calif.
DETROIT OF AIRPLANES	Los Angeles, Calif.
DETROIT OF THE WEST	Oakland, Calif.
DETROIT THE BEAUTIFUL	Detroit, Mich.
DEUTSCH-ATHENS	Milwaukee, Wis.
DIAMOND CITY	Wilkes-Barre, Pa.
DIMPLE OF THE BLUE-GRASS	Lexington, Ky.
DIMPLE OF THE UNIVERSE	Nashville, Tenn.
DISTRIBUTION CENTER OF THE SOUTHEAST	Augusta, Ga.
DISTRIBUTION CENTER OF THE SOUTHEAST	Jacksonville, Fla.
DIVERSIFIED AGRICULTURAL AND INDUSTRIAL COMMUNITY	Pierce City, Mo.
DIVERSIFIED CITY	Waycross, Ga.
DIVERSIFIED COMMUNITY	Frankfort, Ky.
DIVERSIFIED MANUFACTURING COMMUNITY	Framingham, Mass.
DIXIE GATEWAY	Covington, Ky.
DOGWOOD CITY	Atlanta, Ga.
DORMATORY OF NEW YORK	Brooklyn, N. Y.
DORP	Schenectady, N.Y.

DREAM CITY COME TRUE	Hollywood, Fla.
DREAM TOWN	Greenfield, Mass.
DRUID CITY	Tuscaloosa, Ala.
DUAL CITIES	Minneapolis, and St. Paul, Minn.
DUAL CITIES	St. Paul, and Minneapolis, Minn.
DUCKS' PUDDLE	Drakes Branch, Va.
DUDE RANCH CAPITAL OF THE WORLD	Wickenburg, Ariz.
DUKE CITY	Albuquerque, N.M.
DUPONT TOWN	Wilmington, Del.
DUPONTONIA	Wilmington, Del.
DUTCH CITY	Holland, Mich.
DUTCHTOWN	Aurora, Ore.
DYNAMIC CITY	Detroit, Mich.
DYNAMIC DETROIT	Detroit, Mich.
DYNAMIC METROPOLIS OF THE ROCKY MOUNTAIN EMPIRE	Denver, Colo.
DYNAMO OF DIXIE	Chattanooga, Tenn.

E

EARTHQUAKE CITY	Charleston, S.C.
EASTERN CONNECTICUT CENTER	Willimantic, Conn.
EASTERN GATEWAY TO MT. RANIER NATIONAL PARK	Yakima, Wash.
EASTERN GATEWAY TO THE BLACK HILLS	Rapid City, S.D.
EASTERN GATEWAY TO THE MOUNTAINOUS BLACK HILLS WHERE EAST MEETS WEST AND THE FRIENDLY HOSPITALITY	Rapid City, S.D.
EDEN OF OHIO	Sabina, Ohio
EDEN OF THE CLOSEST STATE TO HEAVEN	Fort Collins, Colo.
EDINBURGH OF AMERICA	Albany, N. Y.
EDUCATIONAL CAPITAL	Jackson, Miss.

EDUCATIONAL CENTER OF THE WEST	Emporia, Kans.
EGG BASKET OF THE WORLD	Petaluma, Calif.
EL-AY	Los Angeles, Calif.
ELAY	Los Angeles, Calif.
ELECTRIC CITY	Great Falls, Mont.
ELECTRIC CITY	Schenectady, N.Y.
ELECTRIC CITY	Scranton, Pa.
ELECTRIC CITY OF THE FUTURE	Buffalo, N.Y.
ELECTRICAL CITY	Schenectady, N.Y.
ELECTRONIC CENTER OF THE SOUTHWEST	Fort Huachuca, Ariz.
ELECTRONICS CAPITOL OF THE WORLD	Syracuse, N.Y.
ELM CITY	New Haven, Conn.
ELM CITY	Waterville, Me.
EMBRYONIC CAPITAL	Washington, D.C.
EMPIRE CITY	New York, N.Y.
ENERGY CAPITAL OF THE WEST	Farmington, N.M.
ENGINEERS' TOWN	Coulee City, Wash.
ENTERTAINMENT CAPITAL OF THE WORLD	New York, N.Y.
ENTRANCE TO THE CHAIN-O-LAKES	Elk Rapids, Mich.
ESSEN OF AMERICA	Bridgeport, Conn.
EVERGREEN CITY	Sheboygan, Wis.
EVERGREEN PLAYGROUND	Seattle, Wash.
EVERGREEN PLAYGROUND	Tacoma, Wash.
EXCITING CITY OF WELCOME	Honolulu, Hawaii
EXECUTIVE CITY	Washington, D.C.
EXPOSITION CITY	San Francisco, Calif.

F

FABULOUS CITY IN THE SUN	Miami Beach, Fla.
FAIR CITY	Huron, S.D.
FAIR CITY	Largo, Fla.
FAIR CITY	Syracuse, N.Y.

FAIR LITTLE CITY	Tulsa, Okla.
FAIR PLAY CITY	Jersey Shore, Pa.
FAIR WHITE CITY	Milwaukee, Wis.
FAIRYLAND	Hollywood, Calif.
FAITHFUL CITY	Worcester, Mass.
FALLS	Fall City, Wash.
FALLS	Tumwater, Wash.
FALLS CITIES	Jeffersonville, Ind.
FALLS CITIES	Louisville, Ky.
FALLS CITIES	New Albany, Ind.
FALLS CITY	Louisville, Ky.
FAMED GOLD RUSH TOWN	Nome, Alaska
FAMILY CITY	St. Louis, Mo.
FAMOUS PLAYGROUND OF THE WONDROUS NORTH-WEST	Coeur d'Alene, Idaho
FAMOUS WINTER RESORT FOR NORTHERN INVALIDS AND PLEASURE SEEKERS	Thomasville, Ga.
FAR AWAY ISLAND	Nantucket, Mass.
FAR AWAY LAND	Nantucket, Mass.
FARM MACHINERY CAPITAL OF AMERICA	Moline, Ill.
FASCINATING FOOTHILLS CITY	Fort Collins, Colo.
FAST GROWING INDUSTRIAL COMMUNITY	Richmond, Calif.
FASTEST GROWING CITY IN LOS ANGELES COUNTY	Montebello, Calif.
FASTEST GROWING CITY IN TEXAS	Corpus Christi, Texas
FASTEST GROWING CITY IN THE NORTHWEST	Bismarck, N.D.
FASTEST GROWING CITY IN THE STATE	Hastings, Neb.
FASTEST GROWING COMMUNITY IN MAINE	Norway, Me.
FASTEST GROWING COMMUNITY IN MAINE	Paris, Me.
FASTEST GROWING DEEP WATER SEAPORT IN MAINE	Searsport, Me.
FASTEST GROWING TOWN IN HILLSBORO COUNTY	Merrimack, N.H.

FATHER KNICKERBOCKER	New York, N.Y.
FAVORITE FAMILY SEASIDE RESORT	Hampton Beach, N.H.
FAVORSBURG	Pataha, Wash.
FEDERAL CAPITAL	Washington, D.C.
FEDERAL CITY	Atlanta, Ga.
FEDERAL CITY	Washington, D.C.
FEDERAL SEAT	Washington, D.C.
FEDERAL SITE	Washington, D.C.
FEDERAL TOWN	Washington, D.C.
FIGHTIN'EST TOWN ON THE RIVER	Lancaster, Ore.
FILBERT CENTER OF THE UNITED STATES	Hillsboro, Ore.
FILM CAPITAL	Hollywood, Calif.
FILM CAPITAL OF THE WORLD	Hollywood, Calif.
FILM CITY	Hollywood, Calif.
FILMDOM	Hollywood, Calif.
FILMLAND	Hollywood, Calif.
FINANCE CENTER OF FLORIDA	Jacksonville, Fla.
FINANCIAL CAPITAL OF THE WORLD	New York, N.Y.
FINANCIAL CENTER OF THE WEST	San Francisco, Calif.
FINANCIAL CENTER OF THE WORLD	San Francisco, Calif.
FINE RESIDENTIAL CITY	Fargo, N.D.
FINEST BEACH IN THE WORLD	Old Orchard Beach, Me.
FINEST HOME AND CULTURAL COMMUNITY IN SOUTHERN CALIFORNIA	Whittier, Calif.
FINEST NEW ENGLAND VILLAGE IN THE MIDDLE WEST	Evanston, Ill.
FIRECLAY CAPITAL	Mexico, Mo.
FIRECLAY CAPITAL OF THE WORLD	Mexico, Mo.
FIRST AMERICAN CAPITAL WEST OF THE ROCKIES	Monterey, Calif.

FIRST CAPITAL OF ARIZONA	Prescott, Ariz.
FIRST CAPITAL OF MISSOURI	St. Charles, Mo.
FIRST CAPITAL OF NEW YORK	Kingston, N.Y.
FIRST CAPITAL OF THE REPUBLIC OF TEXAS	West Columbia, Texas
FIRST CAPITAL OF THE STATE	Huntsville, Ala.
FIRST CITY	Ketchikan, Alaska
FIRST CITY	Memphis, Tenn.
FIRST CITY IN TEXAS	Houston, Texas
FIRST CITY OF AMERICA'S FIRST VACATIONLAND	Providence, R.I.
FIRST CITY OF THE FIRST STATE	Wilmington, Del.
FIRST CITY OF THE SOUTH	Savannah, Ga.
FIRST CITY OF THE WORLD	New York, N.Y.
FIRST COTTON PORT	Houston, Texas
FIRST ON THE FUN COAST OF FLORIDA	West Palm Beach, Fla.
FIRST STOP OF THE EAST-WIND	Chatham, Mass.
FIRST TERRITORIAL CAPITAL	Lewiston, Idaho
FIRST TOWN OF AMERICA	Plymouth, Mass.
FIRST TVA CITY	Tupelo, Miss.
FISH CITY	Lake Andes, S.D.
FISHERMAN'S HARBOR	Coyle, Wash.
FISHERMAN'S PARADISE	Belmar, N.J.
FISHERMAN'S PARADISE	Everglades, Fla.
FISHERMAN'S PARADISE OF THE NORTH ATLANTIC	New Shoreham, R.I.
FISHING CAPITAL OF THE OZARKS	Mountain Home, Ark.
FIVE MILES OF HEALTH AND HAPPINESS	Wildwood, N.J.
FIVE STAR CITY IN THE VALLEY OF THE SUN	Chandler, Ariz.
FLICKER CAPITAL	Hollywood, Calif.
FLICKER CITY	Hollywood, Calif.
FLICKER LANE	Hollywood, Calif.

FLOOD CITY	Johnstown, Pa.
FLOOD FREE CITY	Johnstown, Pa.
FLORAL CITY	Cincinnati, Ohio
FLORIDA'S ALL-YEAR RESORT	West Palm Beach, Fla.
FLORIDA'S ATTRACTION SHOWPLACE	Lake Wales, Fla.
FLORIDA'S CENTER FOR SCIENCE, EDUCATION, MEDICINE	Gainesville, Fla.
FLORIDA'S CITY BEAUTIFUL	Orlando, Fla.
FLORIDA'S CONVENTION CITY	Tampa, Fla.
FLORIDA'S EIGHTH CITY	Lakeland, Fla.
FLORIDA'S FINEST AGRICULTURAL, INDUSTRIAL AND RESORT COMMUNITY	Fort Pierce, Fla.
FLORIDA'S GATEWAY CITY	Jacksonville, Fla.
FLORIDA'S GOLFINGEST CITY	Hollywood, Fla.
FLORIDA'S GULF COAST METROPOLIS	Tampa, Fla.
FLORIDA'S HUB OF FUN	Jacksonville, Fla.
FLORIDA'S MAGIC CITY	Miami, Fla.
FLORIDA'S METROPOLITAN DISTRIBUTING CENTER	Tampa, Fla.
FLORIDA'S NEWEST CONVENTION CITY	Clearwater, Fla.
FLORIDA'S NEWEST METROPOLITAN INDUSTRIAL AREA	Daytona Beach, Fla.
FLORIDA'S SHOWCASE COMMUNITY	Coral Gables, Fla.
FLORIDA'S TROPICAL PARADISE	Fort Lauderdale, Fla.
FLORIDA'S YEAR 'ROUND CITY	Tampa, Fla.
FLOUR CITY	Buffalo, N.Y.
FLOUR CITY	Minneapolis, Minn.
FLOUR CITY	Rochester, N.Y.
FLOWER CITY	Rochester, N.Y.
FLOWER CITY	Springfield, Ill.
FLOWER CITY	Springfield, Ohio

FLOWER TOWN IN THE PINES	Summerville, S.C.
FLOWERBOX CITY	Neosho, Mo.
FOAM CITY	Milwaukee, Wis.
FOOD BASKET OF THE WORLD	Fargo, N.D.
FOOD EMPORIUM	Wishram, Wash.
FOOT OF THE ADIRON-DACKS	Amsterdam, N.Y.
FOOTHILLS OF THE CATSKILLS	Walton, N.Y.
FORDTOWN	Detroit, Mich.
FOREST CITY	Cleveland, Ohio
FOREST CITY	Middletown, Conn.
FOREST CITY	Portland, Me.
FOREST CITY	Rockford, Ill.
FOREST CITY	Savannah, Ga.
FOREST CITY	Wausau, Wis.
FOREST CITY OF THE SOUTH	Savannah, Ga.
FOREST PRODUCTS CAPITAL OF AMERICA	Tacoma, Wash.
FORMER CAPITAL OF THE CHEROKEE INDIAN NATION	Tahlequah, Okla.
FORMER CAPITAL OF THE CHICKASAW NATION	Tupelo, Miss.
FORT TOWN	Fort Worth, Texas
FORTUNATE ISLAND	Monhegan, Me.
FOUNDLING CAPITAL	Washington, D.C.
FOUNTAIN CITY	De Soto, Mo.
FOUNTAIN CITY	Fond du Lac, Wis.
FOUNTAIN CITY	Pueblo, Colo.
FOUNTAIN OF YOUTH CITY	St. Augustine, Fla.
FOUR LAKE CITY	Madison, Wis.
FOUR LAKES CITY	Madison, Wis.
FRATERNAL CAPITAL OF THE SOUTHWEST	Guthrie, Okla.
FREE STATE OF BEXAR	San Antonio, Texas
FRIENDLIEST AREA IN NORTHERN LOWER MICHIGAN	Cadillac, Mich.
FRIENDLIEST CITY	Rochester, N.Y.

FRIENDLIEST LITTLE "BIG TOWN" IN KENTUCKY	Murray, Ky.
FRIENDLIEST TOWN IN AMERICA	Tryon, N.C.
FRIENDLIEST TOWN IN NEW ENGLAND	Skowhegan, Me.
FRIENDLY CITY	Albertville, Ala.
FRIENDLY CITY	Algona, Iowa
FRIENDLY CITY	Augusta, Ga.
FRIENDLY CITY	Bradenton, Fla.
FRIENDLY CITY	Chehalis, Wash.
FRIENDLY CITY	Columbus, Miss.
FRIENDLY CITY	Cordova, Alaska
FRIENDLY CITY	Douglas, Ga.
FRIENDLY CITY	Fort Worth, Texas
FRIENDLY CITY	Fortuna, Calif.
FRIENDLY CITY	Jackson, Miss.
FRIENDLY CITY	Johnston, R.I.
FRIENDLY CITY	Johnstown, Pa.
FRIENDLY CITY	Lynchburg, Va.
FRIENDLY CITY	Milwaukee, Wis.
FRIENDLY CITY	New York, N.Y.
FRIENDLY CITY	Porterville, Calif.
FRIENDLY CITY	Scranton, Pa.
FRIENDLY CITY	Spokane, Wash.
FRIENDLY CITY IN THE HEART OF GEORGIA	Macon, Ga.
FRIENDLY CITY IN THE HEART OF THE OLD WEST	Douglas, Ariz.
FRIENDLY CITY IN THE SKY	Denver, Colo.
FRIENDLY CITY OF ENDLESS CHARM	Jacksonville, Fla.
FRIENDLY CITY OF PROGRESS	Goldsboro, N.C.
FRIENDLY CITY ON THE OREGON TRAIL	Baker, Ore.
FRIENDLY COMMUNITY	Grove, Okla.
FRIENDLY COMMUNITY OF BEAUTY AND INDUSTRY	Upper Sandusky, Ohio
FRIENDLY FABULOUS FLAGSTAFF	Flagstaff, Ariz.
FRIENDLY FOLK'S VILLAGE	Plainfield, Ind.

FRIENDLY FRONTIER CITY	Fairbanks, Alaska
FRIENDLY ISLAND	Marthas Vineyard,Mass.
FRIENDLY PROSPEROUS TOWN	Fryeburg, Me.
FRIENDLY RESORT CITY	Bradley Beach, N.J.
FRIENDLY TOWN	Johnston, R.I.
FRIENDLY VILLAGE	Prentice, Wis.
FRISCO	San Francisco, Calif.
FROG AND TOE	New York, N.Y.
FROG LEVEL	Clinchport, Va.
FROG MARKET OF THE NATION	Rayne, La.
FRONT DOOR ENTRANCE TO AN ALASKA VACATION	Anchorage, Alaska
FRONT OFFICE OF AMERICAN BUSINESS	New York, N.Y.
FROSTY CITY	Somerset, Pa.
FRUIT BOWL OF THE NATION	Yakima, Wash.
FUN SPOT OF THE SOUTH-WEST	Fort Worth, Texas
FUN TOWN	Park Falls, Wis.
FURNITURE CAPITAL OF AMERICA	Grand Rapids, Mich.
FURNITURE CITY	Grand Rapids, Mich.
FURNITURE CITY	High Point, N.C.
FURNITURE CITY	Martinsville, Va.
FUTURE GREAT CITY	Pierre, S.D.
FUTURE GREAT CITY OF THE WORLD	St. Louis, Mo.
FUTURE INDUSTRIAL CAPITAL OF THE SOUTH SHORE	Braintree, Mass.
FUTURE MINDED CITY	Chicopee, Mass.

G

GABLE TOWN	Danville, Ind.
GAMBLING QUEEN	Muskegon, Mich.
GAMECOCK CITY	Sumter, S.C.
GANGLAND	Chicago, Ill.
GAP	Pennington Gap, Va.
GARDEN CITY	Basin, Wyo.

GARDEN CITY	Beverly, Mass.
GARDEN CITY	Cedar Falls, Iowa
GARDEN CITY	Chicago, Ill.
GARDEN CITY	Missoula, Mont.
GARDEN CITY	Newton, Mass.
GARDEN CITY	San Jose, Calif.
GARDEN CITY	Savannah, Ga.
GARDEN CITY OF THE SOUTH	Augusta, Ga.
GARDEN SPOT FOR GOLF	Virginia Beach, Va.
GARDEN SPOT OF NORTH-WEST FLORIDA	Monticello, Fla.
GARDEN SPOT OF THE GARDEN STATE	Hammonton, N.J.
GARDEN SPOT OF THE PENINSULA	Palo Alto, Calif.
GARDEN SPOT OF THE SOUTH	Pensacola, Fla.
GARDEN SPOT OF THE WORLD FAMOUS SANTA CLARA VALLEY	Los Altos, Calif.
GARDEN OF MAINE	Houlton, Me.
GAS HOUSE OF THE NATION	Washington, D.C.
GATE CITY	Atlanta, Ga.
GATE CITY	Chattanooga, Tenn.
GATE CITY	Denison, Texas
GATE CITY	Keokuk, Iowa
GATE CITY	Laredo, Texas
GATE CITY	Nashua, N.H.
GATE CITY	Rapid City, S.D.
GATE CITY	San Bernardino, Calif.
GATE CITY	Winona, Minn.
GATE CITY OF FLORIDA	Jacksonville, Fla.
GATE CITY OF THE WEST	Omaha, Neb.
GATE CITY TO THE GREAT NORTHWEST	Pocatello, Idaho
GATE CITY TO THE SOUTH	Atlanta, Ga.
GATE TO THE SPORTS-MAN'S EDEN	Ely, Minn.
GATEWAY	Ashland, Ore.
GATEWAY ARCH CITY	St. Louis, Mo.
GATEWAY CITY	Fargo, N.D.

GATEWAY CITY	Huntington, W. Va.
GATEWAY CITY	Jacksonville, Fla.
GATEWAY CITY	La Crosse, Wis.
GATEWAY CITY	Louisville, Ky.
GATEWAY CITY	Minneapolis, Minn.
GATEWAY CITY	Seward, Alaska
GATEWAY CITY TO THE HILLS	Rapid City, S. D.
GATEWAY CITY TO CANADA	Buffalo, N. Y.
GATEWAY CITY TO THE BREAD BASKET OF THE WORLD	Fargo, N. D.
GATEWAY FROM SOUTH AND WEST TO OZARK PLAYGROUNDS	Pryor, Okla.
GATEWAY OF AMERICA'S SCENIC WONDERLAND	Dickinson, N. D.
GATEWAY OF KANSAS	Shawnee, Kans.
GATEWAY OF LAKE SUPERIOR	Sault Ste. Marie, Mich.
GATEWAY OF SOUTHERN INDIANA	Seymour, Ind.
GATEWAY OF SOUTHERN NEW ENGLAND	Providence, R. I.
GATEWAY OF THE ADIRONDACKS	Utica, N. Y.
GATEWAY OF THE LAKE REGION	Leesburg, Ind.
GATEWAY OF THE SOUTH	Atlanta, Ga.
GATEWAY OF THE SOUTH	Nashville, Tenn.
GATEWAY OF THE SOUTH-EAST	Augusta, Ga.
GATEWAY OF THE WEST	St. Louis, Mo.
GATEWAY OF VAST FARM AND INDUSTRIAL MARKETS	Gary, Ind.
GATEWAY OF WEST TEXAS	Fort Worth, Texas
GATEWAY TO ADVENTURE	Ketchikan, Alaska
GATEWAY TO ALASKA	Seattle, Wash.
GATEWAY TO ALL FLORIDA	Jacksonville, Fla.
GATEWAY TO ALL FLORIDA	Perry, Fla.
GATEWAY TO AMERICA'S WONDERLAND	Billings, Mont.

GATEWAY TO ARIZONA'S SCENIC AND RECREATIONAL AREA	Globe, Ariz.
GATEWAY TO BLUE SHOALS LAKE AND DAM	Flippin, Ark.
GATEWAY TO BROWN COUNTY	Morgantown, Ind.
GATEWAY TO CALIFORNIA	San Diego, Calif.
GATEWAY TO CANADA'S ST. LAWRENCE SEAWAY	Fort Kent, Me.
GATEWAY TO CANDLEWOOD LAKE	Danbury, Conn.
GATEWAY TO COLORADO'S SCENIC REGION	Boulder, Colo.
GATEWAY TO DEATH VALLEY	Beatty, Nev.
GATEWAY TO EASTERN MICHIGAN	Royal Oak, Mich.
GATEWAY TO EGYPT	Centralia, Ill.
GATEWAY TO FLORIDA	Pensacola, Fla.
GATEWAY TO FORT HUACHUCA	Bisbee, Ariz.
GATEWAY TO FOUR OZARK VACATION AREAS	Springfield, Mo.
GATEWAY TO GLACIER BAY NATIONAL MONUMENT	Juneau, Alaska
GATEWAY TO HISTORYLAND	Fredericksburg, Va.
GATEWAY TO HOPILAND AND NAVAJOLAND	Winslow, Ariz.
GATEWAY TO INDIANA DUNES	Gary, Ind.
GATEWAY TO ISLE ROYALE NATIONAL PARK	Grand Portage, Minn.
GATEWAY TO LAKE ERIE	Sandusky, Ohio
GATEWAY TO LAKE OF THE OZARKS	Eldon, Mo.
GATEWAY TO LAKE TAHOE AND YOSEMITE VALLEY	Carson City, Nev.
GATEWAY TO MACKINAC ISLAND AND UPPER PENINSULA OF MICHIGAN	Mackinaw City, Mich.
GATEWAY TO MAINE	Biddeford, Me.
GATEWAY TO MAINE	Kittery, Me.

GATEWAY TO MAINE	Saco, Me.
GATEWAY TO MAINE FROM THE WHITE MOUNTAINS	Bethel, Me.
GATEWAY TO MEXICO	San Antonio, Texas
GATEWAY TO MT. MAGAZINE	Paris, Ark.
GATEWAY TO MOUNT RANIER	Tacoma, Wash.
GATEWAY TO MUIR WOODS	Mill Valley, Calif.
GATEWAY TO NEW ENGLAND	Greenwich, Conn.
GATEWAY TO NIAGARA FALLS	Williamsville, N.Y.
GATEWAY TO NOVA	Edgewater, Fla.
GATEWAY TO OKEFENOKEE SWAMP	Waycross, Ga.
GATEWAY TO OUTDOOR FISHING AND HUNTING ACTIVITIES	Monett, Mo.
GATEWAY TO PICTURED ROCKS	Munising, Mich.
GATEWAY TO PICTUR-ESQUE CANADA	Buffalo, N.Y.
GATEWAY TO RANGELEY AND SUGARLOAF	Farmington, Me.
GATEWAY TO REAL VACATION PLEASURE	Jackman, Me.
GATEWAY TO "SAILFISH ALLEY"	Boynton Beach, Fla.
GATEWAY TO SCENIC BOSTON MOUNTAINS	Fayetteville, Ark.
GATEWAY TO SCENIC SOUTHERN INDIANA	Greater Bloomington, Ind.
GATEWAY TO SLEEPING BEAR DUNES	Honor, Mich.
GATEWAY TO SMUGGLER'S NOTCH	Stowe, Vt.
GATEWAY TO SONOYTA, MEXICO AND THE GULF OF LOWER CALIFORNIA	Ajo, Ariz.

GATEWAY TO SOUTH DAKOTA'S VACATION WONDERLAND	Yankton, S.D.
GATEWAY TO THE (See also under "Gateway of" and "Gateway to")	
GATEWAY TO THE ADIRONDACKS	Lake Luzerne, N.Y.
GATEWAY TO THE ADIRONDACKS	Utica, N.Y.
GATEWAY TO THE ALLAGASH COUNTY	Fort Kent, Me.
GATEWAY TO THE ARCTIC	Fairbanks, Alaska
GATEWAY TO THE BADLANDS NATIONAL PARK	Wall, S.D.
GATEWAY TO THE BASS CAPITAL OF THE WORLD	Crescent City, Fla.
GATEWAY TO THE BEAR RIVER MIGRATORY BIRD REFUGE	Brigham, Utah
GATEWAY TO THE BEAUTIFUL OZARK PLAYGROUND	Fort Smith, Ark.
GATEWAY TO THE BLACK HILLS	Rapid City, S.D.
GATEWAY TO THE CANYONLANDS AND HIGHLAND OF SOUTHEASTERN UTAH	Price, Utah
GATEWAY TO THE CARIBBEAN	Tampa, Fla.
GATEWAY TO THE CATSKILLS	Kingston, N.Y.
GATEWAY TO THE DAKOTAS	Sioux Falls, S.D.
GATEWAY TO THE DELTA	Yazoo City, Miss.
GATEWAY TO THE DESERT AND IDYLLWILD MOUNTAIN RESORT	Banning, Calif.
GATEWAY TO THE EVERGLADES	Fort Lauderdale, Fla.
GATEWAY TO THE FAMOUS GOLD COAST	Hobe Sound, Fla.
GATEWAY TO THE FAR EAST	San Francisco, Calif.

GATEWAY TO THE FISH RIVER CHAIN OF LAKES	Fort Kent, Me.
GATEWAY TO THE GALAXIES	Titusville, Fla.
GATEWAY TO THE GREAT SMOKIES	Gatlinburg, Tenn.
GATEWAY TO THE HEART-LAND OF AMERICA	Buffalo, N.Y.
GATEWAY TO THE HISTORIC NORTHWEST	Glendive, Mont.
GATEWAY TO THE LAKE MEAD RECREATIONAL AREA	Boulder City, Nev.
GATEWAY TO THE LAKE REGION	Webster, S.D.
GATEWAY TO THE LAKES AND STREAMS OF THE THUNDER MOUNTAIN REGION	Crivitz, Wis.
GATEWAY TO THE LAND O'LAKES	Sedalia, Mo.
GATEWAY TO THE LITCHFIELD HILLS	Waterbury, Conn.
GATEWAY TO THE MAMMOTH CAVE	Cave City, Ky.
GATEWAY TO THE MISSILE TEST CENTER	Eau Gallie, Fla.
GATEWAY TO THE NORTHERN INDIANA LAKE REGION	Fort Wayne, Ind.
GATEWAY TO THE NORTHWEST	St. Paul, Minn.
GATEWAY TO THE OHIO LAKE ERIE ISLANDS	Sandusky, Ohio
GATEWAY TO THE OLD WESTERN RESERVE	Youngstown, Ohio
GATEWAY TO THE OLD WESTERN RESERVE	Zanesville, Ohio
GATEWAY TO THE ORANGE EMPIRE	Baldwin Park, Calif.
GATEWAY TO THE ORIENT	Seattle, Wash.

GATEWAY TO THE OZARKS	Dover, Ark.
GATEWAY TO THE PENNSYLVANIA DUTCH COUNTRY	Downingtown, Pa.
GATEWAY TO THE POCONOS	Stroudsburg, Pa.
GATEWAY TO THE POUDRE	Fort Collins, Colo.
GATEWAY TO THE PROPOSED SLEEPING BEAR NATIONAL PARK	Frankfort, Mich.
GATEWAY TO THE RANGELEY LAKES	Farmington, Me.
GATEWAY TO THE SAN FERNANDO VALLEY	North Hollywood, Calif.
GATEWAY TO THE SAN JOAQUIN VALLEY	Stockton, Calif.
GATEWAY TO THE SAND DUNE MOUNTAINS	Mears, Mich.
GATEWAY TO THE SOUTH	Annapolis, Md.
GATEWAY TO THE SOUTH	Columbia, S. C.
GATEWAY TO THE SOUTH	Louisville, Ky.
GATEWAY TO THE SOUTHERN CATSKILLS	Harriman, N. Y.
GATEWAY TO THE SOUTHWEST	Christiansburg, Va.
GATEWAY TO THE SPACE PROGRAM	Eau Gallie, Fla.
GATEWAY TO THE SPORTSMAN'S EDEN	Ely, Minn.
GATEWAY TO THE TEN THOUSAND ISLANDS	Naples, Fla.
GATEWAY TO THE VALLEY OF PERFECT APPLES	Wenatchee, Wash.
GATEWAY TO THE WATER WONDERLAND	Grand Rapids, Mich.
GATEWAY TO THE WATER WONDERLAND	Morley, Mich.
GATEWAY TO THE WEST	Billings, Mont.
GATEWAY TO THE WEST	Dickinson, N. D.
GATEWAY TO THE WEST	Fort Worth, Texas
GATEWAY TO THE WEST	Independence, Mo.

GATEWAY TO THE WEST	Pittsburgh, Pa.
GATEWAY TO THE WEST	St. Louis, Mo.
GATEWAY TO THE WEST	Schenectady, N.Y.
GATEWAY TO THE WEST	Sioux Falls, S.D.
GATEWAY TO THE WEST AND SOUTHWEST	Kansas City, Mo.
GATEWAY TO THE WHITE-MAN AIR FORCE BASE	Knob Noster, Mo.
GATEWAY TO THE WINNESHIEK	Prairie du Chien, Wis.
GATEWAY TO THE WORLD	New Orleans, La.
GATEWAY TO THREE LOCAL SLOGAN STATES, VIRGINIA, TENNESSEE, NORTH CAROLINA	Damascus, Va.
GATEWAY TO TROPICAL FLORIDA	New Port Richey, Fla.
GATEWAY TO UPSTATE	Middletown, N.Y.
GATEWAY TO VACATION-LAND	Provo, Utah
GATEWAY TO VAST FARM AND INDUSTRIAL MARKETS	Gary, Ind.
GATEWAY TO WALLOWA NATIONAL FOREST	Enterprise, Ore.
GATEWAY TO "WANDER-LAND" IN MOHAVE COUNTY, ARIZONA	Kingman, Ariz.
GATEWAY TO WEST TEXAS	Fort Worth, Texas
GEM CITY	Dayton, Ohio
GEM CITY	Laramie, Wyo.
GEM CITY	Palatka, Fla.
GEM CITY	Pulaski, Va.
GEM CITY	Quincy, Ill.
GEM CITY	St. Paul, Minn.
GEM CITY	Salida, Colo.
GEM CITY IN ARIZONA'S VALLEY OF THE SUN	Mesa, Ariz.
GEM CITY IN THE HEART OF THE GREAT MIS-SISSIPPI VALLEY	Quincy, Ill.
GEM CITY OF CEDAR EMPIRE	Coquille, Ore.

GEM CITY OF OHIO	Dayton, Ohio
GEM CITY OF SOUTHERN ALABAMA	Andalusia, Ala.
GEM CITY OF THE FOOTHILLS	Los Gatos, Calif.
GEM CITY OF THE LAKES	Erie, Pa.
GEM CITY OF THE MIDDLE WEST	Quincy, Ill.
GEM CITY OF THE WEST	Quincy, Ill.
GEM OF THE GOLD COAST	Pompano Beach, Fla.
GEM OF THE HILLS	Clermont, Fla.
GEM OF THE JERSEY COAST	Avalon, N.J.
GEM OF THE NOOKSACK VALLEY	Ferndale, Wash.
GEM OF THE OCEAN	Salida, Colo.
GEM OF THE PRAIRIES	Chicago, Ill.
GEM ON THE OCEAN	Lantana, Fla.
GENEROUS PEOPLE	Puyallup, Wash.
GENTILE PEOPLE	Corinne, Utah
GEOGRAPHIC HEART OF THE STATE	Wisconsin Rapids, Wis.
GEOGRAPHICAL CENTER OF MAGIC VALLEY	Jerome, Idaho
GEOGRAPHICAL CENTER OF THE METROPOLITAN BOSTON AREA	Cambridge, Mass.
GEOGRAPHICAL CENTER OF THE SOUTH	Huntsville, Ala.
GEORGE WASHINGTON'S BOYHOOD HOME	Fredericksburg, Va.
GEORGIA VACATIONLAND	Brunswick, Ga.
GEORGIA VACATIONLAND	Sea Island, Ga.
GEORGIA VACATIONLAND	St. Simons Island, Ga.
GEORGIA'S CRADLE OF THE REVOLUTION	Midway, Ga.
GEORGIA'S MOBILE HOME CENTER	Americus, Ga.
GEORGIA'S SECOND OLDEST CITY	Augusta, Ga.
GERMAN ATHENS	Milwaukee, Wis.
GIBRALTAR OF AMERICA	Vicksburg, Miss.
GIBRALTAR OF LOUISIANA	Vicksburg, Miss.

GIBRALTAR OF THE CONFEDERACY	Vicksburg, Miss.
GIBRALTAR OF THE SOUTH	Vicksburg, Miss.
GLASS CAPITAL OF THE WORLD	Toledo, Ohio
GLASS CENTER	Toledo, Ohio
GLEN	Singers Glen, Va.
GLIDER CAPITAL OF THE WORLD	Elmira, N.Y.
GOAT CREEK	Mazama, Wash.
GOLD COAST OF OREGON	Baker, Ore.
GOLDEN AGE HAVEN	Concord, Mass.
GOLDEN BUCKLE ON THE COTTON BELT	Clarksdale, Miss.
GOLDEN BUCKLE ON THE WHEAT BELT	Colby, Kans.
GOLDEN CITY	Sacramento, Calif.
GOLDEN CITY	San Francisco, Calif.
GOLDEN CITY OF THE GOLD COAST	Boca Raton, Fla.
GOLDEN COAST OF FLORIDA	Palm Beach, Fla.
GOLDEN GATE CITY	San Francisco, Calif.
GOLDEN HEART OF ALASKA	Fairbanks, Alaska
GOLDEN HEART METROPOLIS OF THE INTERIOR	Fairbanks, Alaska
GOLDEN HEART OF THE NORTH	Fairbanks, Alaska
GOLDEN ISLES OF GEORGIA	St. Simons Island, Ga.
GOLDEN ISLES OF GEORGIA	Sea Islands, Ga.
GOLDEN RULE CITY	Columbia, S.C.
GOLF CAPITAL OF AMERICA	Augusta, Ga.
GOLFING CAPITAL OF FLORIDA	Sebring, Fla.
GOOD CAMPING GROUND	Mukilteo, Wash.
GOOD PLACE TO KNOW, GO, VISIT, STAY	Willcox, Ariz.
GOOD PLACE TO LIVE	Aberdeen, S.D.

GOOD PLACE TO LIVE AND WORK	Blacksburg, Va.
GOOD PLACE TO LIVE--BETTER	Brandon, Fla.
GOOD PLACE TO LIVE, TO WORK AND TO REAR YOUR FAMILY	East Point, Ga.
GOOD PLACE TO LIVE, WORK AND PLAY	Fremont, Neb.
GOOD PLACE TO VISIT	Sebring, Fla.
GOOD PLACE TO VISIT, A GOOD PLACE TO LIVE	Dickinson, N.D.
GOOD PLACE TO WORK AND LIVE	Grand Island, Neb.
GOOSETOWN	Wilbur, Wash.
GOTHAM	New York, N. Y.
GOVERNMENTAL, EDUCATIONAL, RECREATIONAL CENTER	Albany, N.Y.
GRAND CANYON OF THE EAST	Ausable Chasm, N.Y.
GRAND EMPORIUM OF THE WEST	Washington, D.C.
GRAND METROPOLIS	Washington, D.C.
GRANITE CENTER OF THE WORLD	Barre, Vt.
GRANITE CENTER OF THE WORLD	Elberton, Ga.
GRANITE CITY	Ashland, Ore.
GRANITE CITY	Milbank, S.D.
GRANITE CITY	Quincy, Mass.
GRANITE CITY	St. Cloud, Minn.
GRANITE CITY	Spencer, S.D.
GRASS LANDS	Palouse, Wash.
GRASS ROOTS OF AMERICA	Orfordville, Wis.
GRASSY PLACE	Kennewick, Wash.
GREAT AMERICAN SHRINE	Springfield, Ill.
GREAT DISMAL	Washington, D.C.
GREAT INTERMOUNTAIN TRANSPORTATION CENTER	Billings, Mont.
GREAT PLACE TO LIVE	Gonzalez, Texas
GREAT RIVER CITY	St. Louis, Mo.

GREAT SALT LAKE CITY	Salt Lake City, Utah
GREAT SERBONIAN BOG	Washington, D.C.
GREAT SOUTH GATE	New Orleans, La.
GREAT WHITE CITY	Washington, D.C.
GREATEST ALL-YEAR ROUND VACATION CITY	New York, N.Y.
GREATEST CITY'S GREATEST BOROUGH	Brooklyn, N.Y.
GREATEST LUMBER MARKET IN THE WORLD	Bangor, Me.
GREATEST PRIMARY WINTER WHEAT MARKET	Kansas City, Mo.
GREATEST TOWNE FOR FISHING IN NEW ENGLAND	Marblehead, Mass.
GREEN BEAN CENTER	Stayton, Ore.
GREEN FELT JUNGLE	Las Vegas, Nev.
GREEN MOUNTAIN CITY	Montpelier, Vt.
GREEN SPOT IN ARIZONA'S FAMOUS VALLEY OF THE SUN	Chandler, Ariz.
GREENWICH VILLAGE OF THE WEST	Sausalito, Calif.
GRETNA GREEN	Elkton, Md.
GRETNA GREEN	Ripley, N.Y.
GRETNA GREEN OF MARYLAND	Elkton, Md.
GREYHOUND CITY	Abilene, Kans.
GROWING CITY	Casper, Wyo.
GROWING CITY	Sioux Falls, S.D.
GROWING CITY OF INDUSTRY AND RECREATION	Fort Smith, Ark.
GROWING INDUSTRIAL CENTER OF NORTHWESTERN PENNSYLVANIA	Bradford, Pa.
GULF CITY	Mobile, Ala.
GULF CITY	New Orleans, La.
GULF COAST CITY	Pensacola, Fla.
GYPSUM CITY	Fort Dodge, Iowa

H

H-BOMB'S HOME TOWN	Ellenton, S.C.

HALF WAY AND A PLACE TO STAY	Kinsley, Kans.
HANGMAN CREEK	Latah, Wash.
HANGTOWN	Placerville, Calif.
HAPPY HOLLOW	Roda, Va.
HARBOR CITY	Erie, Pa.
HARBOR OF THE AIR	Inglewood, Calif.
HARBOUR CITY	Eau Gallie, Fla.
HARDWARE CITY	New Britain, Conn.
HARMONY	Hamilton, Va.
HARTFORD OF THE SOUTH	Jacksonville, Fla.
HARTFORD OF THE WEST	Lincoln, Neb.
HAT CITY	Danbury, Conn.
HAT CITY OF THE WORLD	Danbury, Conn.
HAY FEVER RELIEF HAVEN OF AMERICA	Duluth, Minn.
HEAD OF ELK	Elkton, Md.
HEADQUARTERS OF THE BIG HORN NATIONAL FOREST	Sheridan, Wyo.
HEADWATERS OF STOCKTON LAKE	Greenfield, Mo.
HEALTH CITY	Battle Creek, Mich.
HEALTH FOOD CITY	Battle Creek, Mich.
HEART AND HUB OF DELAWARE COUNTY	Walton, N.Y.
HEART OF A GREAT STATE	Columbus, Ohio
HEART OF A HUNTER'S PARADISE	Price, Utah
HEART OF AMERICA	Frankfort, Ky.
HEART OF AMERICA	Kansas City, Mo.
HEART OF AMERICA	Washington, D.C.
HEART OF AMERICA'S INDUSTRIAL WAR FRONT	Kearny, N.J.
HEART OF AMERICA'S WORKSHOP	Akron, Ohio
HEART OF CALIFORNIA	Sacramento, Calif.
HEART OF EASTERN GEORGIA AND WESTERN SOUTH CAROLINA	Augusta, Ga.
HEART OF EASTERN NORTH CAROLINA	Goldsboro, N.C.

HEART OF FLORIDA'S CITRUS INDUSTRY	Winter Haven, Fla.
HEART OF FLORIDA'S FUN-LAND	Ocala, Fla.
HEART OF GEORGIA	Macon, Ga.
HEART OF INDUSTRIAL AMERICA	Delphos, Ohio
HEART OF KENTUCKY	Frankfort, Ky.
HEART OF KENTUCKY'S BLUE GRASS REGION	Lexington, Ky.
HEART OF MARYLAND	Annapolis, Md.
HEART OF MONTANA'S MAGICLAND	Butte, Mont.
HEART OF NEW ENGLAND	Southbridge, Mass.
HEART OF NEW YORK STATE	Syracuse, N.Y.
HEART OF NORTH DAKOTA	Grand Forks, N.D.
HEART OF NORTH MIS-SISSIPPI AND BEAUTIFUL GRENADA LAKE	Grenada, Miss.
HEART OF RHODE ISLAND	East Greenwich, R.I.
HEART OF THE AMERICAN RIVIERA	Foley, Ala.
HEART OF THE ANTELOPE VALLEY	Lancaster, Calif.
HEART OF THE BAY STATE	Worcester, Mass.
HEART OF THE BERKSHIRES	Pittsfield, Mass.
HEART OF THE CITRUS INDUSTRY	Lakeland, Fla.
HEART OF THE COMMON-WEALTH	Harrisburg, Pa.
HEART OF THE COMMON-WEALTH	Worcester, Mass.
HEART OF THE EMERALD EMPIRE IN THE NORTH IDAHO SCENIC LAND	Coeur d'Alene, Idaho
HEART OF THE FABULOUS GULF COAST COUNTRY	Biloxi, Miss.
HEART OF THE FAMOUS NORTH SHORE	Beverly, Mass.
HEART OF THE FLORIDA KEYS	Marathon, Fla.
HEART OF THE FRUIT BELT	Benton Harbor, Mich.

HEART OF THE GOLD COAST	Deerfield Beach, Fla.
HEART OF THE GOLD COAST	Pompano Beach, Fla.
HEART OF THE GREEN MOUNTAINS	Rutland, Vt.
HEART OF THE HARBOR	Wilmington, Del.
HEART OF THE INLAND EMPIRE	Spokane, Wash.
HEART OF THE LEATHER-STOCKING LAND	Cooperstown, N.Y.
HEART OF THE NATION'S HERITAGE	Alexandria, Va.
HEART OF THE NEW ENGLAND TOBACCO FARM-LAND	Windsor, Conn.
HEART OF THE NEW SOUTH	Meridian, Miss.
HEART OF THE OLD DOMINION	Blackstone, Va.
HEART OF THE OLD SOUTHWEST	Tucson, Ariz.
HEART OF THE PACIFIC WONDERLAND	Salem, Ore.
HEART OF THE PALM BEACHES	Lake Worth, Fla.
HEART OF THE PENN-SYLVANIA DUTCH COUNTRY	Lancaster, Pa.
HEART OF THE PIEDMONT	Charlotte, N.C.
HEART OF THE PIONEER VALLEY	Northampton, Mass.
HEART OF THE POTOMAC HIGHLANDS	Cumberland, Md.
HEART OF THE ROCKIES	Salida, Colo.
HEART OF THE ROMANTIC SOUTHWEST IN THE VALLEY OF THE SUN	Mesa, Ariz.
HEART OF THE SCENIC SOUTHWEST	Tucson, Ariz.
HEART OF THE SOUTH GEORGIA EMPIRE	Fitzgerald, Ga.
HEART OF THE SOUTH-EAST	Macon, Ga.

HEART OF THE SUN COUNTRY	Phoenix, Ariz.
HEART OF THE U.S.A.	Effingham, Ill.
HEART OF THE UNITED STATES OF AMERICA	Kansas City, Mo.
HEART OF THE VALLEY	Corvallis, Ore.
HEART OF THE VALLEY THAT WARMS A NATION	Wilkes-Barre, Pa.
HEART OF THE WESTSIDE OF FRESNO COUNTY	Coalinga, Calif.
HEART OF THE WHITE MOUNTAINS	Bethlehem, N.H.
HEART OF THE YELLOW-STONE VALLEY	Sidney, Mont.
HEART OF WESTCHESTER	White Plains, N.Y.
HEIDELBERG OF AMERICA	Dubuque, Iowa
HELL ON WHEELS	Cheyenne, Wyo.
HELLS FORTY ACRES	San Carlos, Ariz.
HIGH GRADE OIL METROPOLIS OF THE WORLD	Bradford, Pa.
HIGH POINT OF LONG BEACH ISLAND	Harvey Cedars, N.J.
HIGHEST INCORPORATED TOWN IN EASTERN AMERICA	Highlands, N.C.
HILL CITY	Lynchburg, Va.
HILL CITY	Portland, Me.
HILL CITY	Vicksburg, Miss.
HILL TOP CITY	Eveleth, Minn.
HILL TOWN	Hillsville, Va.
HISTORIC AND SCENIC LINCOLN	Lincoln, R.I.
HISTORIC BETHLEHEM	Bethlehem, Pa.
HISTORIC CITY	Williamsburg, Va.
HISTORIC CITY OF AMERICA	Natchez, Miss.
HISTORIC CITY OF THE BLACK HILLS	Deadwood, S.D.
HISTORIC FRANKFORT	Frankfort, Ky.
HISTORIC SHOWPLACE OF AMERICA	Newport, R.I.

HISTORIC HOME TOWN OF GENERAL GEORGE WASHINGTON	Alexandria, Va.
HISTORIC TOWN OF THE OLD SOUTH...NOW A PROGRESSIVE CITY	Canton, Miss.
HISTORICAL CITY	Prairie du Chien, Wis.
HISTORICAL CITY OF HOMES	Evanston, Ill.
HOCKEY CAPITAL OF THE NATION	Eveleth, Minn.
HOGOPOLIS	Chicago, Ill.
HOIST CAPITAL OF AMERICA	Forrest City, Ark.
HOLE IN THE GROUND	Albany, Ore.
HOLE IN THE GROUND	Kahlotus, Wash.
HOLIDAY CITY	St. Louis, Mo.
HOLLAND'S CORNER	Holland, Va.
HOLLY CITY OF AMERICA	Millville, N.J.
HOLSTEIN CAPITAL OF AMERICA	Northfield, Minn.
HOLY CITY	Charleston, S.C.
HOLY CITY	Lincoln, Neb.
HOLY CITY	Sunnyside, Wash.
HOME CITY	Brookings, S.D.
HOME CITY	Charlotte, N.C.
HOME FOR YOUR BUSINESS	Portsmouth, R.I.
HOME FOR YOUR FAMILY	Portsmouth, R.I.
HOME MARKET FOR THE GREAT NORTHWEST	Sioux City, Iowa
HOME OF A YANKEE COUNT	Woburn, Mass.
HOME OF ABRAHAM LINCOLN	Springfield, Ill.
HOME OF AMERICA'S GREATEST SPA	Saratoga Springs, N.Y.
HOME OF APLETS, THE CONFECTION OF THE FAIRIES	Cashmere, Wash.
HOME OF ARKANSAS POLYTECHNIC COLLEGE	Russellville, Ark.
HOME OF BAKED BEANS	Boston, Mass.
HOME OF BASEBALL	Cooperstown, N.Y.

HOME OF BUFFALO BILL	North Platte, Neb.
HOME OF DIAMOND PRODUCTS	Tulsa, Okla.
HOME OF DISNEYLAND	Anaheim, Calif.
HOME OF FLORENCE STATE COLLEGE	Florence, Ala.
HOME OF FORT RUCKER, THE ARMY AVIATION CENTER	Ozark, Ala.
HOME OF FRANKLIN DELANO ROOSEVELT	Hyde Park, N.Y.
HOME OF FRIENDLY PEOPLE	Pierre, S.D.
HOME OF FRONTIER DAYS	Cheyenne, Wyo.
HOME OF GORDON COLLEGE	Barnesville, Ga.
HOME OF HEALTH, HISTORY AND HORSES	Saratoga Springs, N.Y.
HOME OF HELEN KELLER	Tuscumbia, Ala.
HOME OF HOSPITALITY	Jasper, Ala.
HOME OF IDAHO'S GREATEST MINES	Kellogg, Idaho
HOME OF ILLUMINATED CASCADES	Jackson, Mich.
HOME OF JAMES FENIMORE COOPER	Cooperstown, N.Y.
HOME OF LATEX RUBBER	Dover, Del.
HOME OF LITTLE STEEL	Warren, Ohio
HOME OF L.B.J.	Stonewall, Texas
HOME OF MINUTE TAPIOCA	Orange, Mass.
HOME OF MORE THAN 4,000 COMMERCIAL TRAVELERS	Springfield, Mass.
HOME OF NATIONAL INDUSTRIES	Camden, N.J.
HOME OF 'OLD HICKORY' HAM AND BACON	Crane, Mo.
HOME OF OLD SEA CAPTAINS	Searsport, Me.
HOME OF ONE OF THE NATION'S LARGEST SKILLED TECHNICAL WORK FORCES	Rochester, N.Y.

HOME OF PROSPEROUS AGRICULTURE BUSINESS AND INDUSTRY	Mc Kinney, Texas
HOME OF RAINBOW SPRINGS	Dunnellon, Fla.
HOME OF SANDWICH GLASS	Sandwich, Mass.
HOME OF SOUTH DAKOTA STATE COLLEGE	Brookings, S. D.
HOME OF STANFORD UNIVERSITY	Palo Alto, Calif.
HOME OF STATE COLLEGE OF WASHINGTON	Pullman, Wash.
HOME OF STETSON UNIVERSITY	De Land, Fla.
HOME OF TEN THOUSAND FRIENDLY PEOPLE	Flagstaff, Ariz.
HOME OF TEXAS TECH	Lubbock, Texas
HOME OF THE ALBEMARLE PIPPIN	Charlottesville, Va.
HOME OF THE APPLE BLOSSOM FESTIVAL	Winchester, Va.
HOME OF THE ATHLETICS	Kansas City, Mo.
HOME OF THE BOLL WEEVIL MONUMENT	Enterprise, Ala.
HOME OF THE CHRISTMAS TREE INDUSTRY	Cook, Minn.
HOME OF THE COLORADO AGGIES	Fort Collins, Colo.
HOME OF THE COMSTOCK LODE	Virginia City, Nev.
HOME OF CONTENTED COWS	Carnation, Wash.
HOME OF THE EVIL SPIRITS	Enumclaw, Wash.
HOME OF THE FABULOUS SUN DEVIL ATHLETIC TEAM AND ARIZONA STATE UNIVERSITY	Tempe, Ariz.
HOME OF THE FAMOUS PLUTO MINERAL SPRINGS	French Lick, Ind.
HOME OF THE FAMOUS SILVER KING TARPON	Punta Gorda, Fla.

HOME OF THE FIRST FULLY AUTOMATIC NON-ATTENDED DIAL TELEPHONE SWITCHBOARD IN THE UNITED STATES	Ketchum, Okla.
HOME OF THE FLORIDA DERBY	Hallandale, Fla.
HOME OF THE GIANT OAHE DAM	Pierre, S.D.
HOME OF THE INTER-NATIONAL PETROLEUM EXPOSITION	Tulsa, Okla.
HOME OF THE JICARILLA APACHE TRIBE	Dulce, N.M.
HOME OF THE LARGEST COPPER PRODUCING SMELTER AND SMOKE-STACK IN THE WORLD	Anaconda, Mont.
HOME OF THE MINING BARONS	Spokane, Wash.
HOME OF THE MISS UNIVERSE PAGEANT	Long Beach, Calif.
HOME OF THE NATIONAL PEANUT FESTIVAL	Dothan, Ala.
HOME OF THE PACIFIC FLEET	Bremerton, Wash.
HOME OF THE PACKERS	Green Bay, Wis.
HOME OF THE PIONEER FLORIDA MUSEUM	Dade City, Fla.
HOME OF THE SNAKE RIVER STAMPEDE	Nampa, Idaho
HOME OF THE TANGERINE	Brooksville, Fla.
HOME OF THE UNIVERSITY OF ARIZONA	Tucson, Ariz.
HOME OF THE UNIVERSITY OF FLORIDA	Gainesville, Fla.
HOME OF THE UNIVERSITY OF GEORGIA	Athens, Ga.
HOME OF THE UNIVERSITY OF SOUTH DAKOTA	Vermillion, S.D.
HOME OF THE UNIVERSITY OF WISCONSIN	Madison, Wis.

HOME OF THE WORLD CHAMPION CLEARWATER BOMBERS	Clearwater, Fla.
HOME OF THE WORLD FAMOUS GLASS BOTTOM BOATS	Silver Springs, Fla.
HOME OF THE WORLD'S LARGEST BASS	Dunnellon, Fla.
HOME OF THE WORLD'S LARGEST BEAR	Kodiak, Alaska
HOME OF THE WORLD'S LARGEST BREWERY	St. Louis, Mo.
HOME OF THE WORLD'S LARGEST SINGLE-UNIT TEXTILE MILL	Danville, Va.
HOME OF THEODORE ROOSEVELT	Oyster Bay, N.Y.
HOME OF VULCAN	Birmingham, Ala.
HOME OF WARTHER MUSEUM	Dover, Ohio
HOME OF WEST VIRGINIA UNIVERSITY	Morgantown, W.Va.
HOME OF WORLD FAMOUS CARTHAGE MARBLE	Carthage, Mo.
HOME OF WORLD FAMOUS SEA CAPTAINS	Searsport, Me.
HOME OF YACHTSMEN	Mystic, Conn.
HOME TOWN IN THE AMERICAN TROPICS	Fort Lauderdale, Fla.
HOME TOWN OF GEORGE WASHINGTON	Alexandria, Va.
HOME TOWN OF SOUTHERN OREGON	Ashland, Ore.
HOMESEEKER'S PARADISE	Brookhaven, Miss.
HOMOCIDE HEADQUARTERS	Memphis, Tenn.
HOMESTEADER'S PARADISE	Palestine, Texas
HONEY CAPITAL OF THE UNITED STATES	Uvalde, Texas
HONEY CAPITAL OF THE WORLD	Uvalde, Texas
HONEYMOON CITY	Niagara Falls, N.Y.
HOOSIER ATHENS	Crawfordsville, Ind.
HOOSIER CAPITAL	Indianapolis, Ind.

HOOSIER CITY	Indianapolis, Ind.
HORNETS' NEST	Charlotte, N.C.
HORSE PLAINS	Hillyard, Wash.
HOSPITALITY CAPITAL OF THE NEW SOUTH	Brookhaven, Miss.
HOSPITALITY CITY	Gulfport, Miss.
HOSPITALITY CITY OF THE ROCKIES	Salida, Colo.
HOST CITY	Norfolk, Neb.
HOST CITY OF THE NATION	Chicago, Ill.
HOST CITY OF THE SUN-LAND EMPIRE	El Paso, Texas
HOST CITY TO CONVEN-TIONS	Harrisburg, Pa.
HOST OF THE WORLD	New York, N.Y.
HOST TO THE WEST'S SCENIC WONDER-WAYS	Provo, Utah
HOST WITHOUT PARALLEL	Springfield, Mass.
HUB	Boston, Mass.
HUB	Casper, Wyo.
HUB	Proctor, Minn.
HUB	Snohomish, Wash.
HUB CITY	Aberdeen, S.D.
HUB CITY	Albany, Ore.
HUB CITY	Alexandria, La.
HUB CITY	Anchorage, Alaska
HUB CITY	Brainerd, Minn.
HUB CITY	Casper, Wyo.
HUB CITY	Centralia, Wash.
HUB CITY	Compton, Calif.
HUB CITY	Robertsdale, Ala.
HUB CITY IN THE HEART OF FLORIDA'S WEST COUNTRY	Crestview, Fla.
HUB CITY OF NORTHWEST FLORIDA	Crestview, Fla.
HUB CITY OF SOUTH TEXAS	Yoakum, Texas
HUB CITY OF SOUTH-WESTERN WASHINGTON	Centralia, Wash.
HUB CITY OF THE DAKOTAS	Aberdeen, S.D.

HUB CITY OF THE SOUTH-EAST	Spartanburg, S.C.
HUB CITY OF THE WORLD	New York, N.Y.
HUB OF A $500,000,000 TRADING AREA	Lima, Ohio
HUB OF ALL SOUTH FLORIDA'S SUN-FUN VACATIONLAND	Miami, Fla.
HUB OF AMERICAN INLAND NAVIGATION	St. Louis, Mo.
HUB OF AMERICAN MERCHANDISING	Chicago, Ill.
HUB OF ARIZONA'S LUMBER INDUSTRY	Flagstaff, Ariz.
HUB OF BANKING AND INSURANCE INTERESTS	Fort Worth, Texas
HUB OF CENTRAL OREGON	Redmond, Ore.
HUB OF FLORIDA'S SCENIC WONDERLAND	Lakeland, Fla.
HUB OF FUN	Jacksonville, Fla.
HUB OF HISTORIC OHIO	Springfield, Ohio
HUB OF HISTORICAL OHIO	Springfield, Ohio
HUB OF LAKE SUPERIOR'S BEAUTIFUL SOUTH SHORE DRIVE	Port Wing, Wis.
HUB OF NASSAU COUNTY	Hempstead, N.Y.
HUB OF NEW ENGLAND	Boston, Mass.
HUB OF NORTH AMERICA	Superior, Wis.
HUB OF NORTHEAST OREGON	La Grande, Ore.
HUB OF NORTHWEST GEORGIA	Rome, Ga.
HUB OF PINELLAS COUNTY	Largo, Fla.
HUB OF PROGRESS	Jacksonville, Fla.
HUB OF TEXAS	Waco, Texas
HUB OF THE AMERICAS	New Orleans, La.
HUB OF THE CHATTAHOOCHEE VALLEY	Phenix City, Ala.
HUB OF THE EMPIRE STATE	Syracuse, N.Y.
HUB OF THE EMPIRE STATE	Utica, N.Y.
HUB OF THE EMPIRE STATE'S CAPITAL DISTRICT	Albany, N.Y.
HUB OF THE FLORIDA PENINSULA	Sebring, Fla.

HUB OF THE GREAT APALACHICOLA VALLEY	Blountstown, Fla.
HUB OF THE GREAT NORTH-CENTRAL INDUSTRIAL AND AGRICULTURAL AMERICA	Fort Wayne, Ind.
HUB OF THE GREAT LEHIGH VALLEY	Bethlehem, Pa.
HUB OF THE GREAT SOUTHWEST	Oklahoma City, Okla.
HUB OF THE HARLEM VALLEY	Brewster, N.Y.
HUB OF THE INTERNATIONAL SOUTHWEST	El Paso, Texas
HUB OF THE INTERSTATE AND U.S. HIGHWAYS	Harrisburg, Pa.
HUB OF THE MAGIC VALLEY	Twin Falls, Idaho
HUB OF THE NATIONWIDE TRANSPORTATION SYSTEM	Indianapolis, Ind.
HUB OF THE NEW HIGH-SPEED INTERSTATE HIGHWAY SYSTEM	St. Louis, Mo.
HUB OF THE OZARKS	Harrison, Ark.
HUB OF THE PLAINS	Lubbock, Texas
HUB OF THE POWERFUL TENNESSEE VALLEY	Huntsville, Ala.
HUB OF THE SCENIC OZARKS	Cassville, Mo.
HUB OF THE SCENIC WEST	Grand Junction, Colo.
HUB OF THE SOLAR SYSTEM	Boston, Mass.
HUB OF THE SOUTHEAST	Atlanta, Ga.
HUB OF THE UNIVERSE	Boston, Mass.
HUB OF THE VALLEY OF PARKS	Corbin, Ky.
HUB OF THE WILLAMETTE VALLEY	Albany, Ore.
HUB OF THE WINTER GARDEN	Carrizo, Texas
HUB TOWN	Boston, Mass.

HUDSON OF THE WEST	Byron, Ill.
HUNTER'S RENDEZVOUS	Blackduck, Minn.

I

ICE MINE CITY	Coudersport, Pa.
IDAHO'S FARM MARKET	Caldwell, Idaho
IDAHO'S OLDEST INCORPORATED CITY	Lewiston, Idaho
IDAHO'S ONLY SEAPORT	Lewiston, Idaho
IDEAL CITY	Malden, Mass.
IDEAL CITY IN ALL SEASONS	New London, Conn.
IDEAL COMMUNITY	Corvallis, Ore.
IDEAL CONVENTION AND VACATION CITY	Madison, Wis.
IDEAL HOME AND RECREATIONAL CENTER	Palo Alto, Calif.
IDEAL HOME COMMUNITY	Evanston, Ill.
IDEAL LIVING CITY IN THE HEART OF FLORIDA	High Springs, Fla.
IDEAL PLACE IN WHICH TO LIVE, WORK AND PLAY	Bethel, Me.
IDEAL PLACE TO STAY OR PLAY	Carthage, Mo.
IDEAL TOWN	Haydenville, Ohio
IDEAL VACATIONLAND	Brunswick, Ga.
IDEAL YEAR ROUND COMMUNITY	Anaheim, Calif.
IDEAL YEAR ROUND RESORT	Daytona Beach, Fla.
IDEAL YEAR ROUND VACATION SPOT	Jacksonville, Fla.
ILLINOIS' CAPITAL CITY	Springfield, Ill.
ILLINOIS' SECOND CITY	Peoria, Ill.
ILLINOIS' SECOND INDUSTRIAL CITY	Rockford, Ill.
IMPERIAL POLK	Lakeland, Fla.
IMPORTANT CONVENTION AND CONFERENCE CITY	Springfield, Ill.
IMPORTANT LIVESTOCK CENTER	Fargo, N.D.
INDIAN CAPITAL	Gallup, N.M.
INDIAN VILLAGE	Upper Sandusky, Ohio

INDIANA'S GATEWAY CITY	Jeffersonville, Ind.
INDUSTRIAL AND DISTRIBUTING CENTER OF THE PACIFIC COAST EMPIRE	Stockton, Calif.
INDUSTRIAL CAPITAL	Jackson, Miss.
INDUSTRIAL CAPITAL OF AMERICA	Bridgeport, Conn.
INDUSTRIAL CAPITAL OF CALIFORNIA	Pittsburg, Calif.
INDUSTRIAL CAPITAL OF CONNECTICUT	Bridgeport, Conn.
INDUSTRIAL CENTER OF THE GREAT SOUTH	Birmingham, Ala.
INDUSTRIAL CENTER OF THE SOUTHEAST	Birmingham, Ala.
INDUSTRIAL CENTER OF WEST FLORIDA	Pensacola, Fla.
INDUSTRIAL CITY	Holyoke, Mass.
INDUSTRIAL CITY	Milwaukee, Wis.
INDUSTRIAL CITY BEAUTIFUL	Birmingham, Ala.
INDUSTRIAL CITY OF DIXIE	Birmingham, Ala.
INDUSTRIAL CITY OF IOWA	Sioux City, Iowa
INDUSTRIAL CITY OF NORTH ALABAMA	Huntsville, Ala.
INDUSTRIAL CITY OF THE SOUTH	Birmingham, Ala.
INDUSTRIAL CITY OF THE WEST	Pittsburg, Calif.
INDUSTRIAL DYNAMO	Islip, N.Y.
INDUSTRIAL FRONTIER OF AMERICA	Oklahoma City, Okla.
INDUSTRIAL FRONTIER OF THE MAGIC LOWER RIO GRANDE VALLEY OF TEXAS	Pharr, Texas
INDUSTRIAL HALF-SISTER	Everett, Mass.
INDUSTRIAL HEART OF MAINE	Auburn, Me.
INDUSTRIAL HEART OF MAINE	Lewiston, Me.

INDUSTRIAL HUB OF THE WEST	Stockton, Calif.
INDUSTRIAL METROPOLIS	Reading, Pa.
INDUSTRIAL PARADISE	Brookhaven, Miss.
INEVITABLE SPA CITY	Saratoga Springs, N. Y.
INLAND METROPOLIS	Birmingham, Ala.
INSURANCE CENTER OF THE SOUTH	Jacksonville, Fla.
INSURANCE CITY	Atlanta, Ga.
INSURANCE CITY	Hartford, Conn.
INTERNATIONAL CITY	Calais, Me.
IOWA'S INDUSTRIAL, SCENIC AND CULTURED CITY	Dubuque, Iowa
IOWA'S OWN CITY	Des Moines, Iowa
IRIS CITY	Nashville, Tenn.
IRON CITY	Bessemer, Ala.
IRON CITY	Pittsburgh, Pa.
IRON CITY ON THE TENNESSEE RIVER	Sheffield, Ala.
IRON MOUNTAIN CITY	Lebanon, Pa.
IRON ORE CAPITAL OF THE WORLD	Hibbing, Minn.
IRON ORE CITY	Connellsville, Pa.
ISLAND CITY OF OLD WORLD CHARM	Key West, Fla.
ISLAND PARADISE	Key Biscayne, Fla.
ISLAND YOU'LL LOVE	Anna Maria, Fla.
ISLE OF PLEASANT LIVING	Alameda, Calif.

J

JACKSONOPOLIS	Jackson, Mich.
JAWBONE FLATS	Clarkston, Wash.
JAX	Jacksonville, Fla.
JEFF CITY	Jefferson City, Mo.
JEWEL CITY	Glendale, Calif.
JEWEL CITY OF CALIFORNIA	San Diego, Calif.
JEWEL CITY OF THE FLORIDA WEST COAST	Fort Myers, Fla.

JEWEL OF THE GEM STATE	Burley, Idaho
JIMTOWN	Jamestown, N.D.
JUMPER'S FLATS	Waterville, Wash.
JUNCTION	Gretna, Va.

K

KANSAS CITY OF ALASKA	Fairbanks, Alaska
KEY CITY	Port Townsend, Wash.
KEY CITY	Vicksburg, Miss.
KEY JUNCTION TO THE SOUTHEAST	Thomasville, Ga.
KEY NATIONAL DEFENSE CENTER	Jacksonville, Fla.
KEY OF THE GREAT VALLEY	New Orleans, La.
KEY SHOPPING AND MANUFACTURING CENTER	Madison, Wis.
KEY SPOT IN THE FUTURE OF KAYSINGER RESERVOIR	Osceola, Mo.
KING CRAB CAPITAL OF THE WORLD	Kodiak, Alaska
KINGDOM OF OPPORTUNITY	Blountstown, Fla.
KINGDOM OF THE SUN	Dunnellon, Fla.
KODAK CITY	Rochester, N.Y.
KRINGLEVILLE	Racine, Wis.

L

L.A.	Los Angeles, Calif.
LADINO CLOVER CENTER OF AMERICA	Oakdale, Calif.
LAKE CITY	Chicago, Ill.
LAKE CITY	Madison, Wis.
LAKE TROUT CAPITAL	Hovland, Minn.
LAMB AND CATTLE CAPITAL OF THE WEST	Fort Collins, Colo.
LAND OF BEAUTIFUL LAKES	Speculator, N.Y.
LAND OF BERRIES	Utsaladdy, Wash.
LAND OF BREAD	Kittitas, Wash.

LAND OF CHEESE, TREES AND OCEAN BREEZE	Tillamook, Ore.
LAND OF CHIEF WABASIS	Belding, Mich.
LAND OF CROSSES	Auriesville, N.Y.
LAND OF FLOWERS	De Land, Fla.
LAND OF FLOWING SPRINGS	Youngstown, Ohio
LAND OF HAZEL NUTS	Tukwila, Wash.
LAND OF INDUSTRIAL OPPORTUNITIES	Long Beach, Calif.
LAND OF LAKES SHOPPING CENTER	El Dorado Springs, Mo.
LAND OF PERPETUAL HARVEST	Glendale, Ariz.
LAND OF PERPETUAL PROSPERITY	Oklahoma City, Okla.
LAND OF PROMISE	Hollywood, Calif.
LAND OF ROMANCE AND RECREATION	Sacramento, Calif.
LAND OF SHINING MOUNTAINS	Billings, Mont.
LAND OF SUNSHINE	De Land, Fla.
LAND OF THE BIG INCH	Houston, Texas
LAND OF THE OLD SOUTH	St. Simons Island, Ga.
LAND OF THE OLD SOUTH	Sea Island, Ga.
LAND OF THE PILGRIMS, SUN AND SAND	Plymouth, Mass.
LAND OF THE PINES	Alberta, Va.
LAND OF THE SKY	Asheville, N.C.
LANDING	Fall City, Wash.
LARGEST CITY FOR ITS SIZE	Taunton, Mass.
LARGEST CITY IN THE LARGEST STATE	Anchorage, Alaska
LARGEST CITY IN THE SOUTH	Houston, Texas
LARGEST CITY IN THE SOUTHWEST	Houston, Texas
LARGEST CITY OF CONTRA COSTA COUNTY	Richmond, Calif.
LARGEST INSURANCE CENTER IN THE WEST	Des Moines, Iowa

LARGEST METROPOLIS IN THE MISSISSIPPI VALLEY	St. Louis, Mo.
LARGEST PECAN SHIPPING CENTER IN AMERICA	Chandler, Okla.
LARGEST SHOPPING CENTER IN THE POMME DE TERRE AREA	Bolivar, Mo.
LARGEST SMALL CITY IN INDIANA	Mitchell, Ind.
LAS DIABLOS	Los Angeles, Calif.
LAS VEGAS ON THE POTOMAC	Colonial Beach, Va.
LAST CAPITAL OF THE CONFEDERACY	Danville, Va.
LAST OUTPOST OF CIVILIZATION	St. Charles, Mo.
LAST PLACE ON THE MAP	Ogden, Kans.
LAUREL CITY	Winsted, Conn.
LAWN CITY	Cedar Falls, Iowa
LEADING CONVENTION CITY IN THE COUNTRY	Chicago, Ill.
LEADING INDUSTRIAL CITY IN ARKANSAS	Fort Smith, Ark.
LEADING INDUSTRIAL CITY OF THE SOUTHWEST	Houston, Texas
LEADING ISLAND CITY OF THE SOUTH	San Bernardino, Calif.
LEADING RESORT CITY	Augusta, Ga.
LEADING SPOT COTTON MARKET	Houston, Texas
LEMON CENTER	Santa Paula, Calif.
LETTUCE CENTER OF THE NATION	Aguila, Ariz.
LEXINGTON OF TEXAS	Gonzalez, Texas
LILAC CITY	Fort Collins, Colo.
LILAC CITY	Lincoln, Neb.
LILAC TOWN	Lombard, Ill.
LINCOLN CITY	Boonville, Ind.
LITERARY EMPORIUM	Boston, Mass.
LITTLE CAPITAL	Denver, Colo.
LITTLE CITY IN THE WOODS	Kingfield, Me.
LITTLE CITY OF CHARM	Mesa, Ariz.

LITTLE DENMARK	Solvang, Calif.
LITTLE HOLLAND	Garibaldi, Ore.
LITTLE ITALY	Independence, La.
LITTLE LAS VEGAS	Gardena, Calif.
LITTLE LOUISVILLE OF THE SOUTHWEST	Seiling, Okla.
LITTLE NEW YORK	Welch, W. Va.
LITTLE PORTAGE	Seattle, Wash.
LITTLE STUMPTOWN	Portland, Ore.
LITTLE SWITZERLAND	Ashfield, Mass.
LITTLE SWITZERLAND	West Portal, N.J.
LITTLE VENICE	Skamokawa, Wash.
LITTLE WHITE HOUSE CITY	Warm Springs, Ga.
LIVESTOCK, GRAIN AND INDUSTRIAL CAPITAL OF THE GREAT NORTHWEST	Sioux City, Iowa
LOCK CITY	Stamford, Conn.
LONESOMEST TOWN IN THE WORLD	Jordan, Mont.
LOOKOUT CITY	Ebensburg, Pa.
LOVELIEST MODERN CITY IN MID-AMERICA	Lincoln, Neb.
LOVELIEST VILLAGE OF THE PLAINS	Auburn, Ala.
LOVELY GATEWAY TO THE PASSES	Salida, Colo.
LOWELL OF THE SOUTH	Augusta, Ga.
LUMBER CAPITAL	Tacoma, Wash.
LUMBER CAPITAL OF AMERICA	Tacoma, Wash.
LUMBER CAPITAL OF THE NATION	Roseburg, Ore.
LUMBER CAPITAL OF THE WORLD	Tacoma, Wash.
LUMBER CITY	Bangor, Me.
LUMBER CITY	Williamsport, Pa.
LUMBER CITY OF THE WORLD	Muskegon, Mich.
LUMBER INDUSTRY'S CAPITAL	Portland, Ore.

LUMBER MANUFACTURING CENTER OF THE PACIFIC NORTHWEST	Portland, Ore.
LUMBER PORT OF THE WORLD	Coos Bay, Ore.
LUMBER QUEEN	Muskegon, Mich.
LUMBER QUEEN OF THE WORLD	Muskegon, Mich.
LUNCHBURG	Lynchburg, Va.
LUNCHSTONE	Blackstone, Va.
LYONS OF AMERICA	Paterson, N.J.

M

MACHINE CITY	Lynn, Mass.
MAGIC CITY	Anacortes, Wash.
MAGIC CITY	Anniston, Ala.
MAGIC CITY	Billings, Mont.
MAGIC CITY	Birmingham, Ala.
MAGIC CITY	Florence, S.C.
MAGIC CITY	Gary, Ind.
MAGIC CITY	Leadville, Colo.
MAGIC CITY	Marceline, Mo.
MAGIC CITY	Miami, Fla.
MAGIC CITY	Minot, N.D.
MAGIC CITY	Moberly, Mo.
MAGIC CITY	Roanoke, Va.
MAGIC CITY	Schenectady, N.Y.
MAGIC CITY	Tulsa, Okla.
MAGIC CITY OF THE GREEN EMPIRE	Bogalusa, La.
MAGIC CITY OF THE PLAINS	Casper, Wyo.
MAGIC CITY OF THE PLAINS	Cheyenne, Wyo.
MAGIC CITY OF THE SOUTH	Birmingham, Ala.
MAGIC CITY OF THE WEST	Cheyenne, Wyo.
MAGIC CITY OF VIRGINIA	Roanoke, Va.
MAGIC MASCOT OF THE PLAINS	Wichita, Kans.

MAGNOLIA CITY	Houston, Texas
MAGNOLIA STATE'S INDUSTRIAL CITY	Laurel, Miss.
MAGNOLIA'S LARGEST INDUSTRIAL CITY	Laurel, Miss.
MAIN STREET OF NORTH-WEST ARKANSAS	Springdale, Ark.
MAINE'S FASTEST GROWING INDUSTRIAL AND RECREATIONAL AREA	Norway, Me.
MAINE'S FASTEST GROWING INDUSTRIAL AND RECREATIONAL AREA	Paris, Me.
MAINE'S MOST FAMOUS COAST RESORT	Bar Harbor, Me.
MANCHESTER OF AMERICA	Lowell, Mass.
MANCHESTER OF AMERICA	Manchester, N. H.
MANUFACTURING AND INDUSTRIAL METROPOLIS OF THE SOUTHEAST	Atlanta, Ga.
MANUFACTURING CITY OF THE PACIFIC	Stockton, Calif.
MANUFACTURING CITY OF THE ROCKY MOUNTAIN REGIONS	Pueblo, Colo.
MAPLE CENTER OF THE WORLD	St. Johnsbury, Vt.
MAPLE CITY	Goshen, Ind.
MAPLE CITY OF MICHIGAN	Adrian, Mich.
MAPLE SUGAR CENTER OF THE WORLD	St. Johnsbury, Vt.
MARBLE CAPITAL OF THE UNITED STATES	Proctor, Vt.
MARBLE CITY	Knoxville, Tenn.
MARBLE CITY	Rutland, Vt.
MARBLE CITY	Sylacauga, Ala.
MARKET OF THREE BARBARIAN TRIBES	San Francisco, Calif.
MARYLAND'S LARGEST CITY	Baltimore, Md.
MEADOW CITY	Northampton, Mass.
MECCA FOR CHAMPIONS IN MANY FIELDS	Palm Beach, Fla.

MECCA FOR HISTORY LOVERS	Gonzalez, Texas
MECCA OF TELEPHONE MEN	New York, N. Y.
MEDICAL CENTER	Fort Worth, Texas
MEDICAL CENTER	Paducah, Ky.
MELTING POT	New York, N.Y.
MEDICAL CENTER OF NORTH AMERICA	Bismarck, N.D.
MEMPHIS OF THE AMERICAN NILE	St. Louis, Mo.
METROPOLIS	New York, N.Y.
METROPOLIS IN A FOREST OF TREES	Buffalo, N.Y.
METROPOLIS OF A FAST GROWING COMMERCIAL AND AGRICULTURAL AREA	Harrison, Ark.
METROPOLIS OF A NEW SOUTH	Atlanta, Ga.
METROPOLIS OF AMERICA	New York, N.Y.
METROPOLIS OF CENTRAL AND NORTHWEST KANSAS	Salina, Kans.
METROPOLIS OF EASTERN NEVADA	Elko, Nev.
METROPOLIS OF EAST TENNESSEE	Knoxville, Tenn.
METROPOLIS OF INDUSTRY	Cedar Rapids, Iowa
METROPOLIS OF ISMS	Los Angeles, Calif.
METROPOLIS OF NEW ENGLAND	Boston, Mass.
METROPOLIS OF NEW MEXICO	Albuquerque, N.M.
METROPOLIS OF NORTH DAKOTA	Fargo, N.D.
METROPOLIS OF NORTH TEXAS	Dallas, Texas
METROPOLIS OF SOUTH-EASTERN FLORIDA	Miami, Fla.
METROPOLIS OF SOUTHERN NEVADA	Las Vegas, Nev.
METROPOLIS OF THE COUNTRY	Washington, D.C.

METROPOLIS OF THE DESERT	Phoenix, Ariz.
METROPOLIS OF THE INLAND EMPIRE	Spokane, Wash.
METROPOLIS OF THE MAGIC VALLEY	Brownsville, Texas
METROPOLIS OF THE MISSISSIPPI DELTA	Greenville, Miss.
METROPOLIS OF THE MISSOURI VALLEY	Kansas City, Mo.
METROPOLIS OF THE NEW SOUTH	Louisville, Ky.
METROPOLIS OF THE NORTHEAST	Bangor, Me.
METROPOLIS OF THE PACIFIC NORTHWEST	Seattle, Wash.
METROPOLIS OF THE PINE RIDGE RESERVATION COUNTRY	Martin, S.D.
METROPOLIS OF THE SOUTHWEST	Dallas, Texas
METROPOLIS OF THE STATE OF OREGON	Portland, Ore.
METROPOLIS OF THE UNSALTED SEAS	Duluth, Minn.
METROPOLIS OF THE WEST	Chicago, Ill.
METROPOLIS OF THE WEST	Houston, Texas
METROPOLIS OF THE WEST	Los Angeles, Calif.
METROPOLIS OF VASHON ISLAND	Vashon, Wash.
METROPOLIS OF WEST FLORIDA	Pensacola, Fla.
METROPOLIS OF WESTERN MASSACHUSETTS	Springfield, Mass.
METROPOLITAN CENTER OF MCKEAN COUNTY	Bradford, Pa.
METROPOLITAN CENTER OF TROPICAL FLORIDA'S FIRST RESORT AREA	West Palm Beach, Fla.
METROPOLITAN CITY	New York, N.Y.
METROPOLITAN CITY	Washington, D.C.
METROPOLITAN COMMUNITY OF OPPORTUNITY	Beloit, Wis.

MICHIGAN'S DYNAMIC CITY	Dearborn, Mich.
MICHIGAN'S FASTEST GROWING CITY	Dearborn, Mich.
MICHIGAN'S FASTEST GROWING COMMUNITY	Dearborn, Mich.
MICHIGAN'S MOST FAMOUS SUMMER RESORT	Benton Harbor, Mich.
MICHIGAN'S MOST RE-NOWNED PHANTOM CITY	White Rock, Mich.
MID-SOUTH RESORT	Southern Pines, N.C.
MID-WAY CITY	Melbourne, Fla.
MIDDLEWEST CENTER FOR DIVERSIFIED MANU-FACTURE	Milwaukee, Wis.
MIDGET CITY	Colby, Wis.
MIDLAND EMPIRE CITY	Billings, Mont.
MIDLAND METROPOLIS	Chicago, Ill.
MIGHTY CAPITAL	Washington, D.C.
MIGHTY MANHATTAN	New York, N.Y.
MIGHTY METROPOLIS	Chicago, Ill.
MILE HIGH CITY	Denver, Colo.
MILE HIGH CITY	Lead, S.D.
MILE HIGH CITY	Prescott, Ariz.
MILE HIGH CITY OF HEALTH	Prescott, Ariz.
MILE SQUARE CITY	Hoboken, N.J.
MILLTOWN	Minneapolis, Minn.
MILWAUKEE THE BEAUTIFUL	Milwaukee, Wis.
MINERAL CITY OF THE SOUTH	Birmingham, Ala.
MINERAL POCKET OF NEW ENGLAND	Cumberland, R.I.
MINERAL SPRINGS CITY	Bedford, Pa.
MINERAL SPRINGS CITY	Bedford, Va.
MINNEAPOLIS OF THE WEST	Spokane, Wash.
MIRACLE CITY OF THE GOLD COAST	Deerfield Beach, Fla.
MISSILE CITY	Titusville, Fla.
MISSILE LAND, U.S.A.	Cocoa Beach, Fla.
MISSION CITY	San Antonio, Texas
MISSISSIPPI'S BEST EXAMPLE OF THE NEW SOUTH	Tupelo, Miss.

MISSISSIPPI'S FINEST EXAMPLE OF THE NEW SOUTH	Tupelo, Miss.
MISSISSIPPI'S GREAT RESORT AND HISTORIC CENTER	Biloxi, Miss.
MISSISSIPPI'S INDUSTRIAL CITY	Laurel, Miss.
MISSISSIPPI'S LARGEST RIVER PORT	Greenville, Miss.
MISSISSIPPI'S THRIVING INDUSTRIAL CENTER	Yazoo City, Miss.
MOBTOWN	Baltimore, Md.
MODEL CITY	Anniston, Ala.
MODEL CITY	Quincy, Ill.
MODEL CITY OF ALABAMA	Anniston, Ala.
MODEL MINING COMMUNITY	Carbonado, Wash.
MODEL MUNICIPALITY	Monroe, Wash.
MODEL VILLAGE	Coleraine, Minn.
MODERN AMERICAN ATHENS	Lowell, Mass.
MODERN ATHENS	Boston, Mass.
MODERN CITY	Commerce, Calif.
MODERN CITY OF GREAT HISTORICAL INTEREST	Philadelphia, Pa.
MODERN CITY WITH A COLONIAL SETTING	Annapolis, Md.
MODERN GOMORRAH	New York, N.Y.
MODERN LITTLE CITY	Belmar, N.J.
MODERN PHOENIX	Cloquet, Minn.
MODERN ROME	Richmond, Va.
MODERN TOWN RICH IN HISTORY	Wiscasset, Me.
MONEY HOLE	Conconully, Wash.
MONEY TOWN	New York, N.Y.
MONTANA'S FRIENDLY COMMUNITY	Cut Bank, Mont.
MONTANA'S LARGEST AND FRIENDLIEST CITY	Great Falls, Mont.
MONTANA'S ONLY BILLION DOLLAR MARKET	Billings, Mont.
MONUMENT CITY	Richmond, Va.
MONUMENTAL CITY	Baltimore, Md.
MORMON CITY	Salt Lake City, Utah

MORMON'S MECCA	Salt Lake City, Utah
MOST AIR-MINDED CITY IN THE WORLD	Anchorage, Alaska
MOST BEAUTIFUL CITY	Detroit, Mich.
MOST BEAUTIFUL CITY IN AMERICA	Washington, D.C.
MOST BEAUTIFUL COLLEGE TOWN IN AMERICA	Princeton, N.J.
MOST BEAUTIFUL LITTLE CITY IN AMERICA	Madison, Wis.
MOST BRIDGED CITY IN THE WORLD	Pittsburgh, Pa.
MOST COLORFUL EXCITING CITY IN THE WORLD	New York, N.Y.
MOST HISTORIC CITY IN THE EAST	Salem, Mass.
MOST HISTORIC CITY IN THE NORTHWEST TERRITORY	Marietta, Ohio
MOST SCENIC CITY ON THE CONTINENT	Seattle, Wash.
MOST TYPICAL WESTERN CITY IN WYOMING	Evanston, Wyo.
MOTHER CITY	Yankton, S.D.
MOTHER CITY OF AMERICA	Boston, Mass.
MOTHER CITY OF GEORGIA	Savannah, Ga.
MOTHER CITY OF THE DAKOTAS	Yankton, S.D.
MOTHER OF COUNTIES	Fayette, Mo.
MOTHER OF THE WEST	Marshall, Mo.
MOTHER OF TOWNS	Farmington, Conn.
MOTOR CAPITAL OF THE WORLD	Detroit, Mich.
MOTOR CITY	Detroit, Mich.
MOUND CITY	St. Louis, Mo.
MOUNT VERNON OF TEXAS	Huntsville, Texas
MOUNT ZION	Montesano, Wash.
MOUNTAIN CITY	Altoona, Pa.
MOUNTAIN CITY	Chattanooga, Tenn.
MOVIE CITY	Los Angeles, Calif.
MOVIE VILLAGE	Hollywood, Calif.
MOVIELAND	Hollywood, Calif.
MUD HEN CITY	Toledo, Ohio

MUD HOLE CITY	Washington, D.C.
MURDER CAPITAL OF AMERICA	Memphis, Tenn.
MURDER CAPITAL OF THE WORLD	Birmingham, Ala.
MURDER CAPITAL OF THE WORLD	Dallas, Texas
MURDER CAPITAL OF THE WORLD	Houston, Texas
MUSHROOM CAPITAL	Mesick, Mich.
MUSHROOM CITY	San Francisco, Calif.
MUSHROOMOPOLIS	Kansas City, Mo.
MUSIC CITY, U.S.A.	Nashville, Tenn.
MUSICAL INSTRUMENT CAPITAL OF THE WORLD	Elkhart, Ind.

N

NAIL CITY	Wheeling, W.Va.
NAPLES OF AMERICA	Munising, Mich.
NATIONAL ANTHEM CITY	Baltimore, Md.
NATIONAL CAPITAL	Washington, D.C.
NATION'S BEST RECRE-ATIONAL AREA-FOUR SEASON FUN	Biddeford, Me.
NATION'S BIRTHPLACE	Plymouth, Mass.
NATION'S CAPITAL	Washington, D.C.
NATION'S FINEST WINTER SPORTS CENTER	Lake Placid, N.Y.
NATION'S FIRST CITY	New York, N.Y.
NATION'S HEADQUARTERS	Washington, D.C.
NATION'S HEALTH RESORT	Hot Springs, Ark.
NATION'S LARGEST BASQUE COLONY	Boise, Idaho
NATION'S LARGEST COM-MUNICATIONS CENTER	New York, N.Y.
NATION'S LARGEST PORT	New York, N.Y.
NATION'S LARGEST WINTER WHEAT MARKET	Kansas City, Mo.
NATION'S MOST BEAUTIFUL CITY	Seattle, Wash.
NATION'S NO. 1 CONVENTION CITY	Chicago, Ill.

NATION'S OLDEST CITY	St. Augustine, Fla.
NATION'S OLDEST SEA-SHORE RESORT	Cape May, N.J.
NATION'S SAFEST BEACH	White Lake, N.C.
NATION'S SEAFOOD CENTER	Biloxi, Miss.
NATION'S SECOND LARGEST MACHINE-TOOL CENTER	Rockford, Ill.
NATION'S SOUTHERNMOST CITY	Key West, Fla.
NATION'S STATE	Washington, D.C.
NATION'S SUMMER CAPITAL	Rehoboth Beach, Del.
NATION'S THOROUGHFARE	Louisville, Ky.
NATION'S WESTERN CAPITAL	San Francisco, Calif.
NATURAL CITY	Huron, S.D.
NATURAL GAS CITY	Bradford, Pa.
NATURAL LOCATION FOR AGRICULTURAL INDUSTRY	Fargo, N.D.
NATURE'S AIRCONDITIONED CITY	Bluefield, Va.
NATURE'S WONDERLAND	Salida, Colo.
NAVAL CENTER	Newport, R.I.
NAVAL CENTER OF THE SOUTH	Jacksonville, Fla.
NAVAL STORES CAPITAL OF THE WORLD	Valdosta, Ga.
NAVY'S FIRST CITY OF THE SEA	Portsmouth, Va.
NEAREST METROPOLITAN CENTER TO ALL FIVE GATEWAYS OF RANIER NATIONAL PARK	Tacoma, Wash.
NEBRASKA'S THIRD CITY	Grand Island, Neb.
NEIGHBORLY FRIENDLY COMMUNITY	Fontana, Calif.
NEIGHBORLY SATISFYING COMMUNITY FOR LIVING	Plant City, Fla.
NERVE CENTER OF ALASKA	Anchorage, Alaska
NEW CAPITAL	Washington, D.C.
NEW CAR CAPITAL OF ARIZONA	Glendale, Ariz.
NEW CITY IN THE OLD SOUTH	Shreveport, La.
NEW CITY OF WASHINGTON	Washington, D.C.

NEW ENGLAND'S TREASURE HOUSE	Salem, Mass.
NEW HELVETIA	Sacramento, Calif.
NEW INDUSTRIAL FRONTIER OF THE SOUTHWEST	Odessa, Texas
NEW JERUSALEM	Salt Lake City, Utah
NEW MARKET	Tumwater, Wash.
NEW PLAYGROUND OF AMERICA	Pompano Beach, Fla.
NEW SETTLEMENT	Washington, D.C.
NEW YORK OF THE SOUTH	Atlanta, Ga.
NEW YORK STATE'S FIRST CAPITAL	Kingston, N.Y.
NEW YORK'S FIRST CAPITAL	Kingston, N.Y.
NEWPORT OF CHICAGO SOCIETY	Lake Geneva, Wis.
NEWPORT OF THE SOUTH	Beaufort, S.C.
NEWPORT OF THE WEST	Colorado Springs, Colo.
NIAGARA OF PENNSYLVANIA	Bushkill, Pa.
NIAGARA OF THE SOUTH	Muscle Shoals, Ala.
NIAGARA OF THE WEST	Great Falls, Mont.
NICE PLACE TO LIVE	Chowchilla, Calif.
NINE HILLS	Richmond, Va.
NINETEEN SUBURBS IN SEARCH OF A METROPOLIS	Los Angeles, Calif.
NORTH CENTRAL FLORIDA'S SHOPPING CENTER	Gainesville, Fla.
NORTH CENTRAL FLORIDA'S SHOPPING HEADQUARTERS	Gainesville, Fla.
NORTH FLORIDA'S GRETNA GREEN	Macclenny, Fla.
NORTH GATEWAY TO THE KAYSINGER DAM AND RESERVOIR AREA	Windsor, Mo.
NORTH SHORE HAVEN	Beaver Bay, Minn.
NORTH STAR CITY	St. Paul, Minn.
NORTHEASTERN GATEWAY TO THE GRAND LAKE RESORT AREA	Seneca, Mo.
NORTHERN GATEWAY TO ALABAMA	Decatur, Ill.
NORTHERN GATEWAY TO BROWARD COUNTY	Deerfield Beach, Fla.

NORTHERN GATEWAY TO THE BLACK HILLS	Belle Fourche, S.D.
NORTHERN GATEWAY TO THE NATURAL PARADISE BAXTER PARK	Patten, Me.
NORTHERN GATEWAY TO THE SHENANDOAH VALLEY	Winchester, Va.
NUMBER ONE HOST OF THE JERSEY COAST	Atlantic City, N.J.

O

OAK CITY	Raleigh, N.C.
OASIS IN THE DESERT	Palm Springs, Calif.
OCEAN CITY	Fernandina Beach, Fla.
OCOSTA BY THE SEA	Ocosta, Wash.
OHIO'S BEAUTIFUL CAPITAL	Columbus, Ohio
OHIO'S CITY OF FRIENDS	Salem, Ohio
OHIO'S OLDEST AND MOST BEAUTIFUL CITY	Marietta, Ohio
OIL CAPITAL	Jackson, Miss.
OIL CAPITAL	Tulsa, Okla.
OIL CAPITAL IN THE HEART OF THE WHEAT BELT	Great Bend, Kans.
OIL CAPITAL OF ARKANSAS	El Dorado, Ark.
OIL CAPITAL OF MISSISSIPPI	Yazoo City, Miss.
OIL CAPITAL OF THE ROCKIES	Casper, Wyo.
OIL CAPITAL OF THE WORLD	Tulsa, Okla.
OIL CENTER FOR MISSISSIPPI	Jackson, Miss.
OIL CENTER OF THE WORLD	Houston, Texas
OIL CITY	Bayonne, N.J.
OIL CITY	Casper, Wyo.
OIL CITY	Glenrock, Wyo.
OIL CITY OF THE SOUTHWEST	Odessa, Texas
OLD CHI	Chicago, Ill.

OLD CITY WITH A NEW FUTURE	Apalachicola, Fla.
OLD DORP	Schenectady, N.Y.
OLD FRENCH TOWN	New Orleans, La.
OLD GARRISON	San Antonio, Texas
OLD GOLD HILL	San Francisco, Calif.
OLD MAID CITY, LOOKING UNDER HER BED EVERY NIGHT FOR AN OCEAN	Duluth, Minn.
OLD MART	Clarksville, Va.
OLD PUEBLO	Los Angeles, Calif.
OLD PUEBLO	Tucson, Ariz.
OLDEST AND QUAINTEST CITY IN THE UNITED STATES	Santa Fe, N.M.
OLDEST CHARTERED CITY IN THE UNITED STATES	Albany, N.Y.
OLDEST CITY IN THE UNITED STATES	St. Augustine, Fla.
OLDEST CITY IN THE UNITED STATES OPERATING UNDER ITS ORIGINAL CHARTER	Albany, N.Y.
OLDEST CONTINUOUS ENGLISH-SPEAKING SETTLEMENT IN AMERICA	Hampton, Va.
OLDEST FRENCH CITY IN THE U.S.	Biloxi, Miss.
OLDEST SETTLEMENT IN MINNESOTA	Grand Portage, Minn.
OLDEST SUMMER RESORT IN AMERICA	Wolfeboro, N.H.
OLDEST TOWN IN NEVADA	Genoa, Nev.
OLDEST TOWN IN WEST VIRGINIA	Shepherdstown, W.Va.
OLDEST WHITE SETTLEMENT IN THE STATE	Salina, Okla.
OLEANDER CITY	Galveston, Texas
OLEANDER CITY BY THE SEA	Galveston, Texas
OLEANDER CITY OF TEXAS	Galveston, Texas
OLEMAN HOUSE	Port Madison, Wash.

ONCE CONFEDERATE CAPITAL OF AMERICA	Cassville, Mo.
ONE HUNDRED SQUARE MILES OF PICTURESQUE PLEASURE	Marthas Vineyard,Mass.
ONE OF AMERICA'S FASTEST GROWING CITIES	Twin Falls, Idaho
ONE OF AMERICA'S FORE-MOST ALL-YEAR RESORTS	Asbury Park, N.J.
ONE OF AMERICA'S GREAT CITIES	Toledo, Ohio
ONE OF AMERICA'S GREAT-EST PLAYGROUNDS	St. Petersburg, Fla.
ONE OF AMERICA'S MOST INTERESTING CITIES	Chattanooga, Tenn.
ONE OF AMERICA'S MOST INTERESTING CITIES	Montgomery, Ala.
ONE OF AMERICA'S MOST UNIQUE CITIES	Butte, Mont.
ONE OF MISSISSIPPI'S FASTEST GROWING CITIES	Greenville, Miss.
ONE OF NEW ENGLAND'S MOST FAMOUS COAST RESORTS	Wells, Me.
ONE OF THE BUSIEST FRESHWATER PORTS IN THE WORLD	Toledo, Ohio
ONE OF THE FASTEST GROWING CITIES IN THE NATION	Jackson, Miss.
ONE OF THE FIRST AMERICAN CITIES OF THE INDUSTRIAL AGE	New Haven, Conn.
ONE OF THE LEADING HEALTH AND TOURIST RESORTS OF THE EAST	Asheville, N.C.
ONE OF THE MOST AC-CESSIBLE CITIES IN THE EASTERN STATES	Springfield, Mass.
ONE OF THE MOST COLOR-FUL CITIES IN AMERICA	Butte, Mont.

ONE OF THE MOST FASHION-ABLE WINTER RESORTS OF THE SOUTH	Aiken, S.C.
ONE OF THE MOST FAVOR-ABLE WINTER RESORTS OF THE SOUTH	Aiken, S.C.
ONE OF THE NATION'S LARGEST SPRING LAMB PRODUCING CENTERS	Lexington, Ky.
ONE OF THE SOUTH'S FASTEST GROWING CITIES	Jackson, Miss.
ONE OF THE SOUTH'S FOREMOST EDUCATIONAL CENTERS	Lexington, Ky.
ONE OF THE WORLD'S GREAT AIRPLANE MANU-FACTURING CENTERS	Wichita, Kans.
ONE OF WISCONSIN'S FASTEST GROWING CITIES	Beloit, Wis.
ONLY CEDARTOWN IN THE U.S.A.	Cedartown, Ga.
ONLY ELECTRIC-LIT CEMETERY IN THE UNITED STATES	Butte, Mont.
ONLY HENNIKER ON EARTH	Henniker, N.H.
ONLY TOWN IN THE UNITED STATES WITH AN APOSTROPHE IN ITS NAME	Coeur d'Alene, Idaho
OPPORTUNITY FOR HISTORY	Gonzalez, Texas
OPTIMIST CITY	Sheridan, Wyo.
ORANGE CAPITAL OF THE WORLD	Eustis, Fla.
ORCHARD CITY	Burlington, Iowa
ORCHID CAPITAL OF HAWAII	Hilo, Hawaii
OREGON'S BEAUTIFUL CAPITAL CITY	Salem, Ore.
ORIGINAL WINTER RESORT OF THE SOUTH	Thomasville, Ga.
OUR LADY OF THE ANGELS	Port Angeles, Wash.

OUTDOORMAN'S PARADISE	Bristol, Tenn.
OUTSTANDING AMERICAN CITY	Cambridge, Mass.
OVERGROWN COUNTRY TOWN	Cleveland, Ohio
OVERGROWN COW TOWN	Kansas City, Mo.
OVERGROWN SMALL TOWN	Detroit, Mich.
OZARK WONDERLAND	Harrison, Ark.
OZARK'S WESTERN GATEWAY	Vinita, Okla.

P

PACIFIC NORTHWEST'S MOST PROGRESSIVE COMMUNITY	Boise, Idaho
PACKERS' TOWN	Green Bay, Wis.
PAINCOURT	St. Louis, Mo.
PALM CITY	Phoenix, Ariz.
PALMETTO CITY	Charleston, S.C.
PANAMA PORT	Pensacola, Fla.
PANHANDLER'S HEAVEN	Boston, Mass.
PANTHER CITY	Fort Worth, Texas
PAPER CITY	Holyoke, Mass.
PAPER CITY	Johnsonburg, Pa.
PAPER CITY	Neenah, Wis.
PARADISE OF FISHING, HUNTING AND SWIMMING	Blountstown, Fla.
PARADISE OF NEW ENGLAND	Salem, Mass.
PARADISE OF THE SOUTH	Miami, Fla.
PARIS OF AMERICA	Cincinnati, Ohio
PARIS OF AMERICA	New Orleans, La.
PARIS OF AMERICA	San Francisco, Calif.
PARISH OF UNITY	South Berwick, Me.
PARK CITY	Bridgeport, Conn.
PARK PLACE	Monroe, Wash.
PARKING LOT CITY	St. Louis, Mo.
PARLOR CITY	Binghamton, N.Y.
PARLOR CITY	Cedar Rapids, Iowa
PAUL BUNYAN'S CAPITAL	Brainerd, Minn.
PEACH BOWL OF THE UNITED STATES	Marysville, Calif.

PEACH BOWL OF THE UNITED STATES	Yuba City, Calif.
PEACH CAPITAL OF TEXAS	Stonewall, Texas
PEANUT CAPITAL OF THE WORLD	Enterprise, Ala.
PEANUT CITY	Suffolk, Va.
PEAR CITY	Medford, Ore.
PEARL CITY	Muscatine, Iowa
PEARL OF THE SOUTH	Anniston, Ala.
PECAN CAPITAL OF THE WORLD	Chandler, Okla.
PEERLESS PRINCESS OF THE PLAINS	Wichita, Kans.
PENN STATE CITY	State College, Pa.
PENN'S TOWN	Reading, Pa.
PENNSYLVANIA ATHENS	Wellsboro, Pa.
PENNSYLVANIA'S ABOVE-AVERAGE MARKET OF INDUSTRY AND AGRICULTURE	Lancaster, Pa.
PENNSYLVANIA'S CAPITAL CITY	Harrisburg, Pa.
PEONY CENTER OF THE WORLD	Faribault, Minn.
PEOPLES' CITY	Demopolis, Ala.
PERFECT PLACE FOR GROWING UP	Brookhaven, Miss.
PERFECT SPOT TO WORK, TO PLAY, TO ENJOY LIFE	Dothan, Ala.
PERMANENT HOME OF THE PINE	Cass Lake, Minn.
PERRY DAVIS' PAIN KILLER CITY	Providence, R.I.
PHEASANT CAPITAL OF KANSAS	Norton, Kans.
PHEASANT CAPITAL OF THE WORLD	Huron, S.D.
PHEASANT CAPITAL OF THE WORLD	Sioux Falls, S.D.
PHILLY	Philadelphia, Pa.
PHOENIX CITY	Chicago, Ill.

PHOTOGRAPHIC AND OPTICAL CENTER OF THE WORLD	Rochester, N.Y.
PICNIC CITY	Mobile, Ala.
PIG'S EYE	St. Paul, Minn.
PIGOPOLIS	Chicago, Ill.
PIGOPOLIS	Cincinnati, Ohio
PINHOOK	Independence, Va.
PIONEER RESORT TOWN	Winslow, Ark.
PITTSBURGH OF NEW JERSEY	Dover, N.J.
PITTSBURGH OF THE BIG WEST	Terre Haute, Ind.
PITTSBURGH OF THE SOUTH	Birmingham, Ala.
PITTSBURGH OF THE WEST	Joliet, Ill.
PIVOT CITY OF THE CENTRAL SOUTH	Shreveport, La.
PIVOT CITY OF THE GREAT LAKES	Toledo, Ohio
PIVOT CITY OF THE SOUTH	Shreveport, La.
PLACE IN THE SUN TO VISIT, TO PLAY, TO WORK, TO LIVE	Edgewater, Fla.
PLACE FOR VACATIONS YEAR 'ROUND AND FOR YEAR 'ROUND LIVING	Fryeburg, Me.
PLACE OF GOOD ABODE	Memphis, Tenn.
PLACE OF MANY WATERS	Walla Walla, Wash.
PLACE TO GO IN FLORIDA	Fort Lauderdale, Fla.
PLACE WHERE LAKE MEETS FOREST	Grand Marais, Minn.
PLANK ISLAND	Aberdeen, Wash.
PLAYGROUND FOR VACATIONERS	Gonzalez, Texas
PLAYGROUND OF PAUL BUNYON	Blaney Park, Mich.
PLAYGROUND OF PRESIDENTS	Superior, Wis.
PLAYGROUND OF SOUTHERN CALIFORNIA	San Bernardino, Calif.

PLAYGROUND OF THE ADIRONDACKS	Schroon Lake, N.Y.
PLAYGROUND OF THE AMERICAS	Miami, Fla.
PLAYGROUND OF THE AMERICAS	Miami Beach, Fla.
PLAYGROUND OF THE DUNES	Gary, Ind.
PLAYGROUND OF THE NORTHWEST	Seaside, Ore.
PLAYGROUND OF THE WORLD	Atlantic City, N.J.
PLAYGROUND OF VACATIONLAND	Old Orchard Beach, Me.
PLAYTOWN, U.S.A.	Decatur, Ill.
PLEASANT ALL YEAR VACATION CENTER	Pensacola, Fla.
PLEASANT PLACE TO VISIT	Mitchell, S.D.
PLOUGH-SHARE CITY	York, Pa.
PLOW CITY	Moline, Ill.
PLUMB LINE PORT TO PANAMA	Charleston, S.C.
PLYMOUTH OF THE PACIFIC COAST	San Diego, Calif.
PLYMOUTH OF THE WEST	San Diego, Calif.
PLYMOUTH OF THE WESTERN RESERVE	Conneaut, Ohio
POINT OF OPPORTUNITY	West Point, Miss.
POKER CITY	Gardena, Calif.
POKER-PLAYING CAPITAL OF THE WEST	Gardena, Calif.
POLISH CITY	Hamtramck, Mich.
POLISH CITY IN TEXAS	Panna Maria, Texas
POLITICAL FRONT	Washington, D.C.
POLK COUNTY'S LARGEST CITY	Lakeland, Fla.
POLO CAPITAL OF THE SOUTH	Aiken, S.C.
POOR MAN'S PARADISE	San Francisco, Calif.
POPULAR CONVENTION CITY	Asheville, N.C.

POPULAR CONVENTION CITY	Duluth, Minn.
POPULAR SUMMER RESORT	Brevard, N.C.
POPULAR VACATION LAND	Jacksonville, Fla.
PORK CITY	Chicago, Ill.
PORKOPOLIS	Chicago, Ill.
PORKOPOLIS	Cincinnati, Ohio
PORKOPOLIS OF IOWA	Burlington, Iowa
PORT AND PLAYGROUND OF THE SOUTHWEST	Galveston, Texas
PORT CITY	Mobile, Ala.
PORT CITY	Portsmouth, N.H.
PORT O' MISSING MEN	San Francisco, Calif.
PORT OF ENTRY	Port Townsend, Wash.
PORT OF FRIENDLINESS	Avalon, Calif.
PORT OF MANY PORTS	New York, N.Y.
PORT OF PERSONAL SERVICE	Wilmington, Del.
PORT OF SEA CAPTAINS	Coupeville, Wash.
PORT OF THE SOUTHWEST	Galveston, Texas
PORTAGE	Granite Falls, Wash.
PORTAGE CITY	Hollidaysburg, Pa.
PORTAL TO ROMANCE	Sitka, Alaska
PORTAL TO THE QUINT STATES	Salida, Colo.
POSTMARK OF DISTINCTIVE TRADEMARKS	Hamilton, Ohio
POST CITY	Lawton, Okla.
POTATO CAPITOL	Shafter, Calif.
POTTERY CITY	Zanesville, Ohio
POWER CITY	American Falls, Idaho
POWER CITY	Keokuk, Iowa
POWER CITY	Niagara Falls, N.Y.
POWER CITY	Rochester, N.Y.
POWER CITY OF SCENIC WONDERS	Niagara Falls, N.Y.
PRAIRIE	Chicago, Ill.
PRAIRIE CITY	Bloomington, Ill.
PREEMINENT VACATION CENTER	Asheville, N.C.
PRETTIEST LITTLE TOWN THIS SIDE OF HEAVEN	Winter Haven, Fla.
PRETZEL CITY	Lancaster, Pa.
PRETZEL CITY	Reading, Pa.

PRIDE OF THE MISSISSIPPI VALLEY	St. Louis, Mo.
PRIDE OF THE PACIFIC	Long Beach, Calif.
PRINCESS CITY OF PUGET SOUND	Edmonds, Wash.
PRISON CITY	Jackson, Mich.
PROGRESS CITY OF THE ROCKIES	Casper, Wyo.
PROGRESSIVE AMERICAN CITY	Springfield, Ill.
PROGRESSIVE CITY	Athens, Tenn.
PROGRESSIVE CITY	Augusta, Ga.
PROGRESSIVE CITY	Eau Gallie, Fla.
PROGRESSIVE CITY	Grand Isle, Neb.
PROGRESSIVE CITY	Memphis, Tenn.
PROGRESSIVE CITY	Peoria, Ill.
PROGRESSIVE CITY	Sioux Falls, S.D.
PROGRESSIVE CITY WITH THE RICH HERITAGE AND CHARM OF THE OLD RIVER DAYS	Davenport, Iowa
PROGRESSIVE COMMUNITY WITH A BRIGHT FUTURE	Belleview, Fla.
PROGRESSIVELY GROWING WELL-SEASONED CITY	Springfield, Ohio
PROUD PORT OF THE PACIFIC	Long Beach, Calif.
PROUDEST SMALL TOWN IN AMERICA	Cadiz, Ohio
PUMPKIN CAPITAL OF THE WORLD	Eureka, Ill.
PURE BRED JERSEY CAPITAL OF AMERICA	Carthage, Mo.
PURITAN CITY	Boston, Mass.
PUSH ROOT	Lander, Wyo.

Q

QUAD CITIES	East Moline, Moline, Rock Island, Ill., and Davenport, Iowa
QUAIL HAVEN	Cedar Vale, Kans.
QUAKER CITY	Newberg, Ore.

QUAKER CITY	Philadelphia, Pa.
QUAKER CITY	Salem, Ohio
QUAKER CITY	Whittier, Calif.
QUAKER CITY OF THE WEST	Richmond, Ind.
QUAKER TOWN	Wilmington, Del.
QUAKERTOWN	Philadelphia, Pa.
QUALITY CITY	Niagara Falls, N.Y.
QUALITY CITY	Rochester, N.Y.
QUEEN CITY	Allentown, Pa.
QUEEN CITY	Bangor, Me.
QUEEN CITY	Charlotte, N.C.
QUEEN CITY	Cincinnati, Ohio
QUEEN CITY	Cumberland, Md.
QUEEN CITY	Davenport, Iowa
QUEEN CITY	Dickinson, N.D.
QUEEN CITY	Manchester, N.H.
QUEEN CITY	San Francisco, Calif.
QUEEN CITY	Seattle, Wash.
QUEEN CITY	Sioux Falls, S.D.
QUEEN CITY	Spearfish, S.D.
QUEEN CITY	Williamsport, Pa.
QUEEN CITY OF ALABAMA	Gadsden, Ala.
QUEEN CITY OF LAKE SUPERIOR	Marquette, Mich.
QUEEN CITY OF NEW HAMPSHIRE	Manchester, N.H.
QUEEN CITY OF THE ARK-LA-TEX AREA	Shreveport, La.
QUEEN CITY OF THE BORDER	Caldwell, Kans.
QUEEN CITY OF THE CHEROKEE STRIP	Enid, Okla.
QUEEN CITY OF THE COOSA	Gadsden, Ala.
QUEEN CITY OF THE COW TOWNS	Dodge City, Kans.
QUEEN CITY OF THE EAST	Bangor, Me.
QUEEN CITY OF THE GAS BELT	Marion, Ind.
QUEEN CITY OF THE GREAT LAKES	Buffalo, N.Y.

QUEEN CITY OF THE HILLS	Spearfish, S.D.
QUEEN CITY OF THE IRON RANGE	Virginia, Minn.
QUEEN CITY OF THE LAKES	Buffalo, N.Y.
QUEEN CITY OF THE LEHIGH VALLEY	Allentown, Pa.
QUEEN CITY OF THE MERRIMAC VALLEY	Manchester, N.H.
QUEEN CITY OF THE MIDLAND EMPIRE	Billings, Mont.
QUEEN CITY OF THE MISSISSIPPI	St. Louis, Mo.
QUEEN CITY OF THE MOUNTAINS	Knoxville, Tenn.
QUEEN CITY OF THE NORTHLAND	Marquette, Mich.
QUEEN CITY OF THE NORTHWEST	Dubuque, Iowa
QUEEN CITY OF THE OHIO	Cincinnati, Ohio
QUEEN CITY OF THE OZARKS	Springfield, Mo.
QUEEN CITY OF THE PACIFIC	San Francisco, Calif.
QUEEN CITY OF THE PACIFIC COAST	San Francisco, Calif.
QUEEN CITY OF THE PANHANDLE	Amarillo, Texas
QUEEN CITY OF THE PLAINS	Denver, Colo.
QUEEN CITY OF THE PLAINS	Fort Worth, Texas
QUEEN CITY OF THE PRAIRIES	Dickinson, N.D.
QUEEN CITY OF THE PRAIRIES	Fort Worth, Texas
QUEEN CITY OF THE RANGE	Virginia, Minn.
QUEEN CITY OF THE SEA	Charleston, S.C.

QUEEN CITY OF THE SHENANDOAH VALLEY	Staunton, Va.
QUEEN CITY OF THE SOUND	New Rochelle, N.Y.
QUEEN CITY OF THE SOUND	Seattle, Wash.
QUEEN CITY OF THE SOUTH	Charleston, S.C.
QUEEN CITY OF THE SOUTH	Richmond, Va.
QUEEN CITY OF THE TECHE	New Iberia, La.
QUEEN CITY OF THE TRAILS	Independence, Mo.
QUEEN CITY OF THE WEST	Cincinnati, Ohio
QUEEN CITY OF THE WEST	Denver, Colo.
QUEEN CITY OF THE WEST	San Francisco, Calif.
QUEEN CITY OF VERMONT	Burlington, Vt.
QUEEN OF COW TOWNS	Dodge City, Kans.
QUEEN OF LAKE ERIE	Cleveland, Ohio
QUEEN OF SUMMER RESORTS	Newport, R.I.
QUEEN OF THE AMERICAN NILE	Memphis, Tenn.
QUEEN OF THE BEACHES	Long Beach, Calif.
QUEEN OF THE BRAZOS	Waco, Texas
QUEEN OF THE COW TOWNS	Dodge City, Kans.
QUEEN OF THE HILLS	Piedmont, Calif.
QUEEN OF THE LAKES	Buffalo, N.Y.
QUEEN OF THE MISSIONS	Santa Barbara, Calif.
QUEEN OF THE MOUNTAINS	Helena, Mont.
QUEEN OF THE NECHES	Beaumont, Texas
QUEEN OF THE OHIO	Cincinnati, Ohio
QUEEN OF THE PACIFIC	San Francisco, Calif.
QUEEN OF THE SOUTH	New Orleans, La.
QUEEN OF THE SPAS	Saratoga Springs, N.Y.
QUEEN OF THE VALLEY	Glendale, Calif.

QUEEN OF THE WEST	Cincinnati, Ohio
QUEEN ON THE JAMES	Richmond, Va.
QUEEN VILLAGE OF THE ADIRONDACKS	Warrensburg, N.Y.

R

RAGTOWN	Cincinnati, Ohio
RAILROAD CITY	Altoona, Pa.
RAILROAD CITY	Atlanta, Ga.
RAILROAD CITY	Indianapolis, Ind.
RAILROAD CITY	St. Albans, Vt.
RAISIN CAPITAL OF THE WORLD	Selma, Calif.
RAPID CITY	Cedar Rapids, Iowa
REAL PARADISE FOR FAMILY LIVING	Crestview, Fla.
REAL WESTERN CITY	Pierre, S.D.
REBEL CAPITAL	Philadelphia, Pa.
RECREATIONAL CENTER	Madison, Wis.
RECREATIONAL CENTER FOR GENERATIONS	Bridgeport, Conn.
RECREATIONAL, EDUCATIONAL AND CULTURAL CENTER OF NORTHEASTERN OHIO	Youngstown, Ohio
RECREATIONAL INDUSTRIAL CITY	Duluth, Minn.
RECREATIONAL SLUM	Lake Tahoe, Calif.
RED LIGHT QUEEN	Muskegon, Mich.
RED ROSE CITY	Lancaster, Pa.
REFUGE FROM RESORTS	Naples, Fla.
RESEARCH CITY	Stamford, Conn.
RESIDENTIAL HAVEN	Islip, N.Y.
RESORT AND CONVENTION PLAYGROUND OF THE ALLEGHENIES	Bedford, Pa.
RESORT OF ENJOYMENT	Asbury Park, N.J.
RESORT TOWN, U.S.A.	Estes Park, Colo.
RESTING PLACE OF THE UNKNOWN AMERICAN SOLDIER	Arlington, Va.
RESTORED COLONIAL CITY	Williamsburg, Va.

RETAIL CENTER OF SOUTHWEST NEBRASKA AND NORTHEAST KANSAS	McCook, Neb.
RETAIL, WHOLESALE, INDUSTRIAL, MEDICAL INSTITUTION CENTER OF KENTUCKY	Lexington, Ky.
RETIREMENT CENTER OF THE NATION	Tucson, Ariz.
RHODE ISLAND'S MOST HISTORIC TOWN	Newport, R.I.
RICE CAPITAL OF LOUISIANA	Crowley, La.
RICE CAPITAL OF LOUISIANA	Lake Charles, La.
RICE CAPITAL OF THE WORLD	Crowley, La.
RICE CENTER OF AMERICA	Crowley, La.
RICE CITY OF AMERICA	Crowley, La.
RICHEST HILL ON EARTH	Butte, Mont.
RICHEST SQUARE MILE ON EARTH	Central City, Colo.
RICHEST TOWN IN THE WORLD	Brookline, Mass.
RICHEST VILLAGE ON EARTH	Hibbing, Minn.
ROBBERS' ROOST	Ellensburg, Wash.
ROBBERS' ROOST	Fruitland, Wash.
ROCK CITY	Nashville, Tenn.
ROCK CITY	Wabash, Ind.
ROCKET CITY	Alamogordo, N.M.
ROCKET CITY	Huntsville, Ala.
ROCKET CITY, U.S.A.	Huntsville, Ala.
RODEO CITY	Ellensburg, Wash.
ROGER WILLIAMS CITY	Providence, R.I.
ROLLICKING, HILARIOUS TENT AND SHACK CITY	Lawton, Okla.
ROMAN GODDESS OF FRUIT TREES	Pomona, Wash.
ROOF GARDEN OF AMERICA	Salida, Colo.
ROOF GARDEN OF PENNSYLVANIA	Somerset, Pa.

ROOF GARDEN OF TEXAS	Alpine, Texas
ROOF GARDEN RESORT OF TEXAS	Alpine, Texas
ROSE CAPITAL	Tyler, Texas
ROSE CAPITAL OF AMERICA	Newark, N.Y.
ROSE CAPITAL OF THE WORLD	Tyler, N.Y.
ROSE CITY	Jackson, Mich.
ROSE CITY	Madison, N.J.
ROSE CITY	Manheim, Pa.
ROSE CITY	Portland, Ore.
ROSE CITY	Thomasville, Ga.
ROSE OF NEW ENGLAND	Norwich, Conn.
ROUND-UP CITY	Pendleton, Ore.
RUBBER CAPITAL OF THE UNITED STATES	Akron, Ohio
RUBBER CAPITAL OF THE WORLD	Akron, Ohio
RUBBER CITY	Akron, Ohio

S

SACTO	Sacramento, Calif.
SADDLE HORSE CAPITAL OF THE WORLD	Mexico, Mo.
SAFE PLACE FOR CHILDREN	Jamestown, R.I.
SAFEST SPOT IN THE WORLD	Fort Collins, Colo.
SAILFISH CAPITAL OF THE WORLD	Stuart, Fla.
ST. ANTHONY'S TOWN	San Antonio, Texas
ST. MORITZ OF THE ROCKIES	Anaconda, Mont.
ST. PETERSBURG OF TOM SAWYER	Hannibal, Mo.
SAINTLY CITY	St. Paul, Minn.
SAINTS REST	Oak Park, Ill.
SALAD BOWL OF THE NATION	Ruskin, Fla.
SALMON CAPITAL OF ALASKA	Ketchikan, Alaska

SALMON CITY	Astoria, Ore.
SALOON QUEEN	Muskegon, Mich.
SALT CITY	Hutchinson, Kans.
SALT CITY	Manistee, Mich.
SALT CITY	Syracuse, N.Y.
SALT WATER PEOPLE	Quilcene, Wash.
SALT WATER TROUT CAPITAL OF THE WORLD	Cocoa, Fla.
SAN BERDOO	San Bernardino, Calif.
SANTA'S WORKSHOP	North Pole, N.Y.
SARATOGA OF THE WEST	Waukesha, Wis.
SATANIC CITY	Devils Lake, N.D.
SATURDAY TOWN	Decatur, Ala.
SAWDUST CITY	Lock Haven, Pa.
SAWDUST CITY	Minneapolis, Minn.
SAWDUST CITY	Oshkosh, Wis.
SCENIC CALIFORNIA'S SCENIC PLAYGROUND	Santa Cruz, Calif.
SCENIC CAPITAL OF CENTRAL PENNSYLVANIA	Williamsport, Pa.
SCENIC CENTER OF THE SOUTH	Chattanooga, Tenn.
SCENIC CITY	Berlin, Pa.
SCENIC CITY OF NIGHT-LESS SUMMER DAYS	Juneau, Alaska
SCENIC CITY OF SOUTHERN MINNESOTA	Redwood Falls, Minn.
SCENIC HEALTH RESORT OF CALIFORNIA	Elsinore, Calif.
SCHOLARSHIP CITY	Fall River, Mass.
SCIENCE CITY	New York, N.Y.
SCRAPPLE CITY	Allentown, Pa.
SCREENLAND	Hollywood, Calif.
SEA GATE TO THE SOUTHWEST	Lake Charles, La.
SEA TURTLE CAPITAL OF THE WORLD	Jensen Beach, Fla.
SEAFOOD CAPITAL OF THE WORLD	Crisfield, Md.
SEAPORT FOR THE LANDLOCKED STATE OF IDAHO	Lewiston, Idaho
SEAPORT VILLAGE	Mystic, Conn.

SEAT OF EMPIRE	New York, N.Y.
SECOND LARGEST AIRCRAFT PRODUCTION CENTER IN THE COUNTRY	Fort Worth, Texas
SECOND LARGEST RAILROAD CENTER IN THE UNITED STATES	Buffalo, N.Y.
SECOND OLDEST SETTLEMENT IN OKLAHOMA	Vinita, Okla.
SECOND ROME	Washington, D.C.
SEDATE CAPITAL OF THE BIBLE BELT	Oklahoma City, Okla.
SENTINEL CITY IN THE PINES	Prescott, Ariz.
SHADE-GROWN TOBACCO CAPITAL	Quincy, Fla.
SHAKE-RAG	Mineral Point, Wis.
SHIP-BUILDING CITY	Chester, Pa.
SHIP HARBOR	Anacortes, Wash.
SHIPPING CITY	Bath, Me.
SHIRE CITY OF WALDO COUNTY	Belfast, Me.
SHOE CITY	Auburn, Me.
SHOE CITY	Hanover, Pa.
SHOE CITY	Johnson City, N.Y.
SHOE CITY	Lynn, Mass.
SHOPPING CENTER OF THE APPALACHIANS	Bristol, Tenn.
SHOPPING CENTER OF THE APPALACHIANS	Bristol, Va.
SHORE VILLAGE	Guilford, Conn.
SHOVEL CITY OF THE WORLD	Marion, Ohio
SHOWBOAT CITY	St. Louis, Mo.
SHRINE OF THE SOUTH	Lexington, Va.
SIERRA "CONEY ISLAND"	Lake Tahoe, Calif.
SILK CITY	Paterson, N.J.
SILVER CITY	Meriden, Conn.
SILVER DOLLAR CITY	Billings, Mont.
SIN CITY	Atolia, Calif.
SINEMA LAND	Hollywood, Calif.
SISTER CITY OF THE SUN	Miami Beach, Fla.
SITE OF THE OAHE DAM	Pierre, S.D.
SKI CAPITAL OF THE EAST	Stowe, Vt.
SKINNER'S MUDHOLE	Eugene, Ore.

SKY CITY	Acoma, N.M.
SLASH TOWN	Ashland, Va.
SLAUGHTER HOUSE	Auburn, Wash.
SLEEPY TOWN	Philadelphia, Pa.
SMALLEST CAPITAL IN AMERICA	Carson City, Nev.
SMALLEST CAPITAL IN THE WORLD	Carson City, Nev.
SMELTER CITY	Anaconda, Mont.
SMILE OF THE GREAT SPIRIT	Winnipesaukee, N.H.
SMOKE ON THE WATER	Skamokawa, Wash.
SMOKELESS COAL CAPITAL OF THE WORLD	Beckley, W.Va.
SMOKY CITY	Pittsburgh, Pa.
SMOOTH WATER	Sequim, Wash.
SOBER-MINDED	Dedham, Mass.
SODOM-BY-THE-SEA	Coney Island, N.Y.
SODOM OF THE SOUTH	Memphis, Tenn.
SOO	Saulte Ste. Marie, Mich.
SOLID CITY	St. Louis, Mo.
SOUR DOUGH FLATS	Waterville, Wash.
SOUTH ARKANSAS' BUSY PORT CITY	Camden, Ark.
SOUTH CAROLINA'S CAPITAL CITY	Columbia, S.C.
SOUTH DAKOTA'S CITY OF OPPORTUNITY	Mitchell, S.D.
SOUTH SEA ISLES OF AMERICA	Miami, Fla.
SOUTHEASTERN ENTRANCE TO THE REDWOOD EMPIRE	Napa, Calif.
SOUTHERN CALIFORNIA'S DESERT PLAYGROUND	Indio, Calif.
SOUTHERN GATEWAY	Moose Lake, Minn.
SOUTHERN GATEWAY OF NEW ENGLAND	Providence, R.I.
SOUTHLAND AT ITS BEST	Tallahassee, Fla.
SOUTH'S FASTEST GROWING CITY	East Point, Ga.
SOUTH'S GREATEST CITY	New Orleans, La.
SOUTH'S LARGEST PRODUCER OF COTTON CLOTH	Spartanburg, S.C.

SOUTH'S MOST BEAUTIFUL AND INTERESTING CITY	Macon, Ga.
SOUTH'S MOST STRATEGIC AND DISTRIBUTION CENTER	Decatur, Ala.
SOUTH'S MOST STRATEGIC INDUSTRIAL AND DISTRIBUTIONAL CENTER	Decatur, Ala.
SOUTH'S OLDEST INDUSTRIAL CITY	Columbus, Ga.
SOUTHWEST'S SIGHTSEEING CENTER	Phoenix, Ariz.
SOYBEAN CAPITAL OF THE WORLD	Decatur, Ill.
SOYBEAN CENTER	Decatur, Ill.
SPACE AGE CITY	Danbury, Conn.
SPACE CAPITAL OF THE NATION	Huntsville, Ala.
SPACEPORT, U.S.A.	Cape Kennedy, Fla.
SPANISH PEANUT CENTER OF THE WORLD	Dawson, Ga.
SPANISH TOWN	Tampa, Fla.
SPANISH VILLAGE	San Clemente, Calif.
SPEARHEAD OF THE NEW SOUTH	Charlotte, N.C.
SPINACH CAPITAL OF THE WORLD	Crystal City, Texas
SPINDLE CITY	Fall River, Mass.
SPINDLE CITY	Lewiston, Me.
SPINDLE CITY	Lowell, Mass.
SPINSTER CITY	Portland, Ore.
SPOKANE OF OREGON	Eugene, Ore.
SPONGE CITY	Tarpon Springs, Fla.
SPORT CENTER OF THE SOUTH	Aiken, S.C.
SPORT PARACHUTING CENTER OF U.S.A.	Orange, Mass.
SPORTLAND OF THE GULF	Mobile, Ala.
SPORTSMAN'S PARADISE	Chincoteague, Va.
SPORTSMAN'S PARADISE	Punta Gorda, Fla.
SPORTSMAN'S PARADISE	Salida, Colo.
SPOT FOR A HOME AND A LIFE OF JOY	Grove, Okla.

SPRING CITY	Waukesha, Wis.
SPRINGS OF HEALTH AND PITS OF WEALTH	Buhl, Minn.
SPRINGTIME CITY	Clearwater, Fla.
SQUAW HARBOR	Anacortes, Wash.
SQUAWKIEWOOD	Hollywood, Calif.
SQUIRE CITY	Springdale, Wash.
STAGE COACH TOWN	Fort Worth, Texas
STAR CITY	Lafayette, Ind.
STAR CITY OF THE SOUTH	Roanoke, Va.
STAR CITY WITH A GREAT FUTURE	Bethlehem, Pa.
STAR OF THE SOUTHLAND	Long Beach, Calif.
STARDOM	Hollywood, Calif.
STARLAND	Hollywood, Calif.
STATE CITY	Harrisburg, Pa.
STEAK CENTER OF THE NATION	Kansas City, Mo.
STEAMTOWN, U.S.A.	North Walpole, N.H.
STEEL CAPITAL OF THE WORLD	Pittsburgh, Pa.
STEEL CITY	Bethlehem, Pa.
STEEL CITY	Gary, Ind.
STEEL CITY	Pittsburgh, Pa.
STEEL CITY	Portsmouth, Ohio
STEEL CITY OF THE WEST	Pueblo, Colo.
STILL WATER	Sequim, Wash.
STONE CITY	Bedford, Ind.
STORYTOWN, U.S.A.	Lake George, N.Y.
STRAWBERRY CAPITAL OF ALASKA	Haines, Alaska
STRAWBERRY CAPITAL OF AMERICA	Hammond, La.
STRAWBERRY CAPITAL OF THE WORLD	Watsonville, Calif.
STRING TOWN	Bremerton, Wash.
STRING TOWN	Manette, Wash.
STRONG WATER	Shelton, Wash.
STUDIOLAND	Hollywood, Calif.
SUB-TREASURY OF THE PACIFIC NORTHWEST	Portland, Ore.

SUMMER AND HEALTH RESORT	Hendersonville, N.C.
SUMMER AND WINTER YEAR 'ROUND RESORT	St. Augustine, Fla.
SUMMER CAPITAL	Portland, Ore.
SUMMER CAPITAL OF AMERICA	Superior, Wis.
SUMMER CAPITAL OF SOCIETY	Newport, R.I.
SUMMER CITY	Duluth, Minn.
SUMMER FUN CAPITAL OF THE SOUTH	Daytona Beach, Fla.
SUMMER RESORT	Newport, R.I.
SUMMER WONDERLAND	Mackinac Island, Mich.
SUMMIT CITY	Akron, Ohio
SUMMIT CITY	Fort Wayne, Ind.
SUMMIT CITY	Kane, Pa.
SUNSHINE CAPITAL OF THE SOUTHWEST	Tucson, Ariz.
SUNSHINE CAPITAL OF THE UNITED STATES	Yuma, Ariz.
SUNSHINE CITY	St. Petersburg, Fla.
SUNSHINE CITY	Tucson, Ariz.
SUNSHINE TOWN	Newport, N.H.
SWEATSHIRT CAPITAL OF THE WORLD	Martinsville, Va.
SWELL PLACE TO LIVE	Tempe, Ariz.
SWISS CHEESE CAPITAL OF THE UNITED STATES	Monroe, Wis.
SWISS CHEESE CENTER OF OHIO	Sugarcreek, Ohio
SWITCHBACK CITY	Mauch Chunk, Pa.
SWITZERLAND OF AMERICA	Afton, Wyo.
SWITZERLAND OF AMERICA	Durango, Colo.
SWITZERLAND OF AMERICA	Terre Haute, Ind.
SWITZERLAND OF MAINE	Jackman, Me.
SWITZERLAND OF THE CATSKILLS	Hancock, N.Y.
SYCAMORE CITY	Terre Haute, Ind.

T

TABLE-LAND	Mesa, Wash.

TABLE WINE CENTER OF THE WORLD	Napa, Calif.
TABLE WINE CENTER OF THE WORLD	St. Helena, Calif.
TAILHOLD	Rogue River, Ore.
TAILHOLT	Carrollton, Ind.
TALLEST TOWN IN OREGON	Lakeview, Ore.
TANNERY CITY	Blossburg, Pa.
TARGET OF OPPORTUNITY	Waco, Texas
TARRARA CITY	Boykins, Va.
TATER TOWN	Gleason, Tenn.
TATERVILLE	Gleason, Tenn.
TELEGRAPHIC HUB	Syracuse, N.Y.
TENNESSEE'S BEAUTY SPOT	Nashville, Tenn.
TENT CITY	Wildwood, N.J.
TENT TOWN	Douglas, Wyo.
TERRACE CITY	Yonkers, N.Y.
TEXTILE CENTER OF THE WORLD	Greenville, S.C.
TEXTILE CITY	Reading, Pa.
THERMOPYLAE OF MIDDLE TENNESSEE	Tullahoma, Tenn.
THOROUGHBRED, STANDARDBRED AND SADDLE HORSE CENTER OF AMERICA	Lexington, Ky.
THREAD CITY	Willimantic, Conn.
THREE FORKS	Pullman, Wash.
THREE SPITS	Bangor, Wash.
THRESHOLD OF THEODORE ROOSEVELT NATIONAL MEMORIAL PARK	Dickinson, N.D.
TIDE-WATER CITY	Troy, N.Y.
TIN HORN VILLAGE	Newton, Mass.
TIP OF CAPE COD	Provincetown, Mass.
TIRE CITY OF THE UNITED STATES	Akron, Ohio
TOBACCO CAPITAL OF THE WORLD	Richmond, Va.
TOMATO CAPITAL OF SOUTH CENTRAL TEXAS	Yoakum, Texas
TOMATO CAPITAL OF THE OZARKS	Green Forest, Ark.

TOURIST AND CONVENTION CENTER	Jacksonville, Fla.
TOURIST'S PARADISE	Index, Wash.
TOUROPOLIS OF AMERICA	Flagstaff, Ariz.
TOWER TREE CITY	Greensburg, Ind.
TOWN BLESSED BY AN IDEAL YEAR 'ROUND CLIMATE	Las Vegas, Nev.
TOWN FOR THOSE IN LOVE WITH LIFE	Marietta, Ohio
TOWN OF HAPPY HOMES	Greenwood, Ind.
TOWN OF HOMES	Westport, Conn.
TOWN OF MANY OPPORTUNITIES	Uvalde, Texas
TOWN OF MILLIONAIRES	Brookline, Mass.
TOWN OF SCHOOLS--AND A COLLEGE	Wellesley, Mass.
TOWN THAT GAVE THE WORLD A GREAT IDEA	Nebraska City, Neb.
TOWN THAT HAS BECOME A UNIVERSITY	Winter Park, Fla.
TOWN THAT "JACK" BUILT	Joplin, Mo.
TOWN THAT MOVED OVERNIGHT	Hibbing, Minn.
TOWN THAT OUTLIVES AND OUTGROWS THE OIL BOOM	Titusville, Pa.
TOWN THAT ROSES BUILT	Pasadena, Calif.
TOWN THE ATOM BUILT	Richland, Wash.
TOWN TOO TOUGH TO DIE	Tombstone, Ariz.
TOWN TWO MILES LONG AND TWO YARDS WIDE	St. Francisville, La.
TOWN WHERE OIL DERRICKS LOOM IN ALMOST ANY YARD	Oklahoma City, Okla.
TOWN WHERE THE OFFICE LEDGER HAS REPLACED THE HORSE PISTOL	Oklahoma City, Okla.
TOWN WHERE SUMMER IS AIR-CONDITIONED	Chatham, Mass.
TOWN WHICH HELD THE KEY	Orondo, Wash.

TOWN WITH A FUTURE	Stratford, Conn.
TOWN WITH A HEART	Salida, Colo.
TOWN WITH A SPLIT PERSONALITY	Islip, N.Y.
TOWN WITH THE MOST TO OFFER INDUSTRY	Columbus, Miss.
TOY TOWN	Winchendon, Mass.
TRADE CENTER OF SOUTHWEST GEORGIA	Albany, Ga.
TRAIL'S END	International Falls,Minn.
TRANSPORT CENTER OF THE NATION	Buffalo, N.Y.
TRANSPORTATION CENTER OF NORTH AMERICA	Superior, Wis.
TRANSPORTATION CITY	Easton, Pa.
TRANSPORTATION KING OF THE MID-EAST	Harrisburg, Pa.
TREASURE ISLAND OF THE SOUTHWEST	Galveston, Texas
TREE CITY	Boise, Idaho
TREMONT	Boston, Mass.
TRI-CITIES	Florence, Sheffield and Tuscumbia, Ala.
TRI-CITIES	Moline and Rock Island, Ill., and Davenport, Iowa
TRI-COUNTY TRADING CENTER	Aurora, Mo.
TRIMOUNTAIN CITY	Boston, Mass.
TROPIC METROPOLIS	Miami, Fla.
TROPICAL FLORIDA'S FIRST RESORT	West Palm Beach, Fla.
TROPICAL ISLAND WONDERLAND IN THE GULF OF MEXICO	Fort Myers Beach, Fla.
TROPICAL WONDERLAND	Fort Lauderdale, Fla.
TRULY COLONIAL TOWN	Clinton, Conn.
TRULY YEAR 'ROUND VACATION LAND	Wells, N.Y.
TUBE CITY	McKeesport, Pa.
TULIP CENTER OF AMERICA	Holland, Mich.
TULIP CITY	Bellingham, Wash.

TULIP CITY	Holland, Mich.
TUNNEL CITY	Greensburg, Pa.
TURKEY CAPITAL	Aitkin, Minn.
TURKEY CAPITAL OF ARKANSAS	Berryville, Ark.
TURKEY CAPITAL OF MINNESOTA	Worthington, Minn.
TURKEY CAPITAL OF THE WORLD	Worthington, Minn.
TUSSELBURGH	Alton, Ill.
TWIN CITIES	Aberdeen, Wash., and Hoquiam, Wash.
TWIN CITIES	Auburn, Me., and Lewiston, Me.
TWIN CITIES	Bangor, Me., and Brewer, Me.
TWIN CITIES	Benton Harbor, Mich., and St. Joseph, Mich.
TWIN CITIES	Biddeford, Me., and Saco, Me.
TWIN CITIES	Brewer, Me., and Bangor, Me.
TWIN CITIES	Central Falls, R.I., and Pawtucket, R.I.
TWIN CITIES	Champaign, Ill., and Urbana, Ill.
TWIN CITIES	Helena, Ark., and West Helena, Ark.
TWIN CITIES	Hoquiam, Wash., and Aberdeen, Wash.
TWIN CITIES	Lewiston, Me., and Auburn, Me.
TWIN CITIES	Menasha, Wis., and Neenah, Wis.
TWIN CITIES	Minneapolis, Minn., and St. Paul, Minn.
TWIN CITIES	Monroe, La., and West Monroe, La.
TWIN CITIES	Neenah, Wis., and Menasha, Wis.
TWIN CITIES	Pawtucket, R.I., and Central Falls, R.I.

TWIN CITIES	Saco, Me., and Biddeford, Me.
TWIN CITIES	St. Joseph, Mich.,and Benton Harbor, Mich.
TWIN CITIES	St. Paul, Minn., and Minneapolis, Minn.
TWIN CITIES	Texarkana, Ark., and Texarkana, Texas
TWIN CITIES	Texarkana, Wis., and Texarkana, Ark.
TWIN CITIES	Urbana, Ill., and Champaign, Ill.
TWIN CITIES	West Helena, Ark., and Helena, Ark.
TWIN CITIES	West Monroe, La., and Monroe, La.
TWIN CITIES	Winston-Salem, N.C.
TWIN CITIES OF THE NORTHERN BLACK HILLS OF SOUTH DAKOTA	Deadwood, S.D.
TWIN CITIES OF THE NORTHERN BLACK HILLS OF SOUTH DAKOTA	Lead, S.D.
TWIN CITIES OF THE OUACHITA	Monroe, La., and West Monroe, La.
TWIN CITIES ON THE RED RIVER IN THE HEART OF LOUISIANA	Alexandria, La., and Pineville, La.
TWIN CITY	Minneapolis and St. Paul, Minn.
TWIN CITY	St. Paul and Minneapolis, Minn.
TWIN CITY	Winston-Salem, N.C.
TWIN LAKES CAPITAL OF THE OZARKS	Forsyth, Mo.
TWIN VILLAGES	Damariscotta and Newcastle, Me.
TWIN VILLAGES	Newcastle and Damariscotta, Me.
TWINS	Minneapolis and St. Paul, Minn.

TWINS	St. Paul and Minneapolis, Minn.
TYPICAL AMERICAN CITY	Middletown, Ind.
TYPICAL AMERICAN CITY	Muncie, Ind.
TYPICAL AMERICAN CITY	Owatonna, Minn.
TYPICAL NEW ENGLAND CITY	Norton, Mass.
TYPICAL OZARK HOME TOWN	Gentry, Ark.
TYPICAL RESORT CITY	Pensacola, Fla.

U

ULTRA MODERN CITY	Palo Alto, Calif.
UNITED NATIONS' CONFERENCE CENTER	San Francisco, Calif.
UNIVERSITY CITY	Cambridge, Mass.
UNIVERSITY CITY	Gainesville, Fla.
UNIVERSITY CITY	Vermillion, S.D.
UNIVERSITY OF TELEPHONY	New York, N.Y.
UNSAINTED ANTHONY	San Antonio, Texas
UNSPOILED BEAUTY SPOT OF NORTHERN MAINE	Patten, Me.
UP AND COMING TOWN	Sanford, Me.
UP-TO-DATE OLDEST TOWN IN LOUISIANA	Natchitoches, La.
URANIUM CAPITAL OF THE WORLD	Grants, N.M.
UTAH ZION	Salt Lake City, Utah

V

VACATION AND HEALTH RESORT	Waynesville, N.C.
VACATION CAPITAL OF THE APPALACHIAN HIGHLANDS	Elkins, W.Va.
VACATION CAPITAL OF THE NATION	Atlantic City, N.J.
VACATION CENTER	Portsmouth, R.I.
VACATION CITY	New York, N.Y.
VACATION CITY	St. Louis, Mo.

VACATION CITY ON CASCO BAY	Portland, Me.
VACATION FUN SPOT OF WESTERN MAINE	Bridgton, Me.
VACATION OR YEAR ROUND HOME CITY	Scituate, Mass.
VACATION WONDERLAND	Morristown, Tenn.
VACATIONER'S PARADISE	Shelter Islands, N.Y.
VACATIONER'S PARADISE	Walker, Minn.
VACATIONLAND OF NORTHERN WISCONSIN	Park Falls, Wis.
VACATIONLAND OF UN-LIMITED ENJOYMENT	Speculator, N.Y.
VACATIONLAND, U.S.A.	Miami Beach, Fla.
VALE OF BEAUTY	Valdosta, Ga.
VALLEY OF THE GARDENS	Santa Maria, Calif.
VAPOR CITY	Hot Springs, Ark.
VARIETY OF RECREATIONAL OPPORTUNITIES	Stockton, Calif.
VATICAN CITY	St. Louis, Mo.
VEHICLE CITY	Flint, Mich.
VENICE OF AMERICA	Annapolis, Md.
VENICE OF AMERICA	Fort Lauderdale, Fla.
VENICE OF AMERICA	Stone Harbor, N.J.
VENICE OF AMERICA	Syracuse, N.Y.
VENICE OF AMERICA	Wickford, R.I.
VENICE OF PUGET SOUND	La Conner, Wash.
VENICE OF THE NORTH-WEST	Willapa, Wash.
VENICE OF THE PACIFIC	Union, Wash.
VENICE OF THE PRAIRIE	San Antonio, Texas
VENICE OF THE SOUTH	Tarpon Springs, Fla.
VERMONT'S MOST HISTORIC TOWN	Bennington, Vt.
VERSATILE CITY	Rome, Ga.
VERY CENTER OF THE SUNSHINE STATE	Lake Weir, Fla.
VERY HEART OF FLORIDA	Orlando, Fla.
VILLAGE BEAUTIFUL	Williamstown, Mass.
VILLAGE OF BREATH-TAKING BEAUTY AND ENCHANTMENT	North Pole, N.Y.
VILLAGE OF CITY CHARM	Manchester, Conn.

VILLAGE OF DESTINY	Gilbert, Minn.
VILLAGE OF ENCHANTMENT	North Pole, N.Y.
VILLAGE OF FRIENDLY FOLK	Plainfield, Ind.
VILLAGE OF GREAT MUSEUMS	Cooperstown, N.Y.
VILLAGE OF THE PLAINS	Auburn, Ala.
VILLAGE WHERE NATURE SMILES	Cooperstown, N.Y.
VIRGIN CAPITAL	Washington, D.C.
VIRGINIA'S ATLANTIC CITY	Virginia Beach, Va.
VIRGINIA'S BIGGEST LITTLE CITY	Harrisonburg, Va.
VIRGINIA COLONY'S ELEGANT OLD CAPITAL	Williamsburg, Va.
VIVID CAPITAL OF THE OLD SOUTH	Jackson, Miss.

W

WALL STREET OF THE SOUTH	Nashville, Tenn.
WALNUT CITY	McMinnville, Ore.
WASHINGTON, B.C. -- BEFORE CORN	Washington, D.C.
WASHINGTON-BY-THE-SEA	Rehoboth Beach, Del.
WATER CITY	Madison, S.D.
WATER POLO CAPITAL OF FLORIDA	Boca Raton, Fla.
WATERFALLS	Tumwater, Wash.
WATERING-POT OF AMERICA	Utica, N.Y.
WATERLOO OF THE REVOLUTION	Yorktown, Va.
WATERMELON CAPITAL	Chiefland, Fla.
WATERMELON CAPITAL	Immokalee, Fla.
WATERMELON CAPITAL OF FLORIDA	Leesburg, Fla.
WATERSTOWN	Pataha, Wash.
WELL-BALANCED COMMUNITY	Greenfield, Mass.
WEST GATE TO THE LAND-O-LAKES	Butler, Mo.

WEST POINT OF THE SOUTH	Fort Benning, Ga.
WESTERN CAPITAL	Denver, Colo.
WESTERN CITY OF SHIPS	Oakland, Calif.
WESTERN GATE	San Francisco, Calif.
WESTERN GATE TO MEXICO	Tucson, Ariz.
WESTERN MECCA FOR ENJOYMENT UNLIMITED	Boise, Idaho
WESTERN METROPOLIS	Chicago, Ill.
WESTERN SHANGRI-LA	Upland, Calif.
WESTERN WATER GATE	Everglades, Fla.
WEST'S MOST WESTERN TOWN	Scottsdale, Ariz.
WHALING CITY	New Bedford, Mass.
WHALING CITY	New London, Conn.
WHIP CITY	Westfield, Mass.
WHISKEY TOWN	Peoria, Ill.
WHITE CITY	Chicago, Ill.
WHITE COLLAR CITY	Denver, Colo.
WHITE ROSE CITY	York, Pa.
WHITE STALLION	Touchet, Wash.
WICKEDEST CITY IN AMERICA	Phenix City, Ala.
WICKEDEST LITTLE CITY IN AMERICA	Dodge City, Kansas
WILDERNESS CAPITAL OF LINCOLN'S LAND	Vandalia, Ill.
WILDERNESS CITY	Washington, D.C.
WILLIAMSBURG OF THE SEA	Mystic, Conn.
WINDY CITY	Chicago, Ill.
WINE AND OLIVE COLONY	Demopolis, Ala.
WINTER AND SUMMER VACATION CENTER OF FLORIDA	Eustis, Fla.
WINTER CAPITAL OF AMERICA	New Orleans, La.
WINTER GOLF CAPITAL OF AMERICA	Pinehurst, N.C.
WINTER GOLF CAPITAL OF THE WORLD	Augusta, Ga.
WINTER HOME OF THE NATIONAL LEAGUE PHILADELPHIA "PHILLIES"	Clearwater, Fla.

WINTER PLAYGROUND OF AMERICA	San Antonio, Texas
WINTER SPORTS CAPITAL OF THE NATION	St. Paul, Minn.
WINTER SPORTS CITY	Kane, Pa.
WINTER STRAWBERRY CAPITAL OF THE WORLD	Plant City, Fla.
WISCONSIN'S BEAUTIFUL CAPITOL CITY	Milwaukee, Wis.
WISCONSIN'S SECOND CITY	Racine, Wis.
WITCH CITY	Salem, Mass.
WITCHCRAFT CITY	Salem, Mass.
WIZARD'S CLIP	Middleway, W. Va.
WONDER CITY	Decatur, Ala.
WONDER CITY	Hopewell, Va.
WONDER CITY	New York, N.Y.
WONDER CITY OF AMERICA	Buffalo, N.Y.
WONDER CITY OF THE WORLD	Miami, Fla.
WONDERFUL CONVENTION CITY	Scranton, Pa.
WONDERFUL PLACE TO LIVE	Augusta, Ga.
WONDERFUL PLACE TO LIVE	Mitchell, S.D.
WONDERFUL PLACE TO LIVE	Sebring, Fla.
WONDERFUL PLACE TO LIVE, TO WORK, TO PLAY	Augusta, Ga.
WONDERFUL WEATHER LAND	Tucson, Ariz.
WONDERLAND OF AMERICA	Boulder, Colo.
WOODS	Boise, Idaho
WOODS	Middletown, R.I.
WOOL CITY	Eaton Rapids, Mich.
WORLD FAMOUS MANUFACTURING CENTER	Dayton, Ohio
WORLD GLIDING CENTER	Bishop, Calif.
WORLD PORT	Seattle, Wash.
WORLD'S BEST BEACH	Cocoa Beach, Fla.
WORLD'S BEST TOBACCO MARKET	Danville, Va.

WORLD'S CAPITAL CITY	New York, N.Y.
WORLD'S CELERY CENTER	Sanford, Fla.
WORLD'S CENTRAL LIVE-STOCK MARKET	Sioux City, Iowa
WORLD'S CITRUS CENTER	Lakeland, Fla.
WORLD'S FAIR CITY	New York, N.Y.
WORLD'S FINANCIAL CAPITAL	New York, N.Y.
WORLD'S FINEST AND SAFEST BATHING BEACH	Wildwood, N.J.
WORLD'S GREATEST HARBOR	Hampton Roads, Va.
WORLD'S GREATEST HARBOR	Newport News, Va.
WORLD'S GREATEST MULE MARKET	Galesburg, Ill.
WORLD'S GREATEST STORE-HOUSE OF RAW MATERIAL	Fort Worth, Texas
WORLD'S GREATEST WORK-SHOP	Philadelphia, Pa.
WORLD'S LARGEST AN-THRACITE COAL MINING CITY	Scranton, Pa.
WORLD'S LARGEST ART POTTERY CITY	Macomb, Ill.
WORLD'S LARGEST BLACK WALNUT FACTORY	Gravette, Ark.
WORLD'S LARGEST COAL-SHIPPING PORT	Toledo, Ohio
WORLD'S LARGEST FAMILY RESORT	Daytona Beach, Fla.
WORLD'S LARGEST IMPORT EXPORT AIR CARGO TERMINAL	Miami, Fla.
WORLD'S LARGEST LOOSE-LEAF TOBACCO MARKET	Lexington, Ky.
WORLD'S LARGEST MINERAL HOT SPRINGS	Thermopolis, Wyo.
WORLD'S LARGEST SAFEST BATHING BEACH	New Smyrna, Fla.
WORLD'S LARGEST SPANISH PEANUT MARKET	Dawson, Ga.

WORLD'S LARGEST SPECIALTY JEWELRY MANUFACTURING CENTER	Plainville, Mass.
WORLD'S LIVELIEST GHOST TOWN	Virginia City, Nev.
WORLD'S LUCKIEST FISH-ING VILLAGE	Destin, Fla.
WORLD'S METROPOLIS	New York, N.Y.
WORLD'S MOST BEAUTIFUL CITY	Washington, D.C.
WORLD'S MOST EXCITING ALL YEAR ROUND VACATION CENTER	New York, N.Y.
WORLD'S MOST FAMOUS BEACH	Daytona Beach, Fla.
WORLD'S OYSTER CAPITAL	Norwalk, Conn.
WORLD'S PLAYGROUND	Atlantic City, N.J.
WORLD'S PREMIER WINTER RESORT	Palm Beach, Fla.
WORLD'S RAILROAD CAPITAL	Chicago, Ill.
WORLD'S RAILROAD MECCA	Chicago, Ill.
WORLD'S SADDLE HORSE CAPITAL	Mexico, Mo.
WORLD'S SPINACH CAPITAL	Crystal City, Texas
WORLD'S SUBMARINE CAPITAL	Groton, Conn.
WORLD'S WORKSHOP	Pittsburgh, Pa.
WYOMING'S YEAR 'ROUND HEALTH AND SCENIC CENTER	Thermopolis, Wyo.

Y

"Y" BRIDGE CITY	Zanesville, Ohio
YANKEE ATHENS	New Haven, Conn.
YANKEE CITY	Newburyport, Mass.
YEAR AROUND LIVING AT ITS BEST	Lake Weir, Fla.
YEAR ROUND CENTER FOR MAJOR SPECTATOR EVENTS	Las Vegas, Nev.
YEAR ROUND PLAYGROUND	Duluth, Minn.

YEAR ROUND PLAYGROUND OF THE AMERICAS	Miami Beach, Fla.
YEAR ROUND PLAYGROUND OF THE PACIFIC	Long Beach, Calif.
YEAR 'ROUND RESORT AND CONVENTION CENTER	Biloxi, Miss.
YEAR ROUND SPORTSMAN'S PARADISE	Okeechobee, Fla.
YEAR ROUND VACATION PLAYLAND	Atlantic City, N. J.
YEAR ROUND VACATION TOWN IN THE WHITE MOUNTAINS	North Conway, N. H.
YEAR ROUND VACATION-LAND	Burlington, Vt.
YOSEMITE OF ARIZONA	Portal, Ariz.
YOUNG CAPITAL	Washington, D. C.
YOUNGEST BIG CITY IN THE UNITED STATES	Phoenix, Ariz.
YOUNGEST OF THE WORLD'S GREAT CITIES	Birmingham, Ala.
YOUR TROPICAL "HOME TOWN"	Englewood, Fla.

Z

ZENITH CITY	Duluth, Minn.
ZENITH CITY OF THE UNSALTED SEAS	Duluth, Minn.
ZION	Salt Lake City, Mo.

All-American Cities

Albuquerque, N. M.	1957
Alexandria, Va.	1963
Allentown, Pa.	1962
Alton, Ill.	1959
Altus, Okla.	1956
Anacortes, Wash.	1961
Anchorage, Alaska	1956
Asheville, N. C.	1951
Atlanta, Ga.	1951
Aztec, N. M.	1963
Baltimore, Md.	1952
Bartlesville, Okla.	1962
Bayonne, N. J.	1949
Bellevue, Wash.	1955
Bemidji, Minn.	1952
Bloomington, Ill.	1955
Bloomington, Ind.	1958
Bloomington, Minn.	1960
Boston, Mass.	1949, 1951, 1962
Brattleboro, Vt.	1956
Brookfield, Ill.	1952
Cambridge, Ohio	1955
Canton, Ohio	1953
Chattanooga, Tenn.	1962
Chicago, Ill.	1954
Cincinnati, Ohio	1949, 1950
Clarksburg, W. Va.	1957
Cleveland, Ohio	1949
Columbia, S. C.	1951
Columbus, Ohio	1958
Compton, Calif.	1952

Dayton, Ohio	1951
Daytona Beach, Fla.	1953
Decatur, Ark.	1954
Decatur, Ill.	1960
Des Moines, Iowa	1949
De Soto, Mo.	1953, 1959
East Providence, R.I.	1960
East St. Louis, Mo.	1959
Elgin, Ill.	1956
Falls Church, Va.	1961
Fargo, N.D.	1959
Flint, Mich.	1953
Galesburg, Ill.	1957
Galveston, Texas	1961
Gastonia, N.C.	1963
Grafton, W.Va.	1962
Grand Island, Neb.	1955
Grand Junction, Colo.	1962
Grand Rapids, Mich.	1949, 1960
Granite City, Ill.	1958
Hartford, Conn.	1950, 1961
Hayden, Ariz.	1958
High Point, N.C.	1962
Highland Park, Ill.	1958
Huntington, W.Va.	1958
Independence, Mo.	1961
Joliet, Ill.	1955
Kalamazoo, Mich.	1951
Kansas City, Mo.	1950, 1951
Ketchikan, Alaska	1957
Knoxville, Tenn.	1962
Lamar, Colo.	1959
Las Vegas, Nev.	1960
Laurinburg, N.C.	1956
Leadville, Colo.	1958

Louisville, Ky.	1963
Lynwood, Calif.	1961
Manhattan, Kans.	1952
Mexico, Mo.	1954
Miami, Fla.	1952, 1957
Middletown, Ohio	1957
Milton, Ore.	1961
Minneapolis, Minn.	1952, 1963
Modesto, Calif.	1954
Montclair, N.J.	1950
Mount Vernon, Ill.	1951
Neosho, Mo.	1957
Newark, N.J.	1954
Newburgh, N.Y.	1952
New Haven, Conn.	1958
New Orleans, La.	1950
Norfolk, Va.	1959
Oakland, Calif.	1956
Oil City, Pa.	1963
Omaha, Neb.	1957
Owensboro, Ky.	1952
Park Forest, Ill.	1953
Pawtucket, R.I.	1951
Peoria, Ill.	1953
Petersburg, Va.	1953
Phenix City, Ala.	1955
Philadelphia, Pa.	1949, 1951, 1957
Phoenix, Ariz.	1950, 1958
Pittsburgh, Pa.	1949
Port Angeles, Wash.	1953
Port Huron, Mich.	1955
Portland, Me.	1950
Poughkeepsie, N.Y.	1949
Pueblo, Colo.	1954
Quincy, Ill.	1962
Radford, Va.	1960
Reading, Pa.	1955

Richfield, Minn.	1954
Richland, Wash.	1960
Richmond, Calif.	1953
Richmond, Va.	1950
Riverside, Calif.	1955
Roanoke, Va.	1952
Rock Island, Ill.	1954
Rockville, Md.	1954, 1961
Roseville, Calif.	1963
St. Louis, Mo.	1956
St. Paul, Minn.	1955
Salem, Ore.	1960
Salisbury, N.C.	1961
San Antonio, Texas	1949, 1951
San Diego, Calif.	1962
San Jose, Calif.	1960
Santa Fe Springs, Calif.	1959
Savannah, Ga.	1955
Scranton, Pa.	1953
Seattle, Wash.	1959
Seward, Alaska	1963
Sheridan, Wyo.	1958
Shreveport, La.	1953
Sidney, Ohio	1963
Sioux City, Iowa	1961
Springfield, Mo.	1956
Tacoma, Wash.	1956
Toledo, Ohio	1950
Torrance, Calif.	1956
Vallejo, Calif.	1959
Vancouver, Wash.	1957
Warren, Ohio	1954
Westport, Conn.	1958
Wichita, Kans.	1961
Winston Salem, N.C.	1959
Woodbridge, N.J.	1963
Woodstock, Ill.	1963
Woonsocket, R.I.	1952
Worcester, Mass.	1949, 1961

Yankton, S.D.	1957
Youngstown, Ohio	1950
Zanesville, Ohio	1956

Geographical Index
States

ALABAMA

The Cornucopia of the South, The Cotton State (cotton plantations), The Heart of Dixie, The Land of Flowers, The Land of Opportunity, The Lizard State (lizards), The Star of the South, The Yellowhammer State (the uniforms of the Confederate soldiers had a home-dyed yellow tinge)

ALASKA

America's Last Frontier, America's Last Outpost, America's Newest Gayest Frontier, The Arctic Treasureland, The Far North Frontier, The Great Land, The Land of Opportunity, The Land of the Midnight Sun, The Land Where the Summer Sun Never Sets, The Last Frontier, The Nation's New Playground, The New Frontier, The Northern Wonderland, Seward's Folly (William Henry Seward, U.S. Secretary of State, advocated and negotiated purchase from Russia for $7,200,000), Uncle Sam's Icebox, The Vacationland of Opportunity, The Wonderland Unsurpassed

ARIZONA

The Apache State (Indian tribes), The Aztec State (Aztec names), The Baby State (48th state, admitted February 14, 1912), The Canyon State, The Copper State (copper production), Friendly Arizona, The Grand Canyon State, The Italy of America (scenic), The Land of Sunshine and Scenic Grandeur, The Land Where the Sun Spends the Winter, One of America's Most Popular Playgrounds, The Sand Hill State (desert), The Sunset Land, The Sunset State, The Vacation State of the Nation, The Valentine State (admitted on Valentine Day, February 14, 1912)

ARKANSAS

The Bear State (bears), The Bowie State (bowie knives used), The Guinea Pig State (proving ground for experiments of Department of Agriculture), The Hot Water State (numerous hot springs), The Land of Opportunity, The Toothpick State (bowie knives in handles), The Wonder State

CALIFORNIA

The El Dorado State, The Eureka State, The Golden State (gold disc. in 1848; golden poppies each spring), The Grape State (grape production), The Land of Gold, The Land of Sunshine and Flowers

COLORADO

America's Vacation Paradise, The Buffalo Plains State, The Centennial State (admitted August 1, 1876- the hundredth anniversary of the Declaration of Independence), The Colorful Colorado, The Glorious Vacation Playground, The Highest State in the Union (average altitude 6,800 feet), The Lead State (lead production), The Silver State (silver production), The Switzerland of America (numerous high mountains), The Top of the Nation (mountain peaks)

CONNECTICUT

The Blue Law State (New Haven blue laws), The Brownstone State (quarries), The Constitution State (1639, first written constitution, the Fundamental Orders), The Freestone State (freestone quarries), The Land of Steady Habits, The Nutmeg State (wooden nutmegs), The Wooden Nutmeg State

DELAWARE

The Blue Hen State (a fighting hen popular in the Revolutionary War for his bravery), The Blue Hen's Chickens State (see above), The Diamond State (because it is small in size yet important), The Economic Sunshine State, The First State (Delaware on December 7, 1787 was the first state to ratify the Constitution), New Sweden (name of fort built in 1638 by Peter Minuit whose expedition was sent out by Queen Christiana), Uncle Sam's Pocket Handkerchief

FLORIDA

The Alligator State (alligators), The Everglades State (everglades), Fabulous Florida, The Gulf State (on Gulf of Mexico), The Land of Flowers, The Land of Fun, Sun and Sand, The Orange State (orange and citrus production), The Peninsula State (geographical), The Scenic Wonderland, The Sunshine State

GEORGIA

The Buzzard State, The Cracker State, The Empire State of the South, The Goober State, The Peach State, The South's Empire State, The Yankee Land of the South

HAWAII

The Aloha State, The Fiftieth State of Enchantment, The Gateway to the Orient, The Gateway to the Pacific, The Island Paradise, The Island State, The Paradise of the Pacific, The Playground of the Pacific, The Scenic Isle, The Window on the East

IDAHO

The Gem State, The Gem of the Mountain States, The Gem of the Mountains, The Land of Pleasure, The State of Shining Mountains, The Vacation Land, The Vacation Land of Your Fondest Dreams, The Vacation Wonderland

ILLINOIS

The Corn State, The Crossroads of America, Egypt, The Garden of the West, The Hub of the Nation, The Land of Lincoln, The Land of the Illini, The Prairie State, The Sucker State, The Vacation Target for Millions of Americans, The Vacationland

INDIANA

The Crossroads of America, The Hoosier State (claimed to originate from early pioneer greeting "Who'shyer")

IOWA

The Greatest Food Producing Area in the World, The Hawkeye State (Indian Chief Hawkeye), The Land of

IOWA (Cont'd)

the Rolling Prairie, The Last Frontier of Industrial Development, The State Where the West Begins and Progress Never Ceases, The Vacation Haven in Mid-Nation

KANSAS

Bleeding Kansas (the seven hectic years, 1854-1861, while slavery was at stake), The Central State (geographical location), The Cyclone State, The Friendly State, The Garden of the West, The Garden State, The Grasshopper State, The Jayhawk State (irregular troops and pillaging bands in Civil War-one of several explanations, a bird), Midway, U.S.A., The Squatter State (squatters who arrived about 1854), The Sunflower State, The Wheat State

KENTUCKY

The Bluegrass State (blueish tinged grass), The Corncracker State (corn-cracker birds), The Dark and Bloody Ground State (battleground of Indian tribes), The Hemp State, The State Where Big Things Are Happening, The Tobacco State

LOUISIANA

The Bayou State, The Bayou Wonderland, The Child of the Mississippi River, The Creole State (creoles of French and Spanish descent), The Holland of America (numerous canals), The Nation's Industrial Frontier, The Pelican State (the brown pelican native to the shore), The Picturesque Historic Land of Early America, The Sportsman's Paradise, The State That Has to be Seen to be Believed, The Sugar State, The Variety Vacationland

MAINE

America's Top Vacation Land, The Border State, The Complete Vacationland, The Convention State, The Great Recreation Center, The Land of Remembered Vacations, The Lumber State, The Old Dirigo State (state motto "Dirigo"), The Pine Tree State (pine tree depicted on the coat-of-arms), The Playground of the Nation, The Polar Star State, The State Where

MAINE (Cont'd)

Every Season is Vacation Time, The Switzerland of America (scenic), The Vacationland

MARYLAND

The Cockade State (a type of hat worn by patricians), The Free State, The Monumental State (because of its monuments, principally in Baltimore), The Old Line State (the dividing line between the crown land grants of William Penn and Lord Baltimore), The Oyster State (oyster fisheries), The Queen State (named for Queen Henrietta Maria), The Star-Spangled Banner State

MASSACHUSETTS

The Baked Bean State, The Bay State (Massachusetts Bay), The Bean Eating State, The Bean State, The Birthplace of American Freedom, The Historic Vacationland, The Most Varied State of the Fifty, The Old Bay State, The Old Colony State, The Puritan State, The Space Center of the World, The Vacationland of Fun and Plenty

MICHIGAN

The Auto State, The Automobile State, The Lady of the Lake (Lake Michigan), The Lake State (touches Lakes Michigan, Superior, Erie, Huron and St. Clair, One of the Great Resort States of the Middle West, The Tourist Empire of the Inland Seas, The Water Wonderland, The Wolverine State

MINNESOTA

The Bread and Butter State (flour and dairy industry), The Gopher State (gophers), The Lake State (14,215 lakes over 10 acres in size), The Land of 10,000 Lakes (see above), The Nation's Vacation Land, The New England of the West, The North Star State (the state seal has the motto L'Etoile du Nord, the star of the north), The Playground of 10,000 Lakes, The United Nations in Miniature, The Wheat State

MISSISSIPPI

A Great Agricultural State, America's State of Opportunity, The Bayou State (bayous, rivulets), The Border-eagle State (eagle depicted on the coat-of-arms), The Cotton Kingdom, The Crossroads of the South, The Eagle State (see above), The Gateway to the Southland, The Groundhog State, The Heart of the Deep South, The Hospitality State, The Magnolia State (magnolia trees), The Mud-cat State (name for catfish), The Mud-waddler State, The State of Opportunity, The Tadpole State (young French settlers; "frogs" being nickname applied to their elders)

MISSOURI

The Bullion State (Thomas Hart Benton, known as Old Bullion), The Cave State (26 caves open), The Family Vacationland, The Fire Clay Capital, The Heart of America, The Heartland of Hospitality, The Iron Mountain State (Iron Mountain), The Lead State (lead production), Little Dixie, The Mother of the West, The Ozark State (Ozark Mountain), The Pennsylvania of the West, The Puke State, The Show Me State, The Vacation Capital of the Midwest, The World's Saddle Horse Capital

MONTANA

The Big Sky Country, The Big Sky Vacationland, The Bonanza State, The Land of Enchantment, The Lead State (lead production), The Singed Cat State, The Stub Toe State, The Treasure State, The Wonderland

NEBRASKA

The Antelope State (antelopes), The Beef State (cattle production), The Black Water State (dark soil which makes water appear dark), The Bug-eating State (bull bats which eat bugs), The Cornhusker State, The Tall Corn State, The Treeplanter State

NEVADA

The Battle Born State (Nevada was made a territory in 1861 and admitted as a state in 1864 during the Civil War), The Entertainment Capital of the World,

NEVADA (Cont'd)

The Mining State, The Sage State (prevalence of wild sage), The Sage-hen State (a common-type of fowl), The Sagebrush State (wild sage), The Silver State (silver mines)

NEW HAMPSHIRE

The Granite State (granite is the bedrock underlying most of the surface), The Land of Scenic Splendor, The Mother of Rivers, The Old Man of the Mountain State (rock formation), The Scenic State, The Switzerland of America (scenic), The White Mountain State (White Mountains)

NEW JERSEY

The Adaptable State, The Camden and Amboy State (Camden and Amboy Railroad), The Clam State (seafood production), The Cockpit of the Revolution (used in 1776), The Foreigner State (see New Spain State), The Garden State, History's Main Road, The Jersey Blue State (blue uniforms worn by Revolutionary Army troops, or blue laws), The Land of Amazing Advantages, The Land of Amazing Industrial Advantages,The Mosquito State, Nature's Showcase, The New Spain State (in 1812, Joseph Bonaparte, king of Spain, fled to Bordentown, N.J., where he bought 1,400 acres), The Pathway of the Revolution (nearly 100 battles were fought on New Jersey soil), The Riviera of America, The Sharpbacks State, The State of Camden and Amboy (see above), The State of Spain (see above), The Vacationland the Year 'Round

NEW MEXICO

The Cactus Land (profusion of cactus), The Land of the Cactus (cactus plants), The Land of Enchantment, The Land of Hearts' Desire, The Land of Opportunity, The Land of Sunshine, The Land of the Delight-Makers (from the book "The Delight Makers" by Adolf Bandelier), The Playground of the Southwest, The Space Age Research Center for the Free World, The Spanish State, The State of Spain State, The Sunshine State, The Vermin State

NEW YORK

The Empire State, The Excelsior State (motto), The Host State for the World's Fair, The Knickerbocker State (short loose trousers worn by the early Dutch settlers), The Nation's Showcase, The Seat of Empire, The State That Has Everything, The Vacation Empire, The Vacation Variety, The World of Scenic Beauty, The Year-Round Vacationland

NORTH CAROLINA

The Dixie Dynamo, The Ireland of America, The Land of Beginnings (site of the first settlement in America, Roanoke Island), The Land of the Sky (many mountain peaks), The Old North State (north of South Carolina), The Rip Van Winkle State, The Second Nazareth, The Tarheel State (a derisive name applied by Mississippi soldiers to North Carolinians who failed to hold their position, and did not put tar on their heels), The Turpentine State (product obtained from the pine trees), The Variety Vacationland The Year 'Round Vacation State

NORTH DAKOTA

The Crossroads of All America, The Flickertail State (the flickertail squirrel), The Friendly State, The Great Central State (center of the wheat belt), The Land of the Dakotas (Dakota Indians), The Land of the North Furrow, The Sioux State (Indian tribe)

OHIO

The Buckeye State (buckeye or horse-chestnut, buckeye resemblance to the seed, both in color, shape and appearance to the eye of the buck), The Gateway State (to the Northwest Territory), The Gateway to the Northwest Territory, The Land of History, The Land of Opportunity, The Modern Mother of Presidents (birthplace of Grant, Hayes, Garfield, B. Harrison, McKinley, Taft and Harding), The Mother of Presidents, The Oldest State West of the Thirteen Original Colonies, The Yankee State (because of its free institutions)

OKLAHOMA

America's Vacation Treasureland, The Boomers' Paradise (the "boomers" who opened Oklahoma, April 22, 1889), The Sooner State ("sooners" were those who entered Oklahoma sooner than the designated legal time), The State of Industry, The Vacation Adventureland

OREGON

America's Finest Vacationland, The Beaver State, The Cool, Green Vacationland, The Hard-case State (rough life of the early settlers), The Land of Opportunity, The Land Where Dreams Come True, Nature's Wonderland, The Pacific Wonderland, The Scenic State, The State of Excitement, The Sunset State, The Threshold of Paradise, The Web-foot State (excessive rain in winter)

PENNSYLVANIA

The Birth State of the Nation (Declaration of American Independence signed, July 4, 1776), The Coal State (coal mines), The Keystone State (central geographical position among the thirteen original colonies), The Nation's Family Playground, The Quaker State (founded in 1680 by William Penn), The State of 1001 Vacation Pleasures, The Steel State (industry)

RHODE ISLAND

America's First Vacationland, The Land of Roger Williams (founded Providence 1636), Little Rhody, The Plantation State (the State of Rhode Island and Providence Plantations), The Southern Gateway of New England

SOUTH CAROLINA

The Iodine State, The Keystone of the South Atlantic Seaboard (wedge shape), The Palmetto State (tree), The Rice State (rice production), The Sand-lapper State (humorous, designation of poor people who lapped up sand for subsistence), The State Where Resources and Markets Meet, The Swamp State (rice fields), The Wonderful Iodine State

SOUTH DAKOTA

The Artesian State (artesian wells), The Blizzard State (gales, storms), The Coyote State (coyotes), The Friendly Land of Infinite Variety, The Land of Infinite Variety, The Land of Plenty, The Land of Wonder, The Pheasant Capital of the World, The Sunshine State, The Swiagecat State

TENNESSEE

America's Central Vacation Land, America's Most Interesting State, The Big Bend State (Indian name for the Tennessee River), The Hog and Hominy State (leader in corn and pork products in the 1830's), The Lion's Den State, The Mother of South-western Statesmen (Jackson, Polk, Andrew Johnson), The Nation's Most Interesting State, The River With the Big Bend (the Tennessee River), The Scenic Wonderland, The State Where Every Season is Vacation Time, The Volunteer State (on May 26, 1847 during the Mexican War, Governor Aaron Vail Brown called for 2,800 volunteers and 30,000 responded)

TEXAS

America's Fun-tier, The Banner State (descriptive word, leading, excelling, etc.), The Beef State (cattle production), The Blizzard State (dust storms and wind storms), The Jumbo State (referring to size, name of large elephant exhibited by P.T. Barnum), The Land of Promise, The Lone Star State (single star in its coat-of-arms and flag), The New World of Adventure, The Republic, The State of the Confederacy

UTAH

The Beehive State (emblem on the coat-of-arms of Utah), The Center of Scenic America, The Colorful Vacation Land, The Deseret State (the name by which Utah was known in 1849-1850), The Friendly State, The Honey State (the product found in beehives), The Land of Color, The Land of Color and Contrasts, The Land of Contrasts, The Land of the Mormons (the Book of Mormon, or Golden Bible written by the prophet Mormon), The Land of the Saints (the Mormons whose official church name is the Church of

Jesus Christ of the Latter-Day Saints), The Magic Land of Colorful Past and Interesting Future, The Mormon State, Nature's Wonderland, The Salt Lake State (the Great Salt Lake, area 1,500 square miles), The World of Scenic Beauty, The Year 'Round Paradise

VERMONT

The Four Seasons' Recreation State, The Green Mountain State (name of the mountain range)

VIRGINIA

America's Historyland, The Ancient Dominion, The Battlefield of the Civil War, The Beckoning Land, The Birthplace of Eight Presidents (Washington, Jefferson, Madison, Monroe, W.H. Harrison, Tyler, Taylor and Wilson), The Birthplace of the Nation, The Cavalier State (cavaliers settled in Virginia aided with the king against the Parliament), The Commonwealth (term applied to Virginia in its first constitution, adopted June 29, 1776), The Mother of Presidents, The Mother of States (the first state to be settled, the 1609 charter embraced West Virginia, Kentucky, Ohio, Illinois, Indiana, Wisconsin and parts of Minnesota), The Mother of Statesmen (Washington, Jefferson, Madison, Monroe, Marshall, Mason, Patrick Henry, Richard Henry Lee, Payton Randolph, Jr.), The Old Dominion State (Charles II called the colony "the old dominion" because of its loyalty to the Crown)

WASHINGTON

The Chinook State (Chinook division of Indians) (for its salmon industry), The Clam Grabbers, The Evergreen State (forests of fir and pine) (green firs), The Exciting State of Contrasts, The Surprising State

WEST VIRGINIA

The Free State, The Little Mountain State (Allegheny Mountains), The Mountain State, The Panhandle State (descriptive of shape), The Switzerland of America (scenic)

WISCONSIN

America's Dairyland, The Badger State (so-called because the early settlers lived underground), The Cheese Capital of the Nation, The Copper State (copper mines), The Nation's Finest Vacationland, The Playground of the Middle West, The Vacation Land For All

WYOMING

The Cowboy State, The Equality State (equal suffrage extended to women in 1869), The Equality Suffrage State, The Gateway to the Scenic Wonders of the Great, The Land of the Purple Sage, The Sagebrush State (wild sage growing in the deserts), The Sanctuary of Peace, The Wonderland of America, Wonderful Wyoming

Nicknames Index
States

A

ADAPTABLE STATE	New Jersey
ALLIGATOR STATE	Florida
ALOHA STATE	Hawaii
AMERICA'S CENTRAL VACATION LAND	Tennessee
AMERICA'S DAIRYLAND	Wisconsin
AMERICA'S FINEST VACATION-LAND	Oregon
AMERICA'S FIRST VACATION-LAND	Rhode Island
AMERICA'S FUN-TIER	Texas
AMERICA'S HISTORYLAND	Virginia
AMERICA'S LAST FRONTIER	Alaska
AMERICA'S LAST OUTPOST	Alaska
AMERICA'S MOST INTEREST-ING STATE	Tennessee
AMERICA'S NEWEST GAYEST FRONTIER	Alaska
AMERICA'S STATE OF OPPORTUNITY	Mississippi
AMERICA'S TOP VACATION LAND	Maine
AMERICA'S VACATION PARADISE	Colorado
AMERICA'S VACATION TREASURELAND	Oklahoma
ANCIENT DOMINION	Virginia
ANTELOPE STATE	Nebraska
APACHE STATE	Arizona
ARCTIC TREASURELAND	Alaska
ARTESIAN STATE	South Dakota
AUTO STATE	Michigan

AUTOMOBILE STATE	Michigan
AZTEC STATE	Arizona

B

BABY STATE	Arizona
BADGER STATE	Wisconsin
BAKED BEAN STATE	Massachusetts
BANNER STATE	Texas
BATTLE-BORN STATE	Nevada
BATTLEFIELD OF THE CIVIL WAR	Virginia
BAY STATE	Massachusetts
BAYOU STATE	Louisiana
BAYOU STATE	Mississippi
BAYOU WONDERLAND	Louisiana
BEAN EATING STATE	Massachusetts
BEAN STATE	Massachusetts
BEAR STATE	Arkansas
BEAVER STATE	Oregon
BECKONING LAND	Virginia
BEEF STATE	Nebraska
BEEF STATE	Texas
BEEHIVE STATE	Utah
BIG BEND STATE	Tennessee
BIG SKY COUNTRY	Montana
BIG SKY VACATIONLAND	Montana
BIRTH STATE OF THE NATION	Pennsylvania
BIRTHPLACE OF AMERICAN FREEDOM	Massachusetts
BIRTHPLACE OF EIGHT PRESIDENTS	Virginia
BIRTHPLACE OF THE NATION	Virginia
BLACK WATER STATE	Nebraska
BLEEDING KANSAS	Kansas
BLIZZARD STATE	South Dakota
BLIZZARD STATE	Texas
BLUEGRASS STATE	Kentucky
BLUE HEN STATE	Delaware
BLUE HEN'S CHICKENS STATE	Delaware
BLUE LAW STATE	Connecticut
BONANZA STATE	Montana
BOOMERS' PARADISE	Oklahoma

BORDER-EAGLE STATE	Mississippi
BORDER STATE	Maine
BOWIE STATE	Arkansas
BREAD AND BUTTER STATE	Minnesota
BROWNSTONE STATE	Connecticut
BUCKEYE STATE	Ohio
BUFFALO PLAINS STATE	Colorado
BUG-EATING STATE	Nebraska
BULLION STATE	Missouri
BUZZARD STATE	Georgia

C

CACTUS LAND	New Mexico
CAMDEN AND AMBOY STATE	New Jersey
CANYON STATE	Arizona
CAVALIER STATE	Virginia
CAVE STATE	Missouri
CENTENNIAL STATE	Colorado
CENTER OF SCENIC AMERICA	Utah
CENTRAL STATE	Kansas
CHEESE CAPITAL OF THE NATION	Wisconsin
CHILD OF THE MISSISSIPPI RIVER	Louisiana
CHINOOK STATE	Washington
CLAM GRABBERS	Washington
CLAM STATE	New Jersey
COAL STATE	Pennsylvania
COCKADE STATE	Maryland
COCKPIT OF THE REVOLUTION	New Jersey
COLORFUL COLORADO	Colorado
COLORFUL VACATION LAND	Utah
COMMONWEALTH	Virginia
COMPLETE VACATIONLAND	Maine
CONSTITUTION STATE	Connecticut
CONVENTION STATE	Maine
COOL GREEN VACATIONLAND	Oregon
COPPER STATE	Arizona
COPPER STATE	Wisconsin
COMPLETE VACATIONLAND	Maine
CORN STATE	Illinois
CORN-CRACKER STATE	Kentucky

CORNHUSKER STATE	Nebraska
CORNUCOPIA OF THE SOUTH	Alabama
COTTON KINGDOM	Mississippi
COTTON STATE	Alabama
COWBOY STATE	Wyoming
COYOTE STATE	South Dakota
CRACKER STATE	Georgia
CREOLE STATE	Louisiana
CROSSROADS OF ALL AMERICA	North Dakota
CROSSROADS OF AMERICA	Illinois
CROSSROADS OF AMERICA	Indiana
CROSSROADS OF THE SOUTH	Mississippi
CYCLONE STATE	Kansas

D

DARK AND BLOODY GROUND STATE	Kentucky
DESERET STATE	Utah
DIAMOND STATE	Delaware
DIXIE DYNAMO	North Carolina

E

EAGLE STATE	Mississippi
ECONOMIC SUNSHINE STATE	Delaware
EGYPT	Illinois
EL DORADO STATE	California
EMPIRE STATE	New York
EMPIRE STATE OF THE SOUTH	Georgia
ENTERTAINMENT CAPITAL OF THE WORLD	Nevada
EQUALITY STATE	Wyoming
EQUALITY SUFFRAGE STATE	Wyoming
EUREKA STATE	California
EVERGLADES STATE	Florida
EVERGREEN STATE	Washington
EXCELSIOR STATE	New York
EXCITING STATE OF CONTRASTS	Washington

F

FABULOUS FLORIDA	Florida
FAMILY VACATION LAND	Missouri
FAR NORTH FRONTIER	Alaska
FIFTIETH STATE OF ENCHANTMENT	Hawaii
FIRE CLAY CAPITAL	Missouri
FIRST STATE	Delaware
FLICKERTAIL STATE	North Dakota
FOREIGNER STATE	New Jersey
FOUR SEASONS' RECREATION STATE	Vermont
FREE STATE	Maryland
FREE STATE	West Virginia
FREESTONE STATE	Connecticut
FRIENDLY ARIZONA	Arizona
FRIENDLY LAND OF INFINITE VARIETY	South Dakota
FRIENDLY STATE	Kansas
FRIENDLY STATE	North Dakota
FRIENDLY STATE	Utah

G

GARDEN OF THE WEST	Illinois
GARDEN OF THE WEST	Kansas
GARDEN STATE	Kansas
GARDEN STATE	New Jersey
GATEWAY STATE	Ohio
GATEWAY TO THE NORTH-WEST TERRITORY	Ohio
GATEWAY TO THE ORIENT	Hawaii
GATEWAY TO THE PACIFIC	Hawaii
GATEWAY TO THE SCENIC WONDERS OF THE GREAT WEST	Wyoming
GATEWAY TO THE SOUTH-LAND	Mississippi
GEM OF THE MOUNTAIN STATES	Idaho
GEM OF THE MOUNTAINS	Idaho
GEM STATE	Idaho

GLORIOUS VACATION PLAY-GROUND	Colorado
GOLDEN STATE	California
GOOBER STATE	Georgia
GOPHER STATE	Minnesota
GRAND CANYON STATE	Arizona
GRANITE STATE	New Hampshire
GRAPE STATE	California
GRASSHOPPER STATE	Kansas
GREAT AGRICULTURAL STATE	Mississippi
GREAT CENTRAL STATE	North Dakota
GREAT LAND	Alaska
GREAT RECREATION STATE	Maine
GREATEST FOOD PRODUCING AREA IN THE WORLD	Iowa
GREEN MOUNTAIN STATE	Vermont
GROUNDHOG STATE	Mississippi
GUINEA PIG STATE	Arkansas
GULF STATE	Florida

H

HARD-CASE STATE	Oregon
HAWKEYE STATE	Iowa
HEART OF AMERICA	Missouri
HEART OF DIXIE	Alabama
HEART OF THE DEEP SOUTH	Mississippi
HEARTLAND OF HOSPITALITY	Missouri
HEMP STATE	Kentucky
HIGHEST STATE IN THE UNION	Colorado
HISTORIC VACATIONLAND	Massachusetts
HISTORY'S MAIN ROAD	New Jersey
HOG AND HOMINY STATE	Tennessee
HOLLAND OF AMERICA	Louisiana
HONEY STATE	Utah
HOOSIER STATE	Indiana
HOSPITALITY STATE	Mississippi
HOST STATE FOR THE WORLD'S FAIR	New York
HOT-WATER STATE	Arkansas
HUB OF THE NATION	Illinois

I

IODINE STATE	South Carolina
IRELAND OF AMERICA	North Carolina
IRON MOUNTAIN STATE	Missouri
ISLAND PARADISE	Hawaii
ISLAND STATE	Hawaii
ITALY OF AMERICA	Arizona

J

JAYHAWKER STATE	Kansas
JERSEY BLUE STATE	New Jersey
JUMBO STATE	Texas

K

KEYSTONE STATE	Pennsylvania
KEYSTONE OF THE SOUTH ATLANTIC SEABOARD	South Carolina
KNICKERBOCKER STATE	New York

L

LADY OF THE LAKE	Michigan
LAKE STATE	Michigan
LAKE STATE	Minnesota
LAND OF AMAZING ADVANTAGES	New Jersey
LAND OF AMAZING INDUSTRIAL ADVANTAGES	New Jersey
LAND OF BEGINNINGS	North Carolina
LAND OF COLOR	Utah
LAND OF COLOR AND CONTRASTS	Utah
LAND OF CONTRASTS	Utah
LAND OF ENCHANTMENT	Montana
LAND OF ENCHANTMENT	New Mexico
LAND OF FLOWERS	Alabama
LAND OF FLOWERS	Florida
LAND OF FUN, SUN AND SAND	Florida
LAND OF GOLD	California

LAND OF HEARTS' DESIRE	New Mexico
LAND OF HISTORY	Ohio
LAND OF INFINITE VARIETY	South Dakota
LAND OF LINCOLN	Illinois
LAND OF OPPORTUNITY	Alabama
LAND OF OPPORTUNITY	Alaska
LAND OF OPPORTUNITY	Arkansas
LAND OF OPPORTUNITY	New Mexico
LAND OF OPPORTUNITY	Ohio
LAND OF OPPORTUNITY	Oregon
LAND OF PLEASURE	Idaho
LAND OF PLENTY	South Dakota
LAND OF PROMISE	Texas
LAND OF REMEMBERED VACATIONS	Maine
LAND OF ROGER WILLIAMS	Rhode Island
LAND OF SCENIC SPLENDOR	New Hampshire
LAND OF STEADY HABITS	Connecticut
LAND OF SUNSHINE	New Mexico
LAND OF SUNSHINE AND FLOWERS	California
LAND OF SUNSHINE AND SCENIC GRANDEUR	Arizona
LAND OF TEN THOUSAND (10,000) LAKES	Minnesota
LAND OF THE CACTUS	New Mexico
LAND OF THE DAKOTAS	North Dakota
LAND OF THE DELIGHT-MAKERS	New Mexico
LAND OF THE ILLINI	Illinois
LAND OF THE MIDNIGHT SUN	Alaska
LAND OF THE MORMONS	Utah
LAND OF THE NORTH FURROW	North Dakota
LAND OF THE PURPLE SAGE	Wyoming
LAND OF THE ROLLING PRAIRIE	Iowa
LAND OF THE SAINTS	Utah
LAND OF THE SKY	North Carolina
LAND OF WONDER	South Dakota
LAND WHERE DREAMS COME TRUE	Oregon
LAND WHERE THE SUMMER SUN NEVER SETS	Alaska

LAND WHERE THE SUN SPENDS THE WINTER	Arizona
LAST FRONTIER	Alaska
LAST FRONTIER OF INDUSTRIAL DEVELOPMENT	Iowa
LEAD STATE	Colorado
LEAD STATE	Missouri
LEAD STATE	Montana
LION'S DEN STATE	Tennessee
LITTLE DIXIE	Missouri
LITTLE MOUNTAIN STATE	West Virginia
LITTLE RHODY	Rhode Island
LIZARD STATE	Alabama
LONE STAR STATE	Texas
LUMBER STATE	Maine

M

MAGIC LAND OF COLORFUL PAST AND INTERESTING FUTURE	Utah
MAGNOLIA STATE	Mississippi
MIDWAY, U.S.A.	Kansas
MINING STATE	Nevada
MODERN MOTHER OF PRESIDENTS	Ohio
MONUMENTAL STATE	Maryland
MORMON STATE	Utah
MOSQUITO STATE	New Jersey
MOST VARIED STATE OF THE FIFTY	Massachusetts
MOTHER OF PRESIDENTS	Ohio
MOTHER OF PRESIDENTS	Virginia
MOTHER OF RIVERS	New Hampshire
MOTHER OF SOUTH-WESTERN STATESMEN	Tennessee
MOTHER OF STATES	Virginia
MOTHER OF STATESMEN	Virginia
MOTHER OF THE WEST	Missouri
MOUNTAIN STATE	West Virginia
MUD-CAT STATE	Mississippi
MUD-WADDLER STATE	Mississippi

N

NATION'S FAMILY PLAYGROUND	Pennsylvania
NATION'S FINEST VACATIONLAND	Wisconsin
NATION'S INDUSTRIAL FRONTIER	Louisiana
NATION'S MOST INTERESTING STATE	Tennessee
NATION'S NEW PLAYGROUND	Alaska
NATION'S SHOWCASE	New York
NATION'S VACATION LAND	Minnesota
NATION'S WONDERLAND	Oregon
NATURE'S SHOWCASE	New Jersey
NATURE'S WONDERLAND	Utah
NEW ENGLAND OF THE WEST	Minnesota
NEW FRONTIER	Alaska
NEW SPAIN STATE	New Jersey
NEW SWEDEN	Delaware
NEW WORLD OF ADVENTURE	Texas
NORTH STAR STATE	Minnesota
NORTHERN WONDERLAND	Alaska
NUTMEG STATE	Connecticut

O

OLD BAY STATE	Massachusetts
OLD COLONY STATE	Massachusetts
OLD DIRIGO STATE	Maine
OLD DOMINION STATE	Virginia
OLD LINE STATE	Maryland
OLD MAN OF THE MOUNTAIN STATE	New Hampshire
OLD NORTH STATE	North Carolina
OLDEST STATE WEST OF THE THIRTEEN ORIGINAL COLONIES	Ohio
ONE OF AMERICA'S MOST POPULAR PLAYGROUNDS	Arizona
ONE OF THE GREAT RESORT STATES OF THE MIDDLE WEST	Michigan

ORANGE STATE	Florida
OZARK STATE	Missouri
OYSTER STATE	Maryland

P

PACIFIC WONDERLAND	Oregon
PALMETTO STATE	South Carolina
PANHANDLE STATE	West Virginia
PARADISE OF THE PACIFIC	Hawaii
PATHWAY OF THE REVOLUTION	New Jersey
PEACH STATE	Georgia
PELICAN STATE	Louisiana
PENINSULA STATE	Florida
PENNSYLVANIA OF THE WEST	Missouri
PHEASANT CAPITAL OF THE WORLD	South Dakota
PICTURESQUE HISTORIC LAND OF EARLY AMERICA	Louisiana
PINE TREE STATE	Maine
PLANTATION STATE	Rhode Island
PLAYGROUND OF TEN THOUSAND LAKES	Minnesota
PLAYGROUND OF THE MIDDLE WEST	Wisconsin
PLAYGROUND OF THE NATION	Maine
PLAYGROUND OF THE PACIFIC	Hawaii
PLAYGROUND OF THE SOUTHWEST	New Mexico
POLAR STAR STATE	Maine
PRAIRIE STATE	Illinois
PUKE STATE	Missouri
PURITAN STATE	Massachusetts

Q

QUAKER STATE	Pennsylvania
QUEEN STATE	Maryland

R

REPUBLIC	Texas
RICE STATE	South Carolina
RIP VAN WINKLE STATE	North Carolina
RIVER WITH THE BIG BEND	Tennessee
RIVIERA OF AMERICA	New Jersey

S

SAGE STATE	Nevada
SAGEBRUSH STATE	Nevada
SAGEBRUSH STATE	Wyoming
SAGE-HEN STATE	Nevada
SALT LAKE STATE	Utah
SANCTUARY OF PEACE	Wyoming
SAND HILL STATE	Arizona
SAND-LAPPER STATE	South Carolina
SCENIC ISLE	Hawaii
SCENIC STATE	Oregon
SCENIC STATE	New Hampshire
SCENIC WONDERLAND	Florida
SCENIC WONDERLAND	Tennessee
SEAT OF EMPIRE	New York
SECOND NAZARETH	North Carolina
SEWARD'S FOLLY	Alaska
SHARPBACKS STATE	New Jersey
SHOW ME STATE	Missouri
SILVER STATE	Colorado
SILVER STATE	Nevada
SINGED CAT STATE	Montana
SIOUX STATE	North Dakota
SOONER STATE	Oklahoma
SOUTHERN GATEWAY OF NEW ENGLAND	Rhode Island
SOUTH'S EMPIRE STATE	Georgia
SPACE AGE RESEARCH CENTER FOR THE FREE WORLD	New Mexico
SPACE CENTER OF THE WORLD	Massachusetts
SPANISH STATE	New Mexico
SPORTSMAN'S PARADISE	Louisiana

SQUATTER STATE	Kansas
STAR OF THE SOUTH	Alabama
STAR-SPANGLED BANNER STATE	Maryland
STATE OF CAMDEN AND AMBOY	New Jersey
STATE OF EXCITEMENT	Oregon
STATE OF INDUSTRY	Oklahoma
STATE OF ONE THOUSAND AND ONE VACATION PLEASURES	Pennsylvania
STATE OF OPPORTUNITY	Mississippi
STATE OF SHINING MOUNTAINS	Idaho
STATE OF SPAIN	New Jersey
STATE OF SPAIN STATE	New Mexico
STATE OF THE CONFEDERACY	Texas
STATE THAT HAS EVERYTHING	New York
STATE THAT HAS TO BE SEEN TO BE BELIEVED	Louisiana
STATE WHERE BIG THINGS ARE HAPPENING	Kentucky
STATE WHERE EVERY SEASON IS VACATION TIME	Maine
STATE WHERE EVERY SEASON IS VACATION TIME	Tennessee
STATE WHERE RESOURCES AND MARKETS MEET	South Carolina
STATE WHERE THE WEST BEGINS AND PROGRESS NEVER CEASES	Iowa
STEEL STATE	Pennsylvania
STUB TOE STATE	Montana
SUCKER STATE	Illinois
SUGAR STATE	Louisiana
SUNFLOWER STATE	Kansas
SUNSET LAND	Arizona
SUNSET STATE	Arizona
SUNSET STATE	Oregon
SUNSHINE STATE	Florida
SUNSHINE STATE	New Mexico
SUNSHINE STATE	South Dakota
SURPRISING STATE	Washington

SWAMP STATE	South Carolina
SWIAGECAT STATE	South Dakota
SWITZERLAND OF AMERICA	Colorado
SWITZERLAND OF AMERICA	Maine
SWITZERLAND OF AMERICA	New Hampshire
SWITZERLAND OF AMERICA	West Virginia

T

TADPOLE STATE	Mississippi
TALL CORN STATE	Nebraska
TARHEEL STATE	North Carolina
THRESHOLD OF PARADISE	Oregon
TOBACCO STATE	Kentucky
TOOTHPICK STATE	Arkansas
TOP OF THE NATION	Colorado
TOURIST EMPIRE OF THE INLAND SEAS	Michigan
TREASURE STATE	Montana
TREEPLANTER STATE	Nebraska
TURPENTINE STATE	North Carolina

U

UNCLE SAM'S ICEBOX	Alaska
UNCLE SAM'S POCKET HANDKERCHIEF	Delaware
UNITED NATIONS IN MINIATURE	Minnesota

V

VACATION ADVENTURE-LAND	Oklahoma
VACATION CAPITAL OF THE MIDWEST	Missouri
VACATION EMPIRE	New York
VACATION HAVEN IN MID-NATION	Iowa
VACATION LAND	Idaho
VACATION LAND FOR ALL	Wisconsin
VACATION LAND OF FUN AND PLENTY	Massachusetts

VACATION LAND OF YOUR FONDEST DREAMS	Idaho
VACATIONLAND OF OPPORTUNITY	Alaska
VACATION STATE OF THE NATION	Arizona
VACATION TARGET FOR MILLIONS OF AMERICANS	Illinois
VACATION VARIETY	New York
VACATION WONDERLAND	Idaho
VACATIONLAND	Illinois
VACATIONLAND	Maine
VACATIONLAND THE YEAR 'ROUND	New Jersey
VALENTINE STATE	Arizona
VARIETY VACATIONLAND	Louisiana
VARIETY VACATIONLAND	North Carolina
VERMIN STATE	New Mexico
VOLUNTEER STATE	Tennessee

W

WATER WONDERLAND	Michigan
WEB-FOOT STATE	Oregon
WHEAT STATE	Kansas
WHEAT STATE	Minnesota
WHITE MOUNTAIN STATE	New Hampshire
WINDOW ON THE EAST	Hawaii
WOLVERINE STATE	Michigan
WONDER STATE	Arkansas
WONDERFUL IODINE STATE	South Carolina
WONDERFUL WYOMING	Wyoming
WONDERLAND	Montana
WONDERLAND OF AMERICA	Wyoming
WONDERLAND UNSURPASSED	Alaska
WOODEN NUTMEG STATE	Connecticut
WORLD OF SCENIC BEAUTY	New York
WORLD OF SCENIC BEAUTY	Utah
WORLD'S SADDLE HORSE CAPITAL	Missouri

Y

YANKEE LAND OF THE SOUTH	Georgia
YANKEE STATE	Ohio
YEAR 'ROUND PARADISE	Utah
YEAR 'ROUND VACATION STATE	North Carolina
YEAR-ROUND VACATION-LAND	New York
YELLOWHAMMER STATE	Alabama